The Bletchley Girls

*War, secrecy, love and loss: the women
of Bletchley Park tell their story*

Tessa Dunlop

**HODDER &
STOUGHTON**

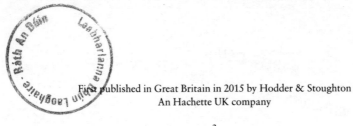

First published in Great Britain in 2015 by Hodder & Stoughton
An Hachette UK company

3

Copyright © Tessa Dunlop 2015

A CIP catalogue record for this title is available from the British Library

Hardback ISBN 978 1 444 79571 4
Trade paperback ISBN 978 1 444 79572 1
Ebook ISBN 978 1 444 79573 8

Printed and bound by Clays Ltd, St Ives plc

Hodder & Stoughton policy is to use papers that are natural, renewable
and recyclable products and made from wood grown in sustainable
forests. The logging and manufacturing processes are expected to
conform to the environmental regulations of the country of origin.

Hodder & Stoughton Ltd
338 Euston Road
London NW1 3BH

www.hodder.co.uk

For the Bletchley Girls

Contents

Introduction

'No, the women have to be alive, otherwise it'll be like all the other Bletchley books.'

The publisher was adamant: this was to be a journey through the lives of the girls who worked for Britain's phenomenal code-breaking organisation; it is their story, they must be here to tell it. He was right; to really understand the human response to these extraordinary experiences we need to hear the women speak for themselves. Boasting an average age of ninety, the fifteen veterans featured in this book are not just Bletchley Girls – they are also the children of the Armistice, the schoolgirls of the thirties, the housewives of the fifties and the grandmothers of the digital age. Born just after the First World War, into a class-bound, cap-doffing era still swathed in imperial pink, their trajectory through a maelstrom of international violence and out the other side into nascent modernity is eye-watering time travel. Before I had even found my first Bletchley girl I felt sure not only of her great age but also of her astonishing resilience. How else could she survive so much change, so many mixed messages?

In keeping with the man's world in which it operated, until recently Bletchley Park's narrative has been predominantly a male one. Moth-ridden, bespectacled boffins enjoying flashes of ingenious inspiration have hogged the Park's unlikely limelight; eccentric Alan Turing, a key code-breaker who is widely regarded as a father of the modern computer, posthumously led the way. This focus on code-breaking's male hierarchy has obscured the reality of Park life. By 1944 women outnumbered men at Bletchley three to one, yet it is only now, at the end of their long lives, that the

1

final few females are enjoying a last hurrah. Having outlived almost all their older male counterparts, the Bletchley narrative is finally their's to own. These are the girls who helped outsmart the enemy within the confines of a Buckinghamshire estate. But for all the celebration of their collective achievements, most female survivors who pop up in the press do just that: they pop up, only to retreat back into their own private realms. All we get is a quick peek at their wartime work, minus the context of the rest of their lives. The indomitable Baroness Trumpington, fuelled by her political and media stature, is a rare exception. A nonagenarian national treasure, she has been able to share her extraordinary life story on a wider stage. But what of the others? Who are these women? Where did they come from? And what did Bletchley really mean to them?

Leading Ladies

Had I seen her on the street I would have recognised Ruth Bourne (née Henry). With pretty lemon-tinted hair and distinctive brown eyes, she is one of Bletchley Park's hardest-working veterans. Her anecdotes pepper many code-breaking books, Wren Henry's sunny face smiles out from the glossy pages of *The Lost World of Bletchley Park* and I have listened to her lucid wartime descriptions on both the Internet and the radio. Perhaps it was Ruth's status that intimidated me as I dialled her number, or maybe just first-time nerves. I had not spoken to a 'Bletchley Girl' before, and I wasn't entirely sure when I had last spoken to someone the same age as our Queen.

'Ha! I am a bit of show-off,' Ruth assured me, 'so it'll be no problem to talk to you.'

I felt a rush of relief. We arranged to meet in her north London home on Valentine's day.

I'd done my homework; I knew Ruth operated one of Bletchley's iconic Bombe machines and I had a mental image of her as a young girl carefully tending its rows of rotating drums, battling to decipher Germany's Enigma encryptions. But I confess to worrying that her Bletchley story was already well known. What more was there for me to discover? The answer came just a few minutes into our chat, when Ruth mentioned her beloved father, Isaac.

'Oh, are you Jewish?'

'Yes,' she smiled, 'I'm a British Jew.'

After that I didn't worry any more. I realised no veteran's war can be fully understood without their background story.

It was Bletchley Park Trust that, after much cajoling, gave me Ruth's contact details. ('The veterans are one of our most precious assets, we do not give out their numbers.') Her active contribution to the Park's heritage centre made her an obvious first choice. Women in their late eighties and nineties can be hard to track down. 'Oh that blankety blank email!' laughs Ruth. She is one of six from the fifteen women featured in this book who braves electronic communication. It is a mistake to presume that operating the world's most cutting-edge technology seventy years ago guarantees lifelong technical savvy. Indeed when it comes to the Bletchley Girls (at least the ones I met), most generalisations are unwise.

Over the last year I have learnt to rebuff numerous assumptions:

'Are all Bletchley ladies really posh?'

'I expect you are speaking to fiercely intelligent women?'

'It must have been really exciting working at Bletchley Park.'

In fact, they are not all posh, nor are they all 'fiercely intelligent' and by no means all of them relished Park life. But they all have stories that demand to be heard.

Years of working in television and radio has taught me the power of the personal story; I was excited about the prospect of talking to women who were players in a past now remembered primarily through a series of big names (Churchill, Hitler, Eisenhower) and iconic events (Dunkirk, the Blitz, the D-Day landings). Our victory in the Second World War has defined Britain's recent national identity; the veterans for whom I searched are now part of a generation celebrated en masse for their selflessness, stoicism and – in the case of Bletchley Park – secrecy. Generalisation threatens to overshadow reality. Only the women could tell me how it really was. But first I had to find them. Ruth could not stand alone.

My search began as a haphazard affair; I fired off letters, contacted museums, gleaned tips and clues from forewords in Bletchley books and memoirs and scanned the papers for relevant articles.

It wasn't long before I struck gold.

I first read about Rozanne Colchester (née Medhurst) in the *Guardian*. The headline was eye-catching: 'Women spies in the Second World War; "It was horrible and wonderful like a love affair."' Rozanne is convinced she didn't say that. 'It sounds so stupid. I would never say a thing like that. A love affair? What does that mean?' And then she laughs; after all, it's in the past now. There is a bell-like quality to her voice as she reminisces about her extraordinary life. Although born in Yorkshire, by the late 1930s Rozanne and her family had moved to Rome. 'Heavens it was exciting but I think you always feel things so much more intensely when you're young. And I loved my time at Bletchley Park, I made such good friends there.'

My ears prick at her mention of Pamela Rose, one of the Park's sophisticated thespian set about whom I had read a couple of heady extracts in Michael Smith's bestselling *Station X*. Surely she wasn't still alive?

'Indeed she is! She's ninety-six. Yes, of course I can forward on a letter, with pleasure.'

Waiting for the post to arrive had never been so fraught with anticipation. How long does a ninety-one-year-old need to deliver a letter? How long does a ninety-six-year-old take to reply to that letter? Suspended in a curious limbo, I began devouring first-person war memoirs. A couple stood out. Gwen Watkins (née Davies) is a skilful writer with an authorial tone that remains delightfully crisp; her latest book, written at ninety, is a memoir about Park life entitled *Cracking the Luftwaffe Codes*. 'Attention is always given to the Enigma machine,' she explains, 'but I and lots of other people had nothing to do with Enigma codes so I decided to set the record straight.'

I find Gwen looking out to sea in front of her pebbledash terrace house in Mumbles, Wales, a faded cotton sunhat perched on her head. She greets me with open arms. 'Now, we could record the interview in the sitting-room, but because of the traffic most journalists prefer to come through the house.'

Gwen, it turns out, is something of a media darling. One of the last people left alive who had a meaningful relationship with Wales' most famous poet, Dylan Thomas, she is quick to attribute her impressive literary connections to Bletchley Park. 'That changed everything, I would not have missed it for all the world.' Before the war Gwen was a mere schoolgirl (albeit a 'fiercely intelligent' one) in Bournemouth. Meeting her confirmed what I had long suspected; my quest was much more than an analysis of code-breaking's component parts. Tucked away in Buckinghamshire, the Bletchley Girls shared a common experience that for some had lifelong repercussions.

At ninety-one, Charlotte Webb (née Vine-Stevens) is almost exactly Gwen's contemporary but unlike Gwen she wasn't a writer. However the depth and breadth of her life's experiences recently compelled Charlotte to put pen to paper.

'Well I started making a few jottings for family, I suppose, that's how it began . . . It's extraordinary how things have taken off.' She looks both surprised and humbled by the attention her memoir *Secret Postings* has attracted.

Invited to spend the night in Charlotte's Worcestershire bungalow, together we are sharing a delicious breakfast of fresh croissants, small pats of butter and sweet marmalade. The jug of milk is carefully covered with a lace doily. Between mouthfuls Charlotte repeats the sentiment in the foreword of her memoir. 'I have been alive for nearly a century, it is extraordinary how things have changed. I am very fortunate to have lived through such interesting times.' In front of me is an astute woman who worked in both Bletchley Park and America's state-of-the-art Pentagon during the Second World War – Charlotte is not the only one feeling fortunate.

To write a Bletchley memoir at the age of ninety is no mean feat, and underlines the special status the Park and war have been accorded in both Gwen and Charlotte's memories. Their books made them easy to find, their tales are ripe for the retelling. However, once again I was aware that I was relying on the testimonies of those who remembered Bletchley Park fondly. No wonder this wartime code-breaking organisation enjoys such a hallowed place in our nation's history – after all, where is the incentive to revisit memory lane if it was no pleasure to walk down in the first place?

Bletchley Park Trust eventually agreed to help me on my quest to find veterans but I didn't want to be over-dependent on a partial source. Numerous personal testimonies in the last forty years have helped bolster the glamorous Bletchley 'brand', which now boasts not only a vast museum, but also several television series and films and countless books. Was there anyone left to counter the prevailing opinion?

———•————

Lady Jean Fforde (née Lady Jean Graham) does not mince her words : 'I had no idea how boring it was going to be. It was excessively boring!'

I couldn't believe my eyes. Tucked away on page 199 of her meaty 383-page memoir, Lady Jean briefly describes how she resented her time at Bletchley Park, before returning to more exciting episodes in her majestic life. Still presiding over the Isle of Arran on the West Coast of Scotland, this ninety-three-year-old Lady was a must-have Bletchley Girl. I immediately penned an enthusiastic missive requesting an interview, citing my Scottish credentials and desire to write a balanced book. My request was politely rebutted.

'I really feel I was not there long enough to make it worth you coming up here.' The letter was a blow. I needed the other side of the story. How could I turn Arran's Lady?

The same day I received Lady Jean's rejection, Rozanne's Park friend, Pamela Rose (née Gibson), left me a telephone message. My letter had arrived. Pamela's voice took me by surprise; it had an authoritative oaky texture and the distinct edge of a trained actress. I returned the call with some trepidation, intuitively understanding that Pamela was important. She was the oldest woman I'd come across; surely the perfect person with whom to begin *The Bletchley Girls*?

We meet in the elegant four-storey London home where she has lived since 1946.

'So you've come to talk about Bletchley?' Her look is almost conspiratorial. 'The mansion was a pretty hideous building. I do think it has been rather overblown; compared with elsewhere it was a cushy berth.'

That was all that was said on the subject of Bletchley during our first meeting. Pamela has lived an extraordinary life – after two full hours of talking we haven't even arrived at 1939, but we've already visited Germany three times.

Team Work

Slotting the stories of my first few Bletchley veterans into the broader history of the Park was incredibly satisfying. Two-dimensional academic descriptions took on a whole new lease of life. During the war each girl was allotted her own highly confidential role within the code-breaking nexus. By 1941 many of the component parts of this intricate process were estab-lished. Every stage had its own specific location and the scale of the operation meant the girls were not always working within the confines of the Park itself. Of course this book cannot represent every role involved. In some cases all the players are dead; the late Mavis Batey (née Lever) was the last of Dilly's Fillies – Alfred Dillwyn Knox's hand-picked team of female code-breakers who worked in Bletchley's research section, located in the Cottage. Other key code-breaking and intelligence roles were generally occupied by better educated, older men. A few older women were present at the Park; Rhoda Welsford, Phoebe Senyard and Claire Harding enjoyed positions of responsibility but they are no longer alive.

The Bletchley Girls featured here were just that, girls. Very young, with simple classroom skills (diligence, obedience and occasionally a language), these female recruits made up the backbone of Bletchley's code-breaking organisation from 1941 onwards. It was young girls who operated the unwieldy machinery, made sense of wireless sound waves, and sorted the decoded messages that would eventually help lead the Allies to victory and the world into the information age. With five and a half Bletchley women on board (I hadn't given up on Lady Jean) I drew a large code-breaking chart circling the jobs already covered – Bombe operator (Ruth); decoders, both German (Gwen) and Italian (Rozanne); registrar (Charlotte); and indexer (Pamela). From Lady Jean's brief description it wasn't immediately clear what role she initially performed, but so far she was the only woman I'd found who worked in Alan Turing's Naval Hut 8. Now I wasn't just looking for any Bletchley Girl who was prepared to talk. I had a specific wish list in mind: at the very least I needed a Colossus operator, a Y-station listener and a brain-box from Bletchley's Enigma-focused heart – Hut 6.

Joanna Chorley (née Stradling) sounds slightly perplexed on the telephone.

'All this hoo-ha because of a photograph. It's a bit silly really.

One paper even said I took the picture, but how could that possibly be? I was in it!'

And so she is: standing near the edge of the frame, her waved hair springing generously from either side of her naval beret. Seventy years on, Joanna's discovery of a sepia photograph featuring thirty-eight Wrens tasked with operating the Bletchley's Colossus machines caused a mini media storm.

'Pictured for the first time: Bletchley Park's women code-breakers who operated the world's first electronic computer during the Second World War' announced the *Daily Mail*, while the *Telegraph* promised: 'WW2 code-breakers – the final secret'. In both cases a contemporary picture of Joanna alongside a revamped Colossus machine in the National Museum of Computing is a reminder of how quickly our world has changed. There were no computers before the Second World War – Joanna has not just lived through an era of unprecedented change, she was part of that change.

Coincidentally she has returned to Buckinghamshire in old age to be near her daughter. The replica Colossus – 'Not entirely the same,' insists Joanna – is only eight miles away in Bletchley. Stony Stratford, the town where she now lives, was once a popular accommodation option for those working at the Park. However, Joanna is unsure about all the media attention. It is a keen sense of duty that compels her to make the occasional appearance for the National Museum of Computing and it takes a while before she is able to talk to me freely about her past. Having kept a secret of national importance for thirty years, Joanna's initial reticence is unsurprising. As she puts it, 'I was born in a time when girls didn't blab about everything.'

In recent years some have found it easier to talk than others. It was historian Asa Briggs' chatty memoir about his time at Bletchley Park, *Secret Days*, that led me to my next veteran. '[Never] had I . . . seen so many machines, or women working them, as I did in the adjacent Machine Room . . . The Machine

Room was the elite room.' Young Briggs was struck not only by the number of women in Hut 6 (the centre for the decryption of Enigma messages from the German Army and Air Force) but also by their intelligence: the hatch and door between him and them did not prevent Asa striking up friendships (and enjoying flirtations) with his female colleagues.

Ann Mitchell (née Williamson) was one such girl. Having studied mathematics at Oxford during the war, Ann was a rare breed. The archivist at Oxford's Lady Margaret Hall sent me her Curriculum Vitae: in an era when women often didn't work it made for intimidating reading. Although now partially sighted, Ann is one of the six women in this book on email. During our lively exchange, I discovered that my Edinburgh-based aunt was her close friend.

'Gosh darling,' boomed Aunt Sally down the phone, 'only the other day I was reading aloud *The Secret Life of Bletchley Park* to Ann. I think that quite enough has already been written on the subject.'

Piqued, I rallied back, 'No Sally! This book will be different,' and duly bought my train ticket north.

Like the other decoding centres in the Park, Hut 6 was dependent on radio interceptions: Asa Briggs remembered: 'it was the basis of all that we could do.' Scattered across Britain with international outposts as remote as New Delhi and Colombia, Y-stations, big and small, improvised and requisitioned, were the nerve centres of an extraordinary eavesdropping operation, intercepting the gobbledygook messages to pass on to Bletchley Park. The RAF, Royal Navy, Army and civilian services all had their own stations, where thousands of invisible listeners hunched night and day over radio sets, their ears straining for enemy output. They were the first vital link in the code-breaking chain and yet history has given Y-station listeners short shrift. Their numbers are not included in the estimated 8,500–10,000 people who worked at Bletchley. Y-stations remained very separate from Station X (the

Park's code name), but veteran listener Betty Gilbert (née Quincey) is in no doubt: 'they couldn't have done it without us. That's what I say.'

She is exceptionally proud of her part in the war and was only too delighted when Bletchley Park put me in contact with her. Over milky tea and a platter of sausage rolls she shows me a large cardboard box full of her wartime memorabilia. We are sitting in her living-room in Higham Ferrers, Northamptonshire.

I've lived 'ere nearly all my life. See we got given this house by the government in 1948. It was one of those new houses they promised. I remember there was no path, nor nothing. Cement floors and couple of chairs and wringer that's all I 'ad.

Betty grins. 'No, I don't own it, no need to.' Then she kneels down with an agility that belies her ninety years and starts to sift through the photographs in the box.

'Ah yes, 'ere it is, me and the rest of the ATS girls.' She pauses before adding, 'You know, up there on that Yorkshire moor, that was the best time of my life.'

Betty's war was very different from that of the other Bletchley Girls, but her role was a vital one; without listeners there would have been no codes to crack. I quickly realised that to rely on her story alone was not enough.

Pat Davies (née Owtram) lives in a charming house in Chiswick, West London. With a clock chiming in the hall she welcomes me into her classy sitting-room. Like Betty, Pat has a box of memorabilia and she too believes that the Y-station story is overlooked.

'The Park do a very good job but for a long time all they gave us was one small display in their museum.'

As far as Pat is concerned, a couple of wireless sets complete with Bakelite headphones was not sufficient. What she then goes on to describe in her commanding voice is a wartime adventure so fluid and full of surprises, I wonder if any museum could capture its essence.

Neither Pat nor Betty ever worked at Bletchley Park, Betty didn't even know of its existence, but they, like all the other women in this book, were integral to Britain's code-breaking phenomenon. They too are Bletchley Girls.

Essential Extras

Bletchley Park has become synonymous with ingenuity, eccentricity and shared endeavour. But Cora Jarman (née Pounds) aspired to be neither eccentric nor ingenious; like most other seventeen-year-old girls she simply wanted to fit in. I found her short testimony on the website of The Second World War Experience Centre:

> I would have been compulsorily 'called up' into one of the Services when I was eighteen, so I volunteered to join the WRNS[1] because the uniform had no buttons to clean and was the nicest to my way of thinking.

Sure enough, accompanying the text is a headshot of the young rating, blonde hair immaculately curled under a dark cap complete with naval insignia.

Now comfortably retired in Hampshire, Cora is still a very elegant woman (with an equally dashing nonagenarian husband) and she has never fully understood exactly what it was she did at the Park. With a coquettish giggle she concedes, 'Well, I was very young.'

She was not, however, as young as Muriel. Muriel Dindol (née Bogush) is sitting waiting for me in Starbucks. She has been waiting for some time, thanks to London's notoriously unreliable Northern Line. When I finally arrive I don't recognise her. I am looking for someone very old – silver haired and perhaps a little unsure in such a noisy place. But the woman with her eye on the

---

1. Women's Royal Naval Service.

door is alert and confident; she has cropped speckled hair and brightly coloured glasses with nails to match.

'Muriel?'

She looks up and smiles and then we hug.

Before I even met her, I knew that Muriel was a find. It was Ruth's Jewish heritage that alerted me to a circle within a Bletchley circle. Historian Martin Sugarman believes there were at least two hundred Jews at the Park, possibly more. He interviewed Muriel years ago and wasn't sure I would get much more out of her. When I mention this, Muriel laughs.

'I can tell you lots of things. I loved Bletchley. But I didn't start work in the actual Park until I was fourteen.'

'Fourteen?'

'Yep, that's when I left school. It was different in those days.'

At a spritely eighty-six, Muriel is the youngest Bletchley Girl.

Now I had eleven women: Ruth, Rozanne, Gwen, Charlotte, Pamela, Joanna, Ann, Betty, Pat, Cora and Muriel (I still hadn't heard from Lady Jean). I might have left it there but something caught my eye in Rozanne's typed reminiscences. 'About two months after arriving in the Park I met a WAAF called Kathleen Godfrey . . . [She is] frequently contacted by the Park because her father's P.A. was Ian Fleming, author of the James Bond books.' According to her daughter Margy, Kathleen Kinmonth Warren (née Godfrey) often handles questions about her father, Admiral John Godfrey, and his working relationship with Ian Fleming. By all accounts M was modelled on Kathleen's intimidating father. Both Godfrey and Fleming were associated with Park life through their roles in Naval Intelligence.

Margy shrugs. 'But it is a bit of a side show. It isn't about my mother.'

Kathleen smiles, and her pale blue eyes light up. Now ninety-one years old it was a long time ago, but wartime Britain still stands tall among her memories. Margy slides a scarlet book across the table. 'Here, borrow this. My mother wrote it ten years ago.'

Shared Lives is a rich personal account of Kathleen's long life; it is her story written in her own voice. Ian Fleming merits just one mention. By writing it all down, Kathleen has made sure she is now the one who is unforgettable.

Having started my search afraid that I wouldn't find sufficient women to sustain a book, I was suddenly in the unexpected position of worrying that I had too many. *No more*, I thought, and then rang one last number.

Doris Moss (née Moller) is an unlikely Bletchley Girl and therein lies her appeal. She began the war in Belgium with a poor grasp of the English language. Today, nurturing a demanding bridge habit and working tirelessly for a local charity aged ninety-two, Doris cuts an energetic figure in her home town of Northampton. In a strong French accent she recalls her epic wartime journey to Britain.

She is my thirteenth veteran but there is no time for superstition. 'Yes! Georgette is still with us! She lives in Texas, I will give you her number. She remembers better than me. Really!'

It just so happens that Doris has an older sister, they worked together at the Park and, aged ninety-four, Georgette McGarrah (née Moller) still loves to talk on the telephone. I had found my fourteenth Bletchley Girl and was ready to write.

It is April 2014 and I should really have started the book. I want it to be finished while all the 'Bletchley Girls' are still alive. Three months into the project and we're in regular communication, they are my newest (and oldest!) friends and I'm keen for them to enjoy the final product. 'I'll try and hold on that long,' says Muriel, staring at the 2015 publication date before giving me a reassuring wink. The seventieth anniversary of the end of the Second World War in 2015 is an additional impetus. But I am not at my desk and I have not started writing. It's Easter week and I'm on a ferry heading for the Isle of Arran clutching a microphone and a homemade cottage pie. If I look to my right across the water I can see Brodick Castle looming above the trees; it was Lady Jean's favourite childhood home. After considerable feudal networking, she has finally granted me an audience. The beginning of the book will have to wait.

1

Children of the Armistice

Pamela was the product of her mother's direct line to God. Dolly had asked for her young husband to be wounded in the left leg during the Great War and her prayers were answered. Thornly returned to England with an injured thigh that, as Dolly had anticipated, removed him from front-line service. The angel of death wreaked havoc among Europe's young men for another two years but Thornly had been saved. Baby Pamela arrived a year later in 1917 – living proof of her father's full recovery.

Despite her protests to the contrary, it is not hard to imagine the striking young woman Pamela once was. At ninety-six she retains an ethereal beauty: startling blue eyes, sculpted features and elegant poise, all wrapped in soft wools and silk. Meeting her for the first time in the 1950s, Pamela's little nephew Adam thought she had fallen off the front of a chocolate box. She jokes that her parents sent their rotund teenage daughter off to Europe one summer in the hope she would return slim and pretty; they can't have been disappointed.

Born into the English Establishment before women were granted a vote, looks mattered for girls like Pamela. But nothing could compete with being a boy. She admits with a chuckle, 'I always knew my brother was the favourite.' The painful hole left by the 722,785 young men who, unlike Pamela's 'blessed' father, never returned from the Great War ensured that in the 1920s a little boy's stock had rarely been higher.

Pamela's parents were not a conventional upper-class Edwardian couple. In the Gibson household music was the governing force. When her father Thornly thought of Germany it was opera that sprung to mind, not Prussian might. He duly abandoned his studies at Oxford to cut his teeth as a professional singer in Berne where his wife-to-be fell in love with his easy-going manner and baritone voice. They married in 1913. Dolly was the quintessential English woman who, as befitted her class, enjoyed artistic pursuits on the Continent. The fact that her father had been a German Jew was rarely mentioned. Since 1890 all restrictions for positions within the British Empire had been removed for Jews,[1] but the whiff of anti-Semitism among the British upper classes would take much longer to disperse. Dolly was simply trying to fit in. And she succeeded. Thornly used his German to translate for Prime Minister Lloyd George at Versailles before he got a sensible job back in England as a stockbroker, ensuring there was time and money for husband and wife to pursue their passion for opera. Pamela remembers musical evenings every Wednesday; a heady mix of professionals and amateurs in front of whom she and her brother, Patrick, occasionally had to perform. It was a privileged, artistic start to life and, just as her mother wished, she grew up every bit a little English girl – albeit with a sprinkling of German.

As an adult, Pamela once danced with the writer and broadcaster J. B. Priestley, 'both being rather small we nearly fell over!' The voice of a generation, he openly coveted the title 'little Englander', noting 'that little sounds the right note of affection. It is little England that I love.'

Pamela sheds light on an expression that has subsequently been associated with bigoted parochialism. 'You see, just after the war people wanted to get back to the safe and familiar, to what they knew and a land they had dreamed of.' Reeling from the protracted horrors of 1914–18, beset with a series of recurrent economic crises and an exhausted, over-stretched empire, Britain's imperial diet of militaristic heroism and tub-thumping had gone right out of fashion. National sentiment changed; there was no place for Victorian bombast in 1920s England.

1. Except that of Monarch.

Unlike the other women featured in this book, Pamela was not a child of the Armistice – she was born during the First World War. But like them, she grew up in a country that struggled to articulate its grief; instead shell-shocked Britain resorted to an annual silence that stopped the empire. Telephone operators, traffic, department stores – everything came to a halt for two minutes once a year on 11 November. Only the children, tight buds of hope, were unable to remember the horror that could never be allowed to happen again. World war must be avoided at all costs.

It was fitting that avuncular pipe-smoking Stanley Baldwin became Prime Minister in 1924 and again in 1926. He helped ensure the nation's swingeing military retrenchment was sugar-coated with a more private, domestic vision of Englishness. In 1926 Baldwin appealed to his St George's Day audience with a pastoral idyll. 'The tinkle of the anvil in the country smithy, the corncrake on a dewy morning, the sight of a plough team coming over the brow of a hill.' Here was a country stripped of all pretension; the perfect place for little English girls to grow up in.

Country Girls

Baldwin's vision of a timeless England chimes perfectly with the picture Charlotte paints of her 1920s childhood. The centre of her universe was a three-acre grassy smallholding sandwiched between the undulating peaks of Herefordshire. In fine summer weather she would take her bed outside and gaze at the stars, dreaming of infinity and beyond. Visitors to the family home may have been startled by a small dark-haired girl hanging by her knees from a tree. The Vine-Stevens ('neither rich nor poor') expected Charlotte to pull her weight; she got up early to tend the pigs, goats and poultry. There was no electricity and no running water and Charlotte's father was away all day in Ludlow where he worked for Lloyds Bank.

In her ninety-second year, Charlotte is still in remarkably good health. A strong sturdy child, she suited the great outdoors, but her little brother wasn't so lucky. Baby David was born disabled into a way of life that demanded robust physical health, miles from any medical help. He died when Charlotte was just four.

'That's my earliest memory – my grandmother coming down the path to meet me. "Where is David?" I asked. I was told to "ssshh!"'

The subject was never mentioned again. To this day Charlotte isn't entirely sure why her brother died. 'You didn't talk about those sorts of things and children didn't ask questions.'

The sentiment behind Charlotte's words is precisely echoed by Betty, born a year later, on George V's birthday.

Her mother Gracie was pregnant with Betty when her husband left. 'He went AWOL. Let's put it like that.' Betty thinks her father was called Albert. He was a policeman in London but she never met him and ninety years on she still doesn't know what happened. 'To say there was another woman would be speculation.' Albert's disappearance left Betty's mother in dire straits; pregnant and with four teenage children, no job, no home and no man she went back to live with her old father in rural Northamptonshire. Gracie took in washing and went out cleaning in the market town of Higham Ferrers where Betty still lives, to supplement the little bits of money her older children were able to earn. Minus their main breadwinner, the Quinceys were dirt poor. 'It was a tough life. Very tough.' But despite the hardship, Betty's father was never mentioned.

Nobody talked about him. 'Oh no, we didn't do that, not ever.' Little Betty grew up in a household with secrets and like Charlotte she knew better than to ask questions. Both girls were schooled in the art of discretion from a very early age.

———— ◆ ————

Charlotte and Betty's families, like much of rural Britain, knew their place in the feudal pecking order. The Vine-Stevens were positioned midway between the Lord of the Manor and the humble cottager. Charlotte remembers 'each class helped the rung below'. Her mother would provide hearty meals for local 'lads and lasses' who lent a hand. Meanwhile further down the social scale, Betty's mother relied on offers of piecemeal work and sustenance for her family's survival.

At the opposite end of society sat the aristocracy. Born in 1920, Lady Jean Graham's arrival was the cross-pollination of two mighty ducal houses – the Hamiltons and the Montroses. The family's lineage can be traced back to King James II[2] and their fiefdoms straddled two enormous Scottish estates, each with its own castle. Lady Jean remembers a lonely childhood; growing up, the only real playmates she had were her second cousins, the Prince of Monaco's children. Among other notable relatives was Germany's Margrave of Baden. So much for little England – this was glorious Scotland.

There was one castle for summer (Arran), and one for winter (Buchanan). Ninety-four years later, step off the ferry onto the Isle of Arran and any local will know her.

'Aye, Lady Jean. Take the short cut across the golf course. She's the born to rule sort, but ach she does a lot for us.'

As she herself explains, 'I was brought up to understand with privilege comes duty.'

A formidable presence in her exquisite drawing room, Arran's spring sunshine bouncing through the bay window, it is immediately clear that Lady Jean learnt much of her life philosophy from the Duchess of Montrose, her indomitable mother. During the First World War, Jean's severely deaf father was only permitted to command a minesweeper in the Clyde; however, the Duchess more than made up for her disabled husband. She threw herself into nursing, occasionally returning at weekends to oversee the staff who looked after her first three children and ran the castles. A hard worker, Jean's mother was soon promoted to

2. James II of England and Ireland and James VII of Scotland.

21

theatre nurse in a mainland hospital before riding straddle-legged (very daring) on a motorcycle to and from Arran's rehabilitation centre. But afterwards, duty done, the war was rarely talked of. Perhaps 'it was just too ghastly,' suggests Lady Jean, born two years later. There was, however, one exception.

> It nearly broke my mother's heart when the cavalry came at the beginning of the war and took away twenty-one of her heavy-weight hunters. All those lovely horses off to the front line never to be seen again. She did speak about that.

If few in Britain could boast a couple of ducal castles, Pat's family, the Owtrams, had made enough money from the cotton-spinning industry in the nineteenth century to fund a gentrified country existence in the north of England. 'My mother said we were squirarchy – one below aristocracy. I grew up in a big sandstone house near Lancaster; it had ten bedrooms including the attic and we had staff.'

Pat's early life was a far cry from her current existence in London's Chiswick. Just as Lady Jean was forced to hunt against her will on Arran, as a child Pat was obliged to beat during pheasant shoots and carry her father's dead game and rabbits. He was a good shot, as was her grandfather. Both men were military minded, but a broken hip ensured her grandfather never got further than the local militia. That did not stop him serving his country. In the First World War, Colonel Herbert Hawksworth Owtram's job was to find horses all over the North West and send them to the front.

Midway through her story, Pat's bright bird-like expression clouds briefly.

> My sister and I thought this was very sad. Horses were killed so fast they always needed replacements. Grandfather contacted farms and country houses and got their poor horses sent off to war. He was awarded an OBE for his services.

Evidently the Duchess of Montrose's sacrifice was a common one.

Pat's father ran the family textile business so had to make do with the Territorial Army in his spare time. He took his military duties very seriously. The Westminster elite could preach peace and retrenchment all they liked but for some the residual hatred of the Hun remained a motivating force in interwar Britain. With a mischievous smile, Pat admits a favourite childhood game was called 'bombing the Germans'.

'My father and uncles played too! Above the house there was a quarry full of old wheelbarrows and metal contraptions. The aim was to throw stones down – a direct hit would send up a tremendous clang.' Only the arrival of her cousin with a German governess in tow put a stop to the 'bombing antics'. Keen military fervour served with a hearty dollop of German xenophobia was not just saved for men in the Owtram household.

In Empire's Wake

In the 1920s, the ink long dried on the Treaty of Versailles, Britain left crippled Germany to its own devices. After all, we had an empire to run.

Kathleen was surely not the only English girl who could claim to be a world traveller by the age of three. (Her earliest childhood memory is watching an enormous crocodile sunning itself as she steamed through the Panama canal.) Great Britain's empire had never been bigger – 1.8 million square miles and 13 million new subjects were added to our imperial reach by the early 1920s. Our depleted Royal Navy had to keep up appearances. Talented young First World War veterans like Kathleen's father, John Godfrey, rose quickly through the ranks. A commander at the age of thirty-two, his career went on to span the globe and by 1925 his wife and family were travelling with him. Little Kathleen would have been forgiven for thinking imperial Britain was unassailable.

Born just days apart at opposite ends of the country, Rozanne was almost Kathleen's twin. While Kathleen's father climbed up the ranks of the Navy, Rozanne's father earned his stripes in the Air Force. The destiny of both families for the next thirty years would depend on their respective fathers' postings.

Relaxed in her 'pink elephant' (the affectionate family name for her large reclining armchair), Rozanne vividly remembers the few First World War stories her father Charles shared.

> They had the most extraordinary aeroplanes with no parachutes. Father was shot down and broke his arm. He always said he was lucky not to have been a soldier. He flew in low over the trenches and saw people stuck on the wire. He knew they couldn't survive.

Charles Medhurst was right, he was lucky. As an airman you were far less likely to die in the First World War than you were as a soldier. Within twenty-five years those statistics would be dramatically reversed; however, in 1918 when the RAF was formed no one anticipated another world war, least of all young Charles. In 1919 he was promoted to captain, by which time he'd already married his childhood sweetheart. Christabel was vivacious, savvy and very beautiful – she longed to leave home and sample the high life; marriage to Charles ensured she could do just that. Rozanne recalls her mother 'had a riot' when they were posted to Baghdad (one of Britain's more expensive First World War acquisitions). As was typical for a woman of her class, Christabel employed nannies to help bring up her three children. This was fortunate as she was 'pretty hopeless with small babies' and in the 1920s there was little incentive to be otherwise. At that time being a good mother meant keeping your distance; received wisdom stated that nannies did a better job of raising the next generation than over-emotional mothers. The influential behaviourist J. B. Watson went further, discouraging all cuddling and even suggesting parents should shake hands with their children in the mornings. Small wonder that amid the ranks of upper-middle-class mothers there was plenty of time for charitable works and frenetic social activities.

⚬

But if hands-off mothering was *de rigueur*, having no mother at all was a very different matter. Joanna Stradling's life was turned upside down before it had really begun. Her father was in the Middle East trying to persuade T. E. Lawrence to stay on after the war. It was a thankless task and Squadron Leader Dick Stradling, an archetypal Edwardian and adjutant to General Trenchard, had little success. 'Father loved a good story; later he told us that "Lawrence of Arabia" would keep bursting into tears.' Things went from bad to worse for Stradling when his wife and baby daughter joined him in Egypt. Joanna was just eighteen months old when her mother contracted typhoid fever and dysentery in Cairo and promptly died. Mad with grief, her father temporarily disappeared and Joanna was returned to England with whooping cough and no parents.

A warm, welcoming woman now in her ninetieth year, it is hard to imagine the trauma that accompanied Joanna's start to life. She was nursed back to health in Cirencester by her grandmother, who having lost a husband and daughter in the same year was determined to save her granddaughter.

Joanna was destined to be an only child, devoted to her nanny, her aunt and her grandmother. Dick Stradling remained out in the Middle East until 1930, returning just once in the interim to visit his small daughter. 'He put his head around my bedroom door and said "Cuckoo!" and I just screamed the house down.' Joanna's father would remain a distant but authoritarian figure in her life. He was a daunting prospect for one lone daughter to deal with.

Interwar Britain had witnessed political sea change. But a move away from 'high Toryism' and national glorification towards an idea of the British as a more private, inward-looking people did

25

not translate into an era of cosy, hands-on fathering. Kathleen probably speaks for many with the description of her high-powered naval father. His

old-fashioned upbringing certainly affected his views on children and their management. Being 'seen and not heard' was imposed on us all. Severe and strict, he insisted on a maze of rules of behaviour; a minefield would be a more accurate analogy, through which it was impossible to tread without incurring wrath and displeasure.

As head of the household, fathers were rarely crossed; respect and deference were expected. Little girls knew their place.

Members of the ruling class like John Godfrey and Charles Medhurst were dedicated professional servicemen who were expected to put duty before family. With a clear division of labour between the sexes, theirs was a public role outside the home. In John's case, there was little energy left for fun with the children. 'For my father, the Navy and his job came first . . . We were always meant to be quiet in the house in order "not to disturb Father", and we never went into his study unless – woe betide – we were summoned.'

However, there were exceptions to the patriarchal norm. Ann's father was not a military man; in 1921 Herbert Williamson retired from the Indian Civil Service and returned to work part-time at Oxford University with his new wife. Ann was born the following year. She remembers a gentle, forward-thinking man. There were Sunday tea parties and numerous visitors to the Williamsons' statuesque Victorian home. Such was the international hue of the family's frequent gatherings, the maid was required to practise the pronunciation of guests' names prior to their arrival. Back in 'little England', Herbert Williamson and his wife Winifred had quickly found their own educated cosmopolitan milieu. Ann, their oldest child, grew up believing the world was her oyster.

Keeping Up Appearances

At ninety Gwen is a tour de force; whether sitting in the kitchen or perilously tending her cliff-side garden in Mumbles she is both frank and ellusive.

> Families were small in the 1920s. What happened was Marie Stopes and her clinics. There was the Dutch Cap that married women could get fitted for free. And the widespread sale of condoms; they were sold secretly in chemists but you could get them!

Marie Stopes' highly controversial clinics targeted the working masses; the upper and middle classes had been limiting the size of their families since the late nineteenth century, with sheaths and coitus interruptus being the most common methods of contraception. But Gwen was not from middle-class stock. 'My grandmother had eight children and a stillbirth of twins. There was no bathroom and no hot water. It was a life of absolute drudgery. That was how it was in our end of West Bromwich, the poor end.' It was Gwen's father Alfred who pulled himself out of this grinding poverty. He studied hard to become a qualified welfare officer and by limiting the size of their family Alfred and his wife Harriet kept costs down and standards up. Gwen remained an only child until she was nine, by which time the Davies' had moved from West Bromwich to the comfortable middle-class town of Bournemouth.

It was in Bournemouth that Cora's father also improved his family's lot. Cecil Pounds developed his father's fledgling business and by the 1930s Charlie's Cars was a reputable luxury motor coach and car hire company. Cecil's timing was perfect; it had never been so in vogue to explore 'little England's' quiet coves and sandy shores but few could afford an automobile. (Ann's mother kept meticulous accounts of her weekly expenditure – in 1939 the largest single item purchased was a Rover for £115.) Even wealthy families thought twice before they bought a set of wheels and Cecil Pounds offered them a cost-effective alternative. 'We never saw father, only at breakfast. He worked every day except Christmas day.' Cecil's hard work paid off. The Pounds family moved into a comfortable two-storey town house with large bay windows, running water and a bathroom.

Between the wars two-thirds of families, including Cora's, had electricity and all sorts of novel mod-cons were emerging on the market for those with money. The Pounds couldn't afford a refrigerator, but by the mid-thirties, in keeping with the majority of British families, they did own a wireless. Across the classes it was the 'must-have' household accessory. Lady Jean's nanny was infatuated with her crystal radio set, although it did complicate family moves between castles.

Each part had to be padded with cotton wool and tissue paper, then placed in an oversized box. Wherever I moved in the nursery there would be a shout, 'Watch out, clumsy, watch out for my wireless!'

Wireless technology transformed the way Britain communicated in the first half of the twentieth century – at home, at work and at war. It was not as a means of military communication that the women of this book came across radio waves, but as a form of intimate mass entertainment. Up and down the country young imaginations were gripped.

Gwen vividly remembers her first encounter with the radio.

My uncle came with a huge pair of earphones and held them over my small ears and said, 'Can you hear anything?'

'What are they saying?'

'Hello everybody! This is Carroll Gibbons from the Savoy Hotel in London.'

'That man is talking hundreds of miles away!'

Five-year-old Gwen was mesmerised. So was the rest of the nation. Across the country families gathered around their wireless sets in the previously sacred space of their living-rooms and 'listened in' to evenings of live entertainment. The newly founded British Broadcasting Corporation conducted the nation's conversation – nothing was left to chance. Working closely with the Government, the BBC aimed to be a Great British unifying force. Cultural, educational and moral standards were set for the majority who could afford to listen to the radio.

Cora was only twelve in 1939. She was dusting her mother's dining-room when she discovered Britain was at war – she didn't need her parents to tell her, she had heard it on the wireless.

Multi-Cultural Britons

In 1919 a $25,000 prize was offered for the first non-stop flight between New York and Paris. Eight years later, American Charles Lindbergh touched down at Le Bourget Aerodrome in front of a vast crowd. He became an overnight celebrity. The world was shrinking, the aviation industry was growing and for Englishmen like John Moller – an aeroplane insurance salesman – life was good.

John had a beautiful Belgian wife Marie-Elisabeth, and three young children including Georgette, who was born in England in 1921, and Doris, born in Paris in 1922.

In her delicious French accent, Doris explains, 'My father was English but I grew up talking French.' Her early memories of life in France centre around a small privileged world of maids, siblings and nannies. 'We drained the glasses after our parents' parties and always asked for presents when they came home.' 1920s Paris sizzled: gaudy flappers, the bounce and jangle of the Charleston, art-deco clubs and casinos dripping with artistes, bohemians and writers, it had much to offer dashing young couples like John and Marie-Elisabeth Moller.

'But we went back to Belgium when I was ten.' Doris pauses. In her ninety-third year it is still difficult to explain. 'Well, I will tell you. My father went bankrupt. He made some bad business decisions. It put a strain on the marriage, yes, I would say so.' John Moller's career in aviation insurance did not survive the Great Depression; in the 1930s he returned to England and took his son, Peter, with him. Doris and her sister Georgette went to Belgium with their mother. The family was split in two, but the girls maintained contact with their father and occasionally they visited him in England on their British passports.

There were no British passports when Ruth's family arrived on Britain's shores in the late nineteenth century. Her paternal grandparents were en route to America, but they didn't get further than Dublin. Her mother's family ended up in Liverpool. Both were part of the 2.7-million-strong Jewish exodus west in the wake of Russian pogroms and atrocities. Between 1881 and 1914 Britain's small Jewish population grew to 250,000 and, propelled by the vitriol of a few publicists and politicians, immigration soon became a heated issue. In 1905 the 'Alien Act' set the precedent for a century of increased immigration controls; British passports were introduced in 1914.

Despite the hype, Britain's new Jewish population integrated quickly. Ruth's father Isaac Henry emerged from 'a pile of children' in Dublin to become a successful doctor in Birmingham and his daughter Ruth grew up feeling every bit a little British girl.

> I felt terribly lucky my grandparents came here. I once asked my grandfather to teach me Russian and he said, 'I won't speak that language; horrible people, horrible people. I want to forget them.'

Unlike the vast majority of people in Britain, Ruth's family understood what it meant to be persecuted.

Muriel's father also arrived in Britain on a boat from Russia. 'He always spoke English with an accent. His brother gave him a box of handkerchiefs to sell; all he could say was "a penny each, a penny each".' Mr Bogush eventually married and settled among the large Jewish community in London's Stamford Hill.

Muriel was born in 1928. Recalling her childhood, she says, 'I don't remember much. Just the usual stuff: I had a whip and a top and I loved my doll and pram – I was really girlie.' As if to underline her point she glances down at her scarlet lacquered nails. 'Oh yes, and I was always annoying my big sister. That's about it, I think.' Muriel grins broadly before admitting that, for her, life really began in 1939, when the family moved to a small village in Buckinghamshire called Bletchley.

2

Educating Girls

Mum,' I said, 'I've passed all my scholarship exams to go to grammar school but I don't wanna go 'cos I know you can't afford it.'

Even at the age of eleven little Betty was a realist. Locked into a life of poverty, with an absentee father and a mother who struggled to make ends meet, Betty knew she was destined for the local shoe factory in Northamptonshire. By the 1920s education was compulsory until the age of fourteen, when the vast majority of working-class girls left school and entered a factory or domestic service until they got married. Although her daughter had won a scholarship, Betty's mother couldn't afford the uniform a smart grammar school would require, and more importantly, Betty was expected to get a job and contribute to the family's modest income.

'No one ever mentioned another word 'bout education after that. But I think perhaps deep down I would've loved to've gone to a grammar school.'

Betty was a highly intelligent girl. She stood out in her overcrowded council school and invariably came top of the class. 'I loved maths, and writing stories. I never got smacked or anything because I behaved. Most of the teachers had canes hanging on the cupboard door and they used them, but not on me!'

Nearly eighty years after her education ended, it is clear from talking to Betty that no matter how brief and elementary her schooling, it had provided an escape from a life of chores and hardship at home. In 1938, aged fourteen, she duly left school and got a job sewing together the leather uppers in shoes. She was paid 11 shillings a week. Had it not been for the outbreak of war the following year, it's likely Betty's intellectual abilities would have remained unrecognised for the rest of her life.

Betty was clever but like most girls of her generation received minimal, state-funded schooling. Only one other woman featured here, Muriel, falls into that category. All the rest received a private education (of sorts). Between the wars there were increasing numbers of impressive girls' schools and for some middle-class families a good academic education for their daughter was important. For others, artistic accomplishments and domestic skills took priority. When it came to educating girls, there was little uniformity. Unbeknown to teachers, politicians and parents of the 1930s, it was from this hotchpotch of standards and accomplishments that the nation would very shortly have to search for a female workforce crucial to its survival.

The Finest Schools in England

In 1920, Katherine's mother, Margaret Godfrey, began her university life aged nineteen at Girton Ladies College, Cambridge. However, within a year she had given up her studies and married John, a naval commander thirteen years her senior.

Writing decades later, Kathleen was struck by her mother's decision. 'To us this seems a terrible sacrifice to have made, but women at that time stood very little chance of marrying as so many thousands of men had been killed in the war.' It is true that in 1920s Britain there was a surfeit of females – unhelpful headlines screamed about the 'Problem of the Surplus Women – Two million who can Never Become Wives . . .' But having decided to exit Cambridge early and get married, Margaret was not giving up as much as Kathleen imagined. As a woman her career prospects were extremely limited. In the 1920s, 80 per cent of female graduates from Oxford and Cambridge became teachers. Margaret became an officer's wife and travelled the world instead of ending up a spinster in the classroom. To her daughter

Kathleen's generation the message was clear: no matter how bright you were, a good marriage was more important than a good education.

However, the paucity of job opportunities available to educated women had an upside. It meant there were plenty of outstanding teachers available to pass on their learning to the next generation of girls.

Gwen is in no doubt that it was these women who transformed her life.

> I cannot thank God enough for my education at Talbot Heath School for Girls; it has been the foundation of my life and the mistresses were wonderful people. My favourite teacher was Dorothy Rowe, a great friend of Dorothy Sayers. And I was taught Latin by Miss Wingate, Major-General Wingate's sister.

Lest there was any doubt as to how important she considered her schooling, Gwen, aged ninety, gamely climbs the stairs with a gammy leg to find Talbot Heath's centenary prospectus.

During the 1920s and 1930s it had become increasingly fashionable for middle-class girls to go to private boarding schools. One of six from her local council school to clinch a scholarship to Talbot Heath, Gwen quickly adapted to life in this prestigious institution. She ironed away her West Bromwich accent and was soon reading literature from countries that she could never have dreamt of visiting on her father's modest Welfare Officer's salary. 'I was a quick learner, I knew the alphabet backwards very early. I had a wonderful French teacher who taught me French and a German teacher.' Gwen's French was far stronger than her German, which she didn't enjoy speaking and was put off learning by the increasingly ugly noises coming from the Continent. However, at Talbot Heath it was considered part of an educated girl's repertoire to have read the poetry and lyrics of Goethe, Schiller and Müller. And so read it she did.

Locally Talbot Heath was a benchmark for high educational

and social standards. For Cora Pounds, another Bournemouth girl, it was her preferred choice. Her father, proud owner of Charlie's Cars, was happy to pay.

Cora is candid about her academic ability. 'I couldn't remember things so I failed my School Certificate and had to retake it. I will never forget going in to see the headmistress and her sighing with relief. She announced, "Cora, you've passed!"' According to Gwen some girls were not allowed to enter their School Certificate at all. 'Miss Stocks would say to outraged parents, "Of course you are at liberty to enter your daughter at any other examination centre, but I cannot allow her to be entered at Talbot Heath."'

Aged seventeen, Cora and Gwen didn't just have their School Certificates, they also had the reputation of Talbot Heath behind them. In the chaos of war it was to prove a valuable currency.

A rise in the number of girls' private schools between the wars reflected the aspirations of the middle classes, who were hoping to give their daughters the best start in life. But this increased emphasis on schooling is not indicative of better opportunities for women elsewhere. From the late nineteenth century, marriage bars banned spouses from numerous professions; for all except the very poor, work remained a transitory experience and the economic depression of the 1930s was a sober reminder that there weren't enough jobs for men, let alone women.

Ruth, an outstanding pupil in her Welsh county school, explains the situation in one succinct sentence: 'It was thought the better educated you were, the better educated the husband you would get.'

But for most women that education did not stretch to university. Even Gwen, who is adamant she would have gone to Oxford ('most likely on a scholarship') had it not been for the war, admits that her father 'probably thought what on earth does a woman want to go to college for?' Others were more forthright. Joanna Chorley's overbearing father, back from the Middle East, spent hours selecting appropriate boarding schools for his only daughter but would not countenance the idea of her going to university. His attitude was clear: 'University for a girl is a waste of money.' Joanna begrudgingly went to domestic science college. Pat's family had a comfortable country seat in Lancashire but apparently there wasn't enough money for their daughter's further education.

> My father explained to my sister and me that my younger brother Bob was to go to Christ Church, Oxford and because it was an expensive college there was no possibility that we could go to university. We could choose between a secretarial course or a domestic science one.

In the end Pat's head teacher argued so hard for her to go to Oxford she might have won, had it not been for the war.

Only one woman in this book made it to university before 1945. The rest would all be selected to work in Britain's giant code-breaking mission without a degree between them.

Ann was the exception.

> As a schoolgirl in the late 1930s, I wanted to specialise in maths. But my headmistress firmly told my parents that mathematics was not a ladylike subject. She herself taught chemistry, which was surely even less ladylike. However, my parents overruled her and I pursued my chosen path.

Ann was passionate about sums and problem-solving but Headington School for Girls (another stellar private girls' school) didn't believe she was talented enough to get into Oxford. Ann proved them wrong and the teacher in question was so embarrassed she hid behind a coat in the school cloakroom.

Even today Ann sees nothing exceptional in her achievement. 'My parents belonged to the Oxford set, I never considered anything but to go to university. I don't remember being aware of the gender issue.'

In 1940 Ann was one of five girls who went to Oxford to study maths, although in her case she simply cycled across town and took up residence in Lady Margaret Hall, one of the University's five female colleges. Ann was on an academic mission – the war would have to wait for her.

The Perfect Woman

If anything, the higher up the social scale the more cavalier the attitude seems to have been towards formal learning for girls. With her father's rapid rise in the Navy, Kathleen's family life (and her education) were dictated by John Godfrey's career. There were seven schools before the age of ten, until she finally settled down as the only day girl in West Heath, a local boarding school. 'The teaching was fearfully uneven, and there was never any thought of a university education for me afterwards. A typical Service upbringing you might say.'

Rozanne Colchester, also a daughter of a serviceman, concedes with a wry smile, 'I wasn't educated very much. In the RAF we were always moving; I went to six schools before I was eleven.'

But what these girls lacked in terms of formal schooling they made up for in other areas; after all, as Jane Austen made so apparent a century earlier, a real lady needed accomplishments. A passion for music and performance, instilled from an early age, was a prominent feature of many of the girls' lives. For Kathleen it was a love inspired by a crush on her music master whose spats and pungent hair cream didn't put her off hitting the highest notes. Even Charlotte, born out in the sticks in Herefordshire and educated at home, was blessed with a musical mother who taught her piano and violin. And there was no question that Pam would be musical; she was the progeny of a talented pair of opera singers who shared musical soirées with John Christie, the man who later founded Glyndebourne Opera House. Performance was in her DNA, elocution lessons were the highlight of her school days and today, aged ninety-six, Pam remains adamant: 'I always wanted to be an actress.'

'I've lived by the skin of my teeth and taking chances at village dances.' This catchy formula, from one of Bletchley Park's most famous female veterans, Baroness Trumpington, speaks volumes. The optimistic 1920s had thrown up a frenzy of new moves and silhouetted shapes, and if by the imperilled 1930s hemlines were back in check, dancing remained a social must. Ballroom dancing – traditional foxtrots and waltzes – was the mainstay in most young girls' repertoires, although in Lady Jean Graham's case an Eightsome Reel, the Gay Gordons and a host of other Scottish dances can be added to that list. (At six foot tall she must have been a formidable sight, but she is quite clear about her ability: 'I was very quick on my feet, I was a good dancer.')

Rozanne danced at every opportunity and she throws her arms out wide to emphasise this point. 'I loved to dance!'

And for Pat, lessons were an integral part of her childhood.

All the local squirarchy children went to dancing classes. There was a class in a neighbouring country house owned by the Fitzherbert Brockholes. They were very posh, they had a ballroom for dancing and someone to wind the clocks.

To underline the class element behind these accomplishments, it is telling that Betty, destined for a shoe factory in Northamptonshire, never learnt to dance, nor could she sing. When she wasn't doing chores, Betty made daisy chains and ran free in Northamptonshire's fields. But for almost all the other girls a firm grounding in classical entertainments and performance was an essential part of a privileged upbringing.

A highlight from Ann's Oxford University days was the annual college dance at Lady Margaret Hall. Her diary entry the day after the event in May 1943 underlines just how important the actual dancing was: 'frustrated. Nothing went wrong but I didn't get the partners I wanted, and my own partner couldn't dance well enough.' Having two left feet was an unforgivable social *faux pas*.

It was not only on the dance floor that one's abilities could be hit-and-miss. By her own account, Lady Jean's private education was fairly idiosyncratic. Ironically her ad-hoc curriculum 'invented' by a devoted nanny and several governesses was not entirely dissimilar to the sort of things Betty would have learnt in her council school. Both posh girls and poor girls were taught conventional domestic skills. There was knitting and sewing at the lower end of the social scale while Lady Jean recalls lace-making, crochet and smocking. Although for Betty these were vital survival skills and for Lady Jean artistic pastimes, the broader aim of preparing a girl for married life cut across the classes.

'I suppose after education one automatically thought one was going to marry someone in the same situation. Yes I think that is it really and I wasn't a keen scholar.'

Lady Jean wasn't given the chance to be a keen scholar, nor was she properly equipped to mix with her peers. Tucked away in a world of Highland aristocrats, governesses and gamekeepers, by the time she was sent to boarding school aged fifteen she believed she was too old to learn how to enjoy it.

But despite her sheltered upbringing, as the daughter of the sixth Duke of Montrose Lady Jean was expected to make a good fist of 'coming out'. Her first London season was in 1939. Pamela was also a debutante (albeit a reluctant one). For both women the experience was a mixed bag. According to Lady Jean, 'I did not know enough young people to really look forward to the parties, being as gauche as I was. I was allowed no make-up, no smoking and no drinking.' She was not even at liberty to choose her own dress, although she did finally persuade her mother that the lesser of all available evils was smoking and was thus permitted a discreet puff or two. By the end of the summer Lady Jean had made a few friends but not found a husband. She recalls that just before the war, men were already at a premium. Her destiny to become a high-society wife would have to wait.

Three years earlier Pam had tolerated her first season for the sake of her parents. 'The express purpose was to find a man. Yes that was the entire point. But I didn't terribly want a man because I wanted to become an actress.' She didn't even stay long enough to meet the new King, Edward VIII, let alone find a husband; instead she left London early to cycle around France. Visiting the Continent, especially France and Germany, was the done thing for girls like Pam. Little did she realise at the time that it was the linguistic accomplishments honed during these excursions, not a society husband, which would jeopardise her budding career as an actress.

Broadening One's Horizons

'I don't think I was political at all. I was terribly unaware about what was going on. I was brought up quite unaware of the Jewish question. I must have been a very stupid child.'

Start a conversation with ninety-six-year-old Pamela and it is immediately apparent that she could never have been stupid. Far from it. So why, when she stayed with family friends in Munich (home of the Nazi Party's Brown House headquarters), did she fail to notice the gravity of Germany's political situation? Like many British people in the interwar period, eighteen-year-old Pamela was predisposed to admire the country, not look for its faults. Fuelled by a growing belief that Germany had been mistreated at Versailles after the First World War, Britain quickly reconnected with its Germanophile tradition. Personal and cultural relationships were soon re-established and Pamela, with several German relations, was well placed to follow suit.

After 1933 any concern about the rise of fascism was tempered with a belief that no-nonsense German bureaucrats would soon bring the Nazis to their senses. Along with a handful of other upper-class English girls, Pamela was simply there to enjoy Germany's musical and theatrical opportunities and improve her language skills. Like her father before her, she was not disappointed. She absorbed all Munich's art scene had to offer and even turned the head of a very grand German, Count Karl Erdmann Henckel von Donnersmarck. But nothing, not even a dashing German aristocrat, could put Pamela off her ambition to be on the stage. She returned to London and enrolled at the Webber Douglas Theatre school, Germany temporarily forgotten.

Kathleen also went back and forth to the Continent. The memories are now somewhat faded but she does recall her stay with the von Richter family near Frankfurt as 'a rather good period just before the war'. She went to a riding school and made a lifelong friend, Maus Bienzele. Like Pamela she remembers no conversation of any sort about the political situation. Thinking back, her pale blue eyes suddenly look anxious – 'If you think of it now I would never have sent my children to Germany!' But in the late 1930s, even at government level, Britain didn't want to believe the horrors our European kinsmen were already committing. Between the wars, the Secret Intelligence Service (SIS) was focused on the threat of Bolshevism; the decryption of messages between Soviet leaders took priority over communications between German fascists. Above all else we didn't want another war, so why not send our daughters off to Germany to help maintain friendship and cultural understanding? People tend to see what they want to see and Pamela and Kathleen's experiences testify there was ample evidence of German kindness at an individual level. Ironically the hospitality the girls received from their hosts would ensure they were better prepared for war than their own government. Unlike Britain's leading politicians, at least Pamela and Kathleen could speak German.

It wasn't just the British elite who enjoyed sojourns in Germany. Charlotte's mother had been a music teacher there when the First World War broke out; stuck as a foreign national in a hostile country with scarcely a word of German, she made it her business to ensure her daughters grew up with the language skills she lacked. Their home education in Herefordshire was supplemented by a German *au pair* and, despite her father's anxiety about the idea, in

1937 at the age of fourteen Charlotte was sent to Saxony on an exchange visit. Her host family, the Pauls, were a humble, deeply religious family who lived in a flat near the Czechoslovakian border. Charlotte clearly remembers a shortage of butter (to rearm at breakneck speed Hitler opted for guns not butter and ordinary people like the Pauls felt the pinch). She overheard snippets of tense conversation she couldn't fully understand but she picked up on her hosts' general anxiety. It must have been difficult for such devout members of the Moravian community that their daughters were obliged to attend Hitler Youth meetings. Charlotte went to the local school for a term with the Pauls' daughter Elizabeth.

'In class we all had to salute the Führer. I waved my arm about to be diplomatic but I didn't say "Heil Hitler". I had a hunch something was up.' Charlotte pauses briefly and stares at the spring flowers bobbing beyond the window, then she adds, 'It's hard to imagine that I was there then.'

Britons carried on being friends with Germans but as the situation became more precarious in Europe it was increasingly difficult to ignore Hitler and his regime. If his 'rants' weren't always taken seriously, his aggressive foreign policy and rapid rearmament were harder to ignore. All eyes and ears were on the German Chancellor. Like the women in this book, Lady Margaret Stirling-Aird worked at Bletchley Park during the war (where she met her childhood friend, Lady Jean). Now well into her nineties, Margaret's story is not featured here because illness has severely depleted her memory. However her daughter confirmed that as a young girl in 1939 Margaret went to finishing school in Germany and still has recollections from that time.

'I remember being very sad because we went to war with them. I loved the place and the people. I remember seeing Hitler go by, standing up in a car.' Even Alzheimer's could not erase the impact of seeing the Führer, nor Margaret's love for a country that was about to become the enemy.

'I had never been abroad before; we went on a train. It was a terrific adventure – the wonderful mountains at night and waking up in the morning having arrived in Rome!'

In 1937 Rozanne's family moved to Italy where Charles Medhurst was the British Air Attaché; his mission was to find out what he could about the Italians rearming. At the tender age of fifteen Rozanne began a new life in the fascist capital. She was soon familiar with Mussolini; on their way to school, all legs and smiles, she and her sister walked past his Villa Torlonia. 'He used to come out at a certain time, just when we were going to school, and wave at us.' With a chuckle Rozanne explains that Mussolini was very fond of girls.

Rozanne loved her time in Italy; the weather, the language and the people. Even the Duce – or Musso, as Rozanne refers to him – had a comical quality.

> He was rather a figure of fun; he took himself very seriously. He would put on a face, throw out his jaw and march about, which was ridiculous. It was ridiculous that the Italians tried to copy Hitler. Middle-aged fat men full of spaghetti trying to do the goose step at the head of their troops. It was the funniest thing!

Then, mid-story, Rozanne pauses, because even at the time she was aware that it wasn't that simple. 'You see there were two levels. There was a terrible tension. You knew what was going on, the Italians were very suspicious of their leader. In the background people were being bumped off.'

One day, walking through Rome's Borgias Gardens, Rozanne and her sister came across a man slumped against a tree. He had been badly beaten; his leg was smashed to pieces. 'A lorry suddenly drove up and three men in fascist uniforms got out. They simply picked him up as if he were a dog – no you wouldn't even treat a dog like that – and they flung him in the van.' The men left the girls with strict instructions. '*Forget what you have seen*. But how could we possibly forget? Something terrible had happened.'

Rozanne's family were in Rome until 1940. Her father desperately urged the British Government to speed up rearmament; fascist Italy was heading in one direction and the Medhurst family were in the thick of it. What came next even seems to surprise Rozanne: 'I met Hitler. I shook his hand.' As a family member of the British diplomatic mission, sixteen-year-old Rozanne was there, waiting on the platform, when in May 1938 Hitler and his retinue of 500 Nazis arrived to woo the Duce. 'There was not a great deal of time to look at him but we did because we had been reading a lot about him in the press.' She closes her eyes briefly to get a better view from all those years ago and when she speaks again her recall is precise. 'He looked much more normal in the flesh. I imagined a Charlie Chaplin-type figure with a black moustache but was amazed to see he was on the blond side!' The sandy tones in the Führer's hair didn't show up in black and white photography. But above all else what stood out for Rozanne were Hitler's eyes. 'I remember his eyes very vividly, they were grey-blue. There was something about his eyes, they looked slightly fanatical.' Mussolini arrived minutes later and the military parade began; the moment had passed.

The following year Italy signed the Pact of Steel with Germany and by 1940 young Rozanne had returned to England, fluent in Italian and capable of differentiating between the Italian people whom she loved and the fascists she would soon be fighting.

Storytelling

On 27 September 1938, Prime Minister Neville Chamberlain addressed the nation by radio:

> How horrible, fantastic, incredible it is that we should be digging trenches and trying on gas masks here, because of a quarrel in a far-off country between a people of whom we know nothing.

Days later, on 30 September 1938, he signed an agreement with Hitler in Munich. Lady Jean remembers the news being received in the Grand Hotel at Charing Cross.

> John Bannerman came into the lounge waving the latest edition of the evening papers showing photographs of Mr Chamberlain arriving back in Britain by air, and large headlines saying 'PEACE IN OUR TIME'. A tremendous cheer went up and there was a completely different tempo in the crowd. Life was great and even Chamberlain had toasts drunk to him.

People still longed for peace, but most realists were taking precautions.

That same year Lady Jean was approached by the family secretary, Miss Merry-Motson (soon to become 'frightfully high up' in the WRNS), to join the newly formed Women's Royal Naval Service, but her parents were not keen. It was the first time the mention of war had entered their house.

Today, with a tinge of regret, Lady Jean still wonders what might have happened had she taken Miss Merry-Motson up on her offer.

It is well known that the Nazi machine swallowed Austria, then Czechoslovakia, while Britain prevaricated. But what is perhaps less well known (and more uncomfortable) is that in the 1930s we were slow to respond to the atrocities being committed against the Jews. Up and down the country people turned a blind eye, but for some families the scary truth was impossible to ignore.

'I was very deeply aware, very deeply of what was happening in Germany.'

In the mid-1930s Ruth found a small rust-coloured book in her father's library – *The Brown Book of the Hitler Terror*. The shocking pages made such an impression on its young Jewish reader that Ruth's recall of its contents nearly eighty years later is almost perfect. 'The book showed a picture of the back of a woman with her buttocks bruised and it said underneath – "this is the way they question women".' That grainy image can be found today in the same book held in the British Library. It is haunting to think of a child taking on board the horrors recorded by a Relief Committee. 'My father had a lot of books I was not supposed to read, but I did, I was a good reader. I read this when I was about nine or ten. And I remember articles in the *Jewish Chronicle*.' While most of Britain was trying hard to pretend everything was going to be all right, Ruth's family were reading regular reports of brutality in fascist Germany. 'So we were aware, certainly I was incredibly aware of what would happen if the Nazis got over here.'

Little Ruth was steeled for trouble long before war was declared.

***

Britain's reaction to the arrival of Jewish refugees was mixed. There were examples of ambivalence and outright hostility but there was also much sympathy and kindness. Citizens of the world, the Williamsons found space in their large, forward-thinking Oxford household for a Jewish schoolgirl. In May 1939, Ellen Feis, a refugee from Hamburg, arrived at short notice with a lot of luggage, including her bedroom furniture. For a year she went to school with Ann. By now, German horror stories were unavoidable; Ellen never saw her mother again.

Pre-eminent among those leading the charge in Britain to save the Jews was Bishop Bell of Chichester. It just so happened he was also governor of Joanna's boarding school. 'The Bishop was instrumental in getting children on the Kindertransport. St Mary's Hall took a lot of Jewish émigrés.'

But perhaps it was Pat in her parents' northern country pile who was most affected by the arrival of Jews from Europe. 'My grandfather couldn't get English cooks and maids in the late 1930s. They didn't want to come to Lancashire so an agency in London found refugee Jewish women who were willing to work.' Before their arrival in 1938, Colonel Owtram gave his granddaughter a series of small brown manila labels – 'These Austrian people are not going to know which are the drinking taps!' Pat duly found her Uncle Tom's German dictionary, looked up the black-letter print and wrote out *wasser für trinken* – drinking water – on each tag. It was her first contact with the German language.

When Lilly Getzl arrived from Vienna she spoke no English, so Pat, as the only family member in possession of a few words of German, was called upon to help. It was through Lilly that Pat's eyes were opened to a whole other world. 'She used to talk about her life in Vienna, the Philharmonic Orchestra and glamorous fur-clad evenings. She thought Lancashire was very dull, damp and dreary.' Lilly confided in Pat; she had come into the country on her sister's passport, pretending her young nephew was her own son and lying about a husband who was a doctor when in fact she wasn't married. Only one in ten Jews who sought asylum in Britain were granted entry – Lilly had taken no chances. And thanks to the stories she told during those long evenings in Lancashire, teenage Pat learnt a whole new language.

Even now, looking back on a remarkable, fulfilled nine decades, Pat still cites her grandfather's command to write instructive labels in German as the pivotal moment in her life.

3

There's a War On

Rozanne was on holiday in Berne when she heard that Britain had declared war on Germany. She was drinking *apfelsaft* and listening to the radio; 3 September 1939 was a gorgeously hot day. She remembers 'an incredible feeling. A mixture – a feeling of excitement and worry as to what was going to happen and sadness at having to leave our Italian friends.' Rozanne's instincts were right: she did have to say goodbye to her friends (by June 1940 Italy was fighting with Germany) and what happened next was exciting.

Rozanne has never forgotten her journey back to England, aged seventeen. She stayed the night in blacked-out France and watched *Goodbye, Mr. Chips* in the cinema. It was the film of the moment – Robert Donat delivering an Oscar-winning victory for timeless England and her stoic people. Surely there was no better morale-boosting formula prior to the Medhursts' departure across the channel?

> The next day we got the ferry, it was extraordinary, the soldier standing guard at the front seemed quite different from when we had come over. There was a wartime feeling. One wondered if one would see a battle.

It was the tail end of the phoney war; Rozanne got home safely, excitement over.

'I have to admit – and perhaps other young people were the same as me – that there was a certain element of adventure in the air,' Lady Jean recalls. Upon hearing the declaration of war, like Rozanne she too felt a 'stir of excitement'. Cushioned from the horrors of the First World War and longing to break free from her confined existence Lady Jean saw the war as a great opportunity.

'One was going to have a purposeful job, one was going to go away and have one's own world, I think that was it.' But excitement was an emotion the older generation did not share. 'Mother came upstairs to the nursery to listen to Nanny's wireless, and the two women had tears pouring down their faces.'

Trenches were burrowed into parks, gas masks were handed out like sweeties and air-raid shelters mushroomed overnight but the conversation about what war really meant was still missing. Abject horror remained the older generation's silent burden. They had not shared their pain and now, their children, optimistic and young, were looking forward. Gwen picked up on her parents' anxiety.

> I remember my mother and father listening to the news for about eighteen months before the actual declaration of war and I would go out of the room simply because I saw they were worried and I couldn't bear them to be worried. But what could you do?

Her father had never talked about his First World War experiences. Meanwhile in her smart private school Gwen had absorbed the glorious euphemisms and noble sentiments of J. M. Barrie, Ernest Raymond and Rupert Brooke. Hers was a censored, sanitised education designed to instil a sense of duty and imperial self-belief and it had worked. 'We had not even any idea that war could involve ordinary clerical work, cleaning, boredom – war meant to us drama and romance and we could not wait to take part.'

Against the advice of her parents, Gwen, one of Talbot Heath's most promising pupils, left school as soon as she could. She applied to join the WAAFs[1] on her eighteenth birthday.

Cora was dusting her parents' sitting-room, Muriel was sitting around the radio with her family in East London, Pat had just returned from

1. Women's Auxiliary Air Force.

a caravanning holiday on the west coast of Scotland and Gwen was at home in Bournemouth. All four vividly remember Chamberlain's declaration on 3 September 1939. Suddenly the small, domestic confines around which most girls' lives had been mapped out from birth were under threat. No wonder they can all recall where they were when war broke out. Rozanne, Lady Jean and Gwen were not alone in looking forward to the great unknown.

Early Days

'We were sat in the front of our house and I remember I heard them talking. "We have to get out of London." That's what they said.'

Muriel's family had already built an air-raid shelter ('the floor was always wet and mother knitted on a bench') and she loved her little gas mask in its own box with her name on it, but fearful of aerial bombing the Government insisted further precautions must be taken. Within the first few months of war one and half million women and children were evacuated from Britain's major cities. However there was no way Muriel's proud Jewish father would let his wife and two daughters leave Stamford Hill without him. 'My father knew somebody in Bletchley. He said, "We'll go there and see if we can rent a property. It will be better than London and safer for the children."'

Muriel remembers the suitcases on the train and her father going off to find the Dindols – the only other Jewish family in the village.

> Father knew him from the markets. He was in drapery and Dad was in jewellery and you know, if you're Jewish, you're akin to each other. They made us something to eat immediately; we felt very welcome.

The Dindols had been in Bletchley since 1927, where the family owned several properties and a large double-fronted drapers shop. During the phoney war many families drifted back to London, but Muriel's stayed put. 'We loved it there.'

Muriel was just eleven when she left her old life behind. She was preoccupied trying to fit in at her new school seven miles away in Wolverton. 'Us evacuees we only did three hours in the morning and out of that we did sewing. I still can't even sew a button on but I can read and write. I was the only Jewish girl there but it wasn't a problem.' Although Bletchley was a small village, the imposing red-brick Victorian house just beyond the station and the constant building work that was taking place in its grounds made no impression on Muriel. 'Well the house didn't mean anything then. I was having fun. Even at twelve years old I was walking up and down, showing off. Dad would be in the market, you know! I was a child.'

But as Muriel would soon discover, in war children grow up very quickly.

———•◦•———

Mr Dindol wasn't the first Jewish person to move to Bletchley. Sir Herbert Leon, a successful Anglo-Jewish stockbroker and Liberal MP, had bought the Park and 581 acres of surrounding Buckinghamshire countryside in 1882. A man who 'made a profession out of being wealthy', he lavished the estate with attention and money. The house sprawled into a modern mansion, and stables, gardens and garages soon adorned the grounds. What Sir Leon lacked in aesthetic vision he more than made up for in scale and endeavour. However, by the 1930s oversized country retreats were no longer cost effective and after Leon's death the estate was sold in lots. By the time Muriel arrived in Bletchley the house and fifty-one acres of grounds were owned and occupied by the Government's Code and Cypher School (GC&CS).

GC&CS was Britain's joint-services code-breaking operation that emerged from the cryptography units of the Admiralty (Room 40) and the War Office after the First World War. Largely based at 54 Broadway, around the corner from Whitehall, the Foreign Office was GC&CS's parent body. To begin with the primary focus was on diplomatic and commercial messages; key among the countries targeted were the Soviet Union and Spain. But during the 1930s the increasingly ominous noises coming from Germany and Japan saw priorities change and by 1938 the government agency had shifted onto a wartime footing. Over a year before the mass evacuation of women and children, GC&CS had already planned its own move out of the capital.

The Chief of the Secret Intelligence Service (SIS, now better known as M16), Admiral Sir Hugh Sinclair, was so convinced of the need to relocate operations to Bletchley he refused to wait for interminably slow government bureaucrats to cough up money for the estate and instead paid the princely sum of £6,000 out of his own pocket. 'Captain Ridley's shooting party' (as the secret team was code-named) was first sent to the Park in 1938 for the duration of the Munich crisis. With a threatening Germany hiding its military communications behind apparently impenetrable Enigma-machine encryptions, a vital information exchange between Polish, French and British cryptanalysts took place outside Warsaw in July 1939 and the recruitment of Britain's finest analytical brains was prioritised. By August 1939, GC&CS's shift to Bletchley Park had been made permanent. With unprecedented speed and secrecy, Sir Herbert Leon's twenty-seven bedrooms, oak-panelled reception rooms and magnificent ballroom suddenly became the nerve centre of a visionary multi-agency operation designed to handle the attack on all enemy ciphers. Embedded at the Park for the duration of the war, Britain's code-breakers were ideally located in an estate which benefited from the proximity of the main north–south telephone lines and was a safe (but workable) distance from London. Here, on the flats of Buckinghamshire, their fledgling operation of just 186 people had space to grow.

◆━━◆━◆━━◆

'For me the start of the Second World War in 1939 – when I was sixteen – meant the end of my childhood. From that moment, our family life became increasingly fractured.'

By 1939, Kathleen's father, Admiral John Godfrey, had been appointed Director of Naval Intelligence. Kathleen remembers 'a distant figure living and working in London'. Admiral Godfrey had a big job on his hands; the Navy had been the victim of political complacency and underfunding for years. He had to build up his own intelligence team at lightning speed and because of Bletchley's joint services remit he was also involved in the setting up of the Park.

With her father already absent in London, the departure from the family home of Kathleen's mother, Margaret Godfrey, just two days before the outbreak of war was keenly felt by her daughters. The Godfreys' house in Kent had to be abandoned. Writing her private memoirs in 2001, Kathleen believed that her Cambridge-educated mother had gone straight to the School of Geography in Oxford to assemble confidential maps and data for the Admiralty. But Kathleen was wrong. Her mother didn't go to work in Oxford until 1940. During the first few months of war Margaret was stationed at Bletchley Park (or BP, as the workers dubbed it). No doubt recommended by her husband for this highly confidential mission, she was one of the first women at BP. The initial handful of cryptanalysts, including Alan Turing, Gordon Welchman and Alfred Dillwyn Knox, were accompanied by 130 civilians, among them Kathleen's mother. No Enigma keys had yet been broken, but the mansion was already bursting at the seams.

Margaret never spoke about her work, and her otherwise meticulously kept diary was left blank during the last four months of 1939, save for the ominous entry 'M to war station' on Friday 1 September. Overnight life had changed for thirty-eight-year-old Margaret; eight days later she wrote to her husband: 'It is now definite that I get £3 per week . . . I feel very rich having never earned anything before in my life.' However, the Godfreys' commitment to wartime service came at a cost. John wrote to his wife, 'There are so many things to be thought out aren't there? And I've no doubt you've reached certain conclusions about K, E and C poor dears. I am afraid we don't give them much of a home these days . . .'

The conclusion reached for their oldest daughter Kathleen took immediate effect.

> My education came to an abrupt halt not much regretted at the time but, looking back on my life, a source of much regret and sometimes envy. I don't remember any discussion about my future and it was decided the easiest thing was to send me to what was called a Domestic Science School.

Aged sixteen, Kathleen had to endure this 'dreadful place'. She rendered down fat from bacon rinds, skinned rabbits and made a pair of satin pants. She rarely saw her sisters and the Godfreys would never return to their family home. So far for Kathleen the war had brought profound change but no excitement.

Early on in the conflict it is no surprise that Charlotte also found herself attending (and resenting) a domestic science course at Shrewsbury's local college. What to do with Britain's young women was a contentious issue. War had always been regarded as a man's business: society was geared to believe in the martial male and peace-keeping female. Women in military uniform threatened domestic norms and social stability. And wasn't that precisely what men were fighting to preserve? Although women serving in the forces, in factories and on farms proved essential in the First World War, it had been a temporary expedient. By the mid-1930s the women's auxiliary services were no nearer full incorporation in the military structure than they had been in 1917.

The War Office continued to drag its feet over the issue of a women's reserve. It was women themselves who forced a rethink, besieging local authority offices after the Munich crisis, clamouring to undertake some form of national service. (With a leadership of 'county ladies' they were predominantly hearty middle-class sorts.) In 1939, 43,000 women had volunteered for the three women's auxiliary services, well in excess of the Government's 25,000 target. Needless to say, the Services were not ready for them and ambivalence at the top level remained. In September 1939, an Air Ministry Official stated 'there is no need for any recruiting drive in the case of the WAAF'. Few thought service women would play a big part in the war.

Gwen, who had forgone university to join the WAAFs, was promptly knocked back for being too young – deferred entrance saw her kill time in a dull clerical job at the Home Office. Together with her boyfriend she had danced and listened to 'I wear a pair of silver wings'. He went off and learnt to fly, she meanwhile had to wait.

In 1939 few could have predicted the mass conscription of women that would later follow. Recruitment posters didn't appear until 1941. At the start of the war, a semblance of normality was a national priority; *Woman's Own* reminded its readers 'we are standing by our posts as the men are standing by theirs'. For the time being this was still a man's war, albeit one with very little fighting. While German generals began transferring units from Poland to the West and Britain sent a 'symbolic' expeditionary force to France, back at home men and women felt cheated by the hype. Petrol rationing, lights out, food restrictions, leaking sandbags, black curtains and no action – the phoney war was a damp squib.

———•———

'I hope your acting is better than your nursing!'

Pam was listlessly sweeping the floor in her Red Cross uniform when a male patient teased her. Twenty-one years old at the outbreak of war, she had already done her VAD (Voluntary Aid Detachment) training. ('Despite my German links I was ready to sign up and serve. Everybody was very anti-Hitler.') But acting, not sweeping the floor, was her first love.

Pam had been working for a trendy little theatre called the Mercury when fears of bombing prompted the Government to close the nation's entertainment venues. Suddenly Pam was out of work and not a single incendiary had been dropped.

'What agent of Chancellor Hitler is it who has suggested we should all cower in darkness and terror "for the duration"?' complained George Bernard Shaw in a letter to *The Times*. Needless to say the closure didn't last long. After two weeks provincial venues were re-opened and the London theatres within a month. Pam hung up her nurse's whites and trod the boards in Bournemouth, then Birmingham. Later, as war intensified, the fight against Nazi Germany was increasingly framed as no ordinary conflict – this was a conflict between ideologies. Britain couldn't afford to cut off its own cultural heritage; theatres and cinemas were now placed at the vanguard of our national struggle. Bombs or not, the actors performed.

> I was in Birmingham during the Blitz. I remember seeing the flames, it was quite alarming. I was in a hostel with a troupe of Polish dancers from the Prince of Wales Theatre. There was a big air raid and we all went down to the cellar. They all seemed to be absolutely hysterical, I felt terribly grown up and English.

Pam pauses and adds as an aside, 'I now think people who are unafraid are very ignorant and stupid.'

Pam entertained the troops through ENSA (Entertainments National Services Association) and also benefited from an artistic world that was supported with government funds for the first time. The CEMA (Council for the Encouragement of Music and Arts) was founded in January 1940 with a general aim of boosting morale through the provision of art. Pam was on a roll, serving her country and doing a job she loved. Her sights were set on London's West End stage; having survived the Blitz, surely nothing could get in her way?

'Keep Calm and Carry On'

'We packed one suitcase and took a tin of condensed milk, a bit of bread and our dog.'

It was May 1940 and Belgium was in the process of being wiped off the map by the advancing Germans. The phoney war was officially over. It took Hitler eighteen days to smash this small country. For the second time in three decades the Belgians were victims in a greater game; nearly two million panicked civilians fled west, among them Doris, her sister Georgette, her mother Marie-Elisabeth and their dog. They 'saw Tommys going in the other direction', but the roads were so blocked with refugees, British and French soldiers struggled to move East.

Doris remembers a train with 'masses and masses of people and no corridors and no loos. There was a mother with her son; she became so deranged they left the carriage, after that we had more room.' Another girl was disorientated; she too went back to Belgium. 'But we had no choice. The British government told us we had to go or we would be interned by the Germans.'

'Oh yes,' agrees Georgette the elder sister (shouting loudly down the phone from Dallas, Texas), 'others ended up with their heads in the oven; we had to go.'

Crucially Doris and Georgette had somewhere to go to – they were British after all (despite their limited English). But stuck on a train, with bombs dropping in the station (Doris recalls seeing dead bodies and buildings on fire), Britain was a long way off.

'Mother put a case against the window, my sister dived under the seat, she came back up black as soot and I remember mother combing her hair. No matter what, we had to look nice.'

Leaving Belgium just ahead of the Germany Army, the train was destined for Paris. 'We had tickets but we never got there. At one stop we had to lie on the ground to avoid being shot down.' The heat was stifling; for six days they lived on bread and kindness passed through windows. Georgette arrived in Moissac, Southern France, with swollen ankles. 'But it was worse for Mummy.'

Sitting in her solid town house in Northampton decades later, Doris jumps between the two sisters' adventure ('When we left Belgium, I was seventeen, my sister was eighteen, we were very attractive girls although I say it myself!') and the nightmare endured by their conservative mother. Marie-Elisabeth abandoned Belgium in the First World War; history was repeating itself and this time she had been forced to leave her own mother behind. They would never see each other again.

Having survived the train journey, Marie-Elisabeth and her daughters found refuge in a French farmhouse, sharing basic quarters with a badly burnt airman and an Army officer. High jinks broke up the boredom. 'We tied their pyjama legs and used warming pans to spread bed bugs!' The men retaliated by stealing off with the sisters' clothes when they were swimming in the Tarn River and dressing up as girls. The menial living, poverty and lack of certainty were much harder for Marie-Elisabeth. 'Mother fainted. We were in one room with a fire; we could cook but the fumes were bad.' The family's suitcase was always packed and each day brought fresh disappointment: the visas they needed to travel through neutral Spain and Portugal remained tantalisingly out of reach. It was a long year. The girls knitted for pin money, converted to Catholicism (dear God!) and waited. What else could they do?

Belgium was one of many. Norway, the Netherlands, Luxembourg, France: the German Blitzkrieg produced a domino effect, toppling country after country. Soon island Britain was on her own. With the Germans now sitting across the Channel, the threat of the jackboot on British soil was terrifyingly real. Belligerent Churchill became Prime Minister, but the signs weren't promising. The desperate retreat from Dunkirk at the beginning of June 1940 was followed by the Battle of Britain overhead and the bombing of British cities down below. Despite Churchill's determination that 'we shall never surrender!' London burnt and the fate of the nation seemed to rely on a handful of Spitfires and Hurricanes.

On 20 August 1940 Churchill famously declared that 'Never in the field of human conflict was so much owed by so many to so few.' And that 'many' included millions of girls: volunteering, fire-watching, knitting, cooking, nursing and waiting.

If listening to Chamberlain's solemn pronouncement on 3 September 1939 had caused a frisson of anticipation among Britain's young women, for many the next couple of years was a frustrating anticlimax. This was not their war to fight, but it dislocated lives and left girls feeling lonely and bewildered. Still dependent on their parents and increasingly dictated to by the state, time dragged. Charlotte on her domestic science course in Shropshire was exasperated. It was 'difficult to remain enthusiastic about cooking colourless food from simplified wartime recipes'.

'Illness exacerbated my dissatisfaction.' Bouts of measles and chickenpox were the last straw. Isolated, except for radio bulletins detailing the Blitz, it wouldn't be long before eighteen-year-old Charlotte decided to take matters into her own hands. After all, this was total war; British women were also under attack. Surely they too should fight back?

Pat had wanted to join the uniformed war effort from the moment it broke out.

> In the first year of war there were news reports and photos of female ambulance drivers in France. I got my mother to take me to a recruiting office in Lancaster and asked if I could become an ambulance driver in France. They said they didn't want a sixteen-year-old ambulance driver. I left in floods of tears.

Pat did not get her dream job but, unlike Charlotte and Kathleen, at least she was given a choice: domestic science college or a secretarial course.

Pat arrived in London in the middle of the Blitz on a mission to type. ('It was really rather good of my mother to let me go.') The Triangle Secretarial School had in fact been moved from Bond Street to Gerrards Cross. But in comparison with Lancashire this was the thick of it. 'I was being shown my bedroom when a landmine came down outside. The window bulged like a bubble, glass smashed everywhere and I dived under the bed with the house-keeper.' Secretarial school proved an eye-opener for rural Pat. 'A Russian girl was pointed out to me as a lesbian. "Do be careful!" the older girls said and there were troops stationed in woods. I remember finding a magazine full of pornography.' Pat had 'no idea what it was all about' and popped it in the dustbin. Like most British girls, she was still a bystander amid the chaos and felt as much. 'Really I was biding time until I was old enough to join the Wrens.'

Male conscription worsened the waiting game. Susceptible sweethearts were in for a long hard road ahead, bumping between bouts of leave, ad-hoc letters and small symbolic signs of survival and affection. War didn't discriminate. David Bevan, a midship-man aged eighteen, was Rozanne's first boyfriend. 'His father had been the naval attaché in Italy. We met on a skiing holiday with our parents. It was more innocent back then; we were great friends but you felt it was getting warmer.'

Rozanne smiles wistfully. This tentative young relationship never went any further. Along with the rest of his crew David drowned in the autumn of 1940. 'He was lost early when his ship was torpedoed in the Mediterranean, it was terribly sad.' Over seventy years later she recalls the immediate shock and sadness and then the feeling 'that there is a war on, one must not indulge oneself. He had been killed on duty, a sort of noble death . . . All I could do was grit my teeth, but I was howling inside.'

Hiding under the dining-room table in Kensington, ducking the falling bombs, was no longer fun. Rozanne and her younger brother were packed off to their grandparents in Yorkshire. 'After David and the Blitz I was longing to be involved. Not to be just a bystander; from then on one was longing to be old enough to get into the Services.'

Destruction and death steeled nerves and heightened resolve. Kathleen had left domestic science college behind; she was a pink-cheeked Land Girl, making hay and driving tractors when the dreaded letter arrived.

Ralph, our favourite uncle, had been killed in the Battle of Britain . . . Ralph had been married to Diana just eleven months when he was shot down over Croydon, South London. He stayed at the controls until his plane was near an open space in order not to crash into houses. By that time, it was skimming over tree-tops, too low for his parachute to open.

Suddenly haymaking wasn't enough. 'After Ralph's heroic death, I decided that I too would join up.' Kathleen didn't act alone: 'None of the girls were being called up, we all just rushed into the fray.'

Long before government acts and snappy propaganda dictated their course, a lot of girls had already made up their minds. Only active service would suffice. Heroes needed heroines.

4

A Civilian Service

Well before a designer had been hired to streamline the uniform, Lady Jean longed to join the Wrens. It was the elite service for women, and as the six-foot daughter of a duke, Lady Jean was an elite woman with impeccable sea-faring connections. Her father had founded the Royal Naval Volunteer Reserve and she had been born and brought up close to a prestigious naval base – mighty capital ships, HMS *Repulse*, HMS *King George* V and even HMS *Hood* made an appearance at Arran's Lamlash. Once war broke out, as far as Lady Jean was concerned her destination was the Women's Royal Naval Service. She promptly let her mother know as much.

But the Duchess, having anticipated the departure of her vast staff, insisted Lady Jean first helped co-ordinate voluntary work parties on the island.

Prodigious numbers of locals knitted, fed evacuees and gathered moss; large bins of garments were sent to the Services, little heads were checked for lice and sphagnum moss was cleaned and converted into medical dressings. Lady Jean dutifully oversaw Arran's local war efforts for six months before she went back to the Duchess. 'I said that I thought I'd got everything organised. I would now like to leave and join the Wrens.' Perhaps one of the great naval dockyards – Portsmouth, Plymouth, Chatham – or even a posting overseas, Lady Jean didn't know where the Wrens might take her, but the prospect of independent adventure was at last around the corner. The service was flooded with applicants but as a well-connected woman Jean was immediately accepted subject to a medical. She even knew the local naval medical officer; they played tennis together.

He said, 'Just a formality! Look at you, a strapping healthy girl.' And he proceeded to enquire after Lady Jean's health. Measles and mumps and chickenpox were duly struck off the list. 'What on earth have you had?' enquired the jocular officer.

'And without thinking I said, "Oh! Just three goes of TB and one of colitis."'

That was the end of Lady Jean's dream. Bovine tuberculosis in the bones (osteomyelitis) had blighted her childhood at a time when there was no vaccination against this potentially fatal disease. The Wrens rejected her.

'I nearly cried. It just broke my heart. However there was nothing I could do but pull myself together and get on. So I went back to Mother and told her she'd have me for quite a long time to come.'

It wasn't all bad. Island life became much more exciting when 8,000 Commandos arrived a few months later. Britain was on the defensive but the collapse of the Belgian and French resistance had taught Churchill a valuable lesson; it was vital that the military retained an aggressive attacking element in its wartime strategy. He demanded amphibious 'raiding forces' of 'specially trained troops of the hunter class' which could deliver a 'vigorous enterprising and ceaseless offensive against the whole German-occupied coastline'. And where better to train than rugged Arran?

Thousands of young men besieged the island; attractive, uniformed and brave, the Commandos rigorously 'learned all methods to kill' on Arran's rocks and shores. However, there was still time for light relief: Dad's Army antics with the local home guard, officers begging baths and beds in the castle and a steely moment with the Duchess when the local deer came under attack from the gung-ho visitors. 'The poor officer thought he had been invited in for a drink and instead Mother reprimanded him. "How are your men going to fare in Africa if you can't control them on Arran?"'

Away from the Duchess's disapproving eyes, the village hall hosted dances: the St Bernard's waltz, the slow foxtrot and the quickstep. An unexpected party had come to Arran and Lady Jean was at the centre of it.

The Commandos were soon gone – taking the fight to Norway, Syria, North Africa, Burma, France and the Channel Islands – but it is clear they made a huge impression on young sheltered Jean. When asked she gently admits that a certain Johnny in No. 3 Commando changed everything. 'Yes, we were in love and we would have married. He was highly amusing and very popular.' We are standing in her large bright kitchen; she is leaning against the Aga, her modest gold jewellery set off against a citron-coloured jersey, her face prettily made-up in blues and pinks. Lady Jean is still an impressive sight to behold. There is a brief pause and then she starts talking and suddenly it is easy to imagine them arm in arm, Jean with her stream of gold hair, Johnny in his Commando beret, striding out across the handsome Scottish island. She deliberately chose not to write about their relationship in her book; she did however write about his death. Operation Claymore, the British Commando raid on the Lofoten Islands in Norway, was a success – several wheels from a German Enigma machine were captured (a vital 'pinch' for Bletchley Park's code-breakers). However, the campaign cost Johnny his life.

He attacked a house and shot four Germans, but did not notice a fifth man go out of the back door and come round to the front waiting for him to come out. He was shot in the head as he came through the door. His brother rushed to him, cradling his skull while his life blood drifted away. Johnny was a great loss to all men who admired him very much. He was tall, a boxing Blue, rowing Blue – a courageous man. Johnny did not come back.

What use is love in war? Lady Jean was 'devastated'. Young men arrived, trained to fight to the death, and left again. Meanwhile

Jean was still stuck volunteering on Arran. It wasn't enough. Her twenty-first birthday came and went – how she longed 'to *do* something. It would have been awful if one had done nothing during the war.' Her hunger to be an official part of the military effort had been exacerbated by Johnny's death. The Duke, her doting father, eventually decided to make a few enquiries. He had a word with his friend and fellow Lord, Naval Commander Mountbatten. 'My girl can't get into the Wrens as she's had TB. Do you know of anything she could do?' It was Mountbatten who suggested that Lady Jean should go and work at a place called Bletchley Park. 'He thought my health would stand it if I had a good billet.' Her interest piqued, Lady Jean set off for Glasgow to do a crash course in touch-typing – apparently a crucial skill for what promised to be a very 'hush hush' mission.

Growing Pains

The story of how Lady Jean came to be selected for Bletchley chimes perfectly with the 'privileged daughters and debs' stereo-type that dominates the Park's image. Lady Jean had been a debu-tante and her father, the Duke, helped his daughter find her first job. Inevitably perhaps, Establishment Britain began recruiting from their own sort for their most secret operations centre. While Lady Jean keenly underlines the *noblesse oblige* prevalent among the upper classes, from Bletchley's perspective the key factor was that these girls belonged to families well known in the relatively small, compact 'ruling class'. That one of the first women sent to Bletchley Park, Kathleen's mother Margaret Godfrey, also happened to be the wife of Admiral Godfrey, Head of Naval Intelligence, and related to Neville Chamberlain is a case in point. 'Posh' girls had fathers and husbands who knew each other and from kinship springs trust. Above all else Bletchley's employees had to be trustworthy. The German military must never know that Britain was in the process of achieving what Hitler believed to be the impossible.

It was in January 1940 that 'in a small bleak wooden hut with nothing but a table and three chairs, the first bundle of Enigma decodes appeared'. By the time the vast majority of Bletchley personnel were being recruited, the first inroads into reading the enemy's Enigma encrypted messages had already been made. The fact that Bletchley was harbouring a vital national secret was reflected in its obsession with security. In a world wary of aliens and spies, Lady Jean's credentials were very reassuring: her family could be traced back to royalty. Bright and trustworthy, she passed the interview and was at last en route to wartime service, albeit without a uniform.

The timing of Lady Jean's invitation to the Park at the end of 1941 is significant. She was one of the first women in this book to be directly involved in the code-breaking process and it's no coincidence that she arrived in Buckinghamshire when GC&CS was dramatically scaling up its operations – thousands of new recruits would soon transform the Park. The eccentric atmosphere that defined Bletchley in the first years of war – trestle tables in corridors, Dilly Knox and his researchers hugger-mugger in the cottage, the air section making do in the dining-room, teleprinters filling the ballroom and academic new recruits 'dropping in with the slightly unexpected effect of carrier pigeons' – was a relatively short transitional period. Months before any Enigma code was cracked on British soil, cryptanalyst Gordon Welchman had predicted that the quantity of enemy communications ('traffic') would soon demand the application of standardised techniques and machinery. The cryptographic task was duly separated into sections, each overseen by its own specialist. Huts with specific remits became entities in their own right.

Welchman ran Hut 6, which dealt with German Army and Air Force traffic, and it was Alan Turing who famously focused on the development of an electronic testing machine designed to locate Enigma key settings: the Bombe (inspired by the 'Bomba', an earlier device designed by the Polish Cypher Bureau). Their ingenious work paid off, but successful code-breaking and intelligence analysis demanded ever greater resources. The need to again 'gear-up' the operation and move it onto a mass-production footing became acute.

In 1940 Bletchley could do nothing to prevent disaster in Norway and the summer debacle in France.

By then numerous Luftwaffe signals were being read, but a lack of secure procedures for handling the sensitive material in the field hampered the use of broken enemy codes. That changed in 1941 when Signals Intelligence, the end product of Bletchley's deciphering and analysis, began to make a real difference on the ground; saving lives and pre-empting the enemy in Greece, North Africa and at sea. Then, as anticipated, the sheer quantity of traffic became unmanageable. The workers crammed into a handful of wooden huts and scattered over a manor house were not sufficient to log, copy, decode, translate, index and analyse millions of messages. In October 1941 Gordon Welchman and three other early Bletchley recruits – Alan Turing, Hugh Alexander and Stuart Milner-Barry – wrote an uncompromising letter to Churchill demanding additional resources. The so-called 'Wicked Uncles', whose bold missive undermined the authority of the Park's then Director Alastair Denniston, had a dramatic effect. Churchill's unequivocal and immediate response –'action this day' – led to a comprehensive reorganisation of the Park's operations and a dramatic scaling up of resources and personnel in January 1942. The world's first code-breaking factory had emerged from fledgling Oxbridge-Establishment origins and above all else this cerebral-industrial hybrid demanded additional manpower. Or rather woman power.

Bletchley Park was not the only wartime body to acknowledge the need for an organisational rethink. By 1941, His Majesty's Coalition Government had come to a revolutionary conclusion. Fighting a war alone across two continents and two oceans had stretched Britain's empire and resources to breaking point. It was (reluctantly) agreed that the war could not be won without the comprehensive engagement of Britain's women, no matter how distasteful the thought was to many British statesmen. The female Labour MP Agnes Hardie spoke for many of them when she argued 'war is not a woman's job . . . women share the bearing and rearing of children and should be exempt from war' before going on to claim 'barrack life and camp life is not suited for women'. But Britain was not in a position to quibble over the potential moral pitfalls of compulsory service; extreme measures were needed to stop Nazism. The National Service (No. 2) Act was passed in December 1941. For the first time in British history women were obliged to work for King and country. In munitions factories, on farms, in hospitals and in the uniformed auxiliary services, what had been voluntary now became compulsory – the Government could call up all unmarried women between the ages of twenty and thirty. It was an unprecedented decision; the scale of female involvement in Britain's war effort wasn't matched in any other country. But if the Establishment were initially reluctant about compelling women to work, for the girls in this book and thousands of others across Britain, conscription was a welcome decision, one which many had already anticipated. Mary Grieve, the editor of *Woman* magazine, recalled that 'in the end the government took the plunge and the operation went wonderfully smoothly'. The vast majority of women agreed 'emphatically' that the fairer sex should do war work.

Godparents

Long before conscription for women was even contemplated, GC&CS employed females in clerical posts. However, it wasn't until 1941 that women began to noticeably outnumber men at the Park. The Foreign Office (GC&CS's parent body) continued to use familiar networks to reach appropriate girls. This informal, confidential recruitment procedure remained a Bletchley hallmark throughout the war.

From good squirarchy stock, it is not surprising that Pat was approached by a well-meaning relative as early as 1940.

I was biding my time at secretarial school when godmother Eleanor who was married to a diplomat in the Foreign Office wrote to my mother. 'A lot of FO girls are going to work at a place called Bletchley Park and it would be so nice if Pat applied to go there because she would be with crowds of jolly girls.'

But Pat had other ideas. 'I wanted to join the Wrens. My uncle was a destroyer captain and helped sink the first German U-boat, U-39. He said girls in the family must go into the Wrens.' This was a girl who grew up 'bombing' the Germans in her local quarry cheered on by her military father – only the best uniformed service would do! She moved swiftly to nip her godmother's idea in the bud, sending her mother an unambiguous night telegram that began: 'HATE CROWDS JOLLY GIRLS'.

Over seven decades later it is not without a hint of triumph that Pat nods her silver bob and declares 'and that took care of that suggestion!' Courtesy of her forthright behaviour, it would be another two years before Pat provided those 'jolly girls' with vital assistance.

In Pamela's case it was her godfather's wife who was interfering. Mrs Eleanor Mary Holland-Martin was the mother of a senior Royal Naval officer and when retelling her story Pam gives Eleanor an upper-class, authoritative voice. 'I know you are doing splendid work dear, entertaining the troops, but there is a place where they want girls exactly like you and if you feel perhaps you would be interested here's the address . . .' Acting was a reserved occupation and Pam was having fun serving her nation, although she concedes that some of the ENSA productions were below par. 'I think quite often they played down to the troops.' But by 1941 it wasn't just the quality of the drama that was needling Pam. Patrick, her only brother, to whom she was devoted, had gone missing. 'It was horrid; I was depressed at the time.' Patrick survived (their mother once again made good use of her direct line to God), but in April 1941, as part of the first Benghazi campaign in North Africa, he'd been captured and taken prisoner. Meanwhile, back in Britain, his German-speaking sister was beginning to have doubts about her acting career. 'I thought perhaps I was fiddling while Rome burnt.'

Then suddenly the moment came that Pamela had been waiting for all her life. 'I got an offer through an agent of a very small part and understudy role in my first West End play *Watch on the Rhine*. It was potentially a big break. The West End was the West End!' *Watch on the Rhine* – a timely emotional drama featuring offshoots of Nazism in an American setting – had been a massive Broadway hit in 1941. Following acclaimed reviews there and sell-out shows, London's West End was keen for a slice of the action. Flamboyant Emyln Williams was confirmed as director and a good run was anticipated at the Aldwych Theatre. This was Pamela's big break. Retelling the story years later the excitement of that moment still catches in her voice. Then she remembers. 'But the thing was, I had already sent off a letter of application to a place called Bletchley Park.'

Fathers and Uncles and Sisters

As Pamela's experiences show, Bletchley Park's covert network ran right through the top echelons of British society. Rozanne was similarly 'tapped up', but on this occasion the contact was even closer to home. Her bittersweet summer of 1940 (a first party in the Savoy, David's sudden death at sea, ducking bombs in Kensington) had ended with a humdrum job in Yorkshire. Sent out of harm's way and still only eighteen years old, she was killing time as a typist for Northern Command. The winters were freezing; Rozanne had a bicycle and controversial pair of slacks which she wore to pedal through the snow. Her over-secretary did not approve.

'You can't wear those trousers, you must wear a little black dress!'

Rozanne protested: 'I haven't got a little black dress.'

Fortunately timing was on her side; the Command's General Hog entered the room and declared: 'I love your slacks!'

Rozanne laughs in her comfy pink chair at the memory. 'So all was well.' It was a small but important victory for an independent woman who was longing to be nineteen. 'Then I knew I would be called up. I wanted to be in the WAAFs. A uniform would say something.' Rozanne had her sights fixed firmly on the Women's Auxiliary Air Force; after all, her 'darling' father, Air Commodore Charles Medhurst (whose photograph gazes down from the wall), was a leading light in the RAF. Flying machines were in the blood. But as Head of Intelligence at the Air Ministry, and with Italy now fighting against Britain, Charles knew his daughter's language skills could not be squandered on square-bashing. (As early as 1922 the Italian language had virtually disappeared from British Secondary Education.) Rozanne possessed a valuable national asset. He duly intervened.

'Father explained to me there was a place called Bletchley Park and they needed Italian speakers.'

But first there would be an interview in London. It all sounded thrilling. Needless to say, the lack of uniform no longer mattered.

Georgette and Doris Moller would arrive at Bletchley Park three months before Rozanne, but as late as August 1941 the odds were stacked against the Belgian refugees even getting to Britain. By now they were in neutral Portugal but had failed to board the British cargo ship SS *Avoceta*, which was docked at Lisbon waiting to take European refugees to Gibraltar. 'Every day we congregated at the British Recreation club in Lisbon but when the ship arrived, we were not on the list. Mother complained but it wasn't our time.'

Georgette is still on the telephone in Texas and this is an important part of the story so she is talking fast, her French accent sometimes hard to make out down the line. 'We would have died. Women and children we knew died.'

Doris confirms her sister's account. 'A fortnight after we arrived in Lisbon, a ship [SS *Avoceta*] left with refugees and it was sunk crossing from Gibraltar by a German submarine.' Luck, fate, call it what you will, but on that night, 26 September 1941, the Moller sisters were not among the thirty-two women and twenty children who died at sea.

Doris sighs. 'I remember women with babies, we had all been waiting together.'

SS *Auguila*, *Avoceta*'s sister ship, had already been sunk by a wolf pack days earlier; 152 civilians drowned.

Meanwhile, the Moller sisters were stuck in neutral Lisbon. 'But the food was good. I was nearly eleven stone when I eventually got to England!' Doris laughs.

Their escape to Britain came six months later. On one sheet of A4 paper the sisters have sketched out their journey. The cargo boat that ferried them from Lisbon to Gibraltar did not survive the war, nor a destroyer that escorted their ship to Britain. Tellingly both Sir Samuel Hoare, the British Ambassador in Spain, and Viscount Gort, the Governor of Gibraltar, came to 'say good bye to us that Christmas' on board MS *Batory*, the large ocean liner destined for Scotland. MS *Batory* was one of Poland's most famous ships, she went faster than SS *Avoceta* and would have two destroyers escorting her, but this was war and no journey was without risk.

Doris is torn between memories of seasonal dinner dances in Gibraltar – 'we went to a dance at the sergeant's mess, my mother was the chaperone . . . there was a Christmas cocktail party but one girl ruined it for the rest of us! The next night we had to spend on the ship' – and with the ever present fear of the onwards journey.

'I remember a boat drill, life jacket fittings. I was nervous.'

It's Georgette who ups the ante for the crossing.

'We were pursued by U-boats, we had to go on deck and stand by our lifeboats. Our passports were in plastic wallets, we didn't sleep. We heard depth charges going off! Is the ship going to be hit or not?!' She is shouting now; her story is terrifying even seven decades later.

Doris shakes her head. 'Very tired, that is how I remember feeling when we got on the train. Very tired.'

In early January 1942, two years after the sisters left their suburban apartment in Brussels, MS *Batory* docked in Greenock, Scotland and the girls headed south to their Uncle Bill's Edwardian home in Kent. There was a delicious Sunday lunch waiting for them, but their respite didn't last long.

'We had to do something didn't we?' It is Doris's turn to be indignant. 'We were young able girls, we had been waiting for two years, we wanted to fight the enemy, we saw what they had done. We were going to join the Wrens. We would show people our British passports.' Doris expands on the family's naval connections, an ancestor who fought with Nelson, cousins who were in the Navy, but it didn't matter. The Wrens' stringent application procedure meant they did not want novices over nineteen years old and Doris did not want to be split from her sister. 'We had been together through thick and thin. We wanted to stay together. What could we do?' It was Uncle Bill who came up with a solution. 'Immediately he got us an interview in London.' In fact, they had only been in the UK a few days when both girls set off to the Admiralty together. Thanks to Uncle Bill ('Yes, you would say he was upper class and he had a son in the navy'), Georgette and Doris were destined for Bletchley Park's Naval Section.

———◦———

Born in France, brought up in Belgium and finally bounced across neutral Europe into Britain, the Moller sisters still managed to find themselves at Bletchley Park. The clue is right there at the tail end of their story – good old Uncle Bill, their very own personal link to the British Establishment, a connection which would give two 'foreign' girls a new life in wartime Britain. But if upper-middle-class contacts were prevalent among Bletchley Park's civilian employees, they weren't a prerequisite.

Muriel is from working-class Jewish stock, and yet she also served at Bletchley Park. By the time Muriel was leaving her neighbouring council school in Wolverton, she recalls the Park was swarming with men, women, motorcycles, automobiles, buses, civilians and uniforms . . . and her sister.

> Yep, she was older than me, she worked at the Park before me. We shared a room and Anita would leave in the middle of the night. But no, I never asked any questions, I was a kid. I wasn't interested – boring – it was just my sister!

Muriel and Anita's landlords, the Dindols, were well established in the local community. 'Mr Dindol was quite friendly with the local police – he probably verified my sister. You had to be a British citizen of good character, nothing against your parents or anything.' So another Bletchley Park recruitment network, this time a local one. 'But my sister never told me anything. All I knew was she worked in this beautiful place and I wanted to work there too. I wanted to leave school, it didn't interest me.'

Beyond Muriel's scarlet-rimmed spectacles and close-cut salt and pepper hair, you can still glimpse the child she once was. The petite, curvaceous girl in the photo she shows me shares the same impish grin. 'I wasn't interested in the war but I wanted to work. I wanted money, you see, for make-up. Bits and pieces. I made my own lipstick, I melted down dead ends in an egg cup until it was soft. Yes, then I poured it in a container.'

And Bletchley Park?

'Yes, my sister put in a word. That's right, that's how come I got a job there. Through my sister. I was only fourteen.'

Oxford

Bletchley Park has become affectionately remembered as a place heaving with boffins and crossword puzzle solvers; it is a benign and unlikely image for one of Britain's key weapons against Hitler.

Certainly just before the war there was a deliberate focus on the recruitment of 'men of the professor type'. These were academics, mainly from Oxford and Cambridge and, as the stipulation suggests, almost entirely male.[1] Hugh Alexander, Alan Turing, Gordon Welchman, Harry Hinsley and Stuart Milner-Barry have been immortalised as members of an elite group who worked out how to break the codes. And as Bletchley's eccentric image suggests, some did exhibit odd personal habits (a coffee mug chained to the radiator, other mugs thrown absent-mindedly into the lake, gas masks worn on bicycles, peculiar physical twitches and idiosyncratic clothing). It was the presence of these talented other-worldly cryptanalysts that explains Bletchley's early link with Oxbridge; an association that has subsequently acquired almost mythical proportions in the code-breaking story. In some quarters it's even believed that Bletchley was selected as a site because of its good rail links with England's two most prestigious university cities. That is not true. Nor is it true that most of Bletchley's staff were cryptanalysts. As Pamela is quick to point out, 'You must understand very few of us at Bletchley were actually responsible for cracking the codes.' And after its rapid expansion in 1941–2 only a small minority of employees at the Park could claim an Oxbridge education. But an early blueprint had been established; precise, analytical minds were the ideal, no matter how humdrum some of the work. It is no surprise therefore that Oxford and Cambridge remained fertile recruiting grounds throughout the war.

1. Among the cryptanalysts there were a handful of women including Joan Clarke, Ruth Briggs, Margaret Rock and Mavis Lever. No female cryptanalysts are still alive today.

Having 'gone up' in 1940 to study maths, Ann was having a ball at Oxford. There was coffee at Fullers and Browns, performances at the Playhouse, singing with the Bach Choir and meetings to organise the University's Musicians' Club. When she felt tired or needed her laundry done, Ann left the comfort of her college set and cycled past the university's parks to her parents' large house. The war hardly got a look in. Of that we can be certain, because for fourteen months Ann kept a diary almost every day. The thoughts, pleasures, flirtations and anxieties of this bright twenty-year-old are captured between its gold-leaved pages in a tiny blue spidery hand. Now over ninety, Ann lives with her husband Angus in Edinburgh's Inverleith. 'The only thing I am suffering from,' she says, 'is extreme old age.'

Ann's sight is restricted, but on hearing extracts from her diary, she smiles. 'For me this brings it all back. Yes it is nostalgic.'

There is a tendency to over-hype our nation's efforts during the Second World War; its importance to our collective national identity has distorted both history and memory – the common narrative is of a 'greatest generation' swathed in nostalgic patriotism, all of them selflessly united in the face of a common enemy in a war that dominated their whole lives. Reading Ann's diary is a refreshing reality check. It is clear that the war did not overshadow or reduce her university experience. Rather, another, sometimes inconvenient, layer was added to her student life.

Having lost the family's domestic help to the war effort, her mother was particularly tired and Ann had to do her share of the housework – the darning was never-ending. '3 September 1943: Four years of war already! And yet it seems aeons since it all started. Mended fourth brassiere . . .' Her younger brother Mark had moved to America (an evacuee scheme available to university families) and occasionally Ann had to fire watch. An annual highlight was cooking for a camp of schoolboys who worked on the farms. She refers to Britain's progress in the war just twice. '10 July 1943: Sicily was invaded today – hurrah!' '8 September 1943: UNCONDITIONAL SURRENDER OF ITALY announced 5.30.'

War was simply a background presence, the norm around which she existed. However in 1943, having completed both her Maths Mods and her Sections, she had no choice but to move it to the foreground. By now, war work was compulsory. Ann was ambitious. She didn't intend to do any old job.

> I didn't want to go into uniform. I thought it would be horrible to wear a uniform and march up and down and drill. I thought I would have to start at the bottom. My father said go to the University Appointments Board and ask for advice. He knew I needed to get into something interesting.

Backed by her enlightened father, Ann successfully solicited the university's assistance. '2 June 1943: I'm now applying for a temporary assistant in the Foreign Office at Bletchley.' Unlike most of Britain, Ann was *au fait* with the term Bletchley. In her diary she refers to graduates who worked there and her colleague Frances had already thought of applying. '27 May 1943: Frances had a letter from the Appointments Committee suggesting a Foreign Office job at Bletchley. How grand if we both went there!!' But it was only a combination of Ann's tenacity (ringing Bletchley directly) and her father's influence at the university that ensured Francis remained in line for a job at the Park.

> 29 June 1943: F[rances] went to see Mr Peacock at Ministry of Labour Office. V doubtful about job front until she mentioned she was staying with us and wanted to work with me and he said he would do his best! Then I saw him and he promised 'to pull strings' because Daddy works in the office! Will phone Bletchley in the morning and hope that Frances and I will both go there! Also said I can name my own date if I am accepted.

Ann and her friend Frances were courting Bletchley and Bletchley was considering them. It is clear from Ann's diary extract that Oxford credentials alone were not always sufficient to clinch a place at the Park. Good personal connections were equally important.

Ann's persistence paid off. On 13 July 1943 she travelled by train to Bletchley for an interview, wearing 'a light costume'. She had no idea what kind of work she would be asked to do. But ever the optimist, Ann was not put off by less than favourable reports. '14 June 1943: Met Yvonne Buckoke (ATS) on leave, I gather from near Bletchley. She says Foreign Office work there is deadly dull, but still perhaps I'd get something better.' Only time would tell. First Ann had to pass the Park's security checks.

5

Service Girls

Before they had even arrived at the Park, civilian employees Lady Jean, Pam, Rozanne, Muriel, Doris, Georgette and Ann were destined to become a minority. By 1944 most of the girls at Bletchley were military personnel in one of the women's auxiliary services. The early history of BP has fed us an image of curious academics supported by a bevy of debutantes when the reality was that in later years the Park came to be dominated by female service staff in military uniforms. It is not surprising that impressionable young Muriel dressed for work in a pressed white blouse and navy skirt. 'I was eventually put in the same hut as the Wrens and I wanted to look like them.' At fourteen a white shirt was the nearest she could get to being a Wren. In fact, she was doing the same job as they were.

In 1922 the GC&CS was transferred from the Admiralty to work under the Foreign Office, and during the war the Foreign Office continued to employ Bletchley's civilian workers directly. But as a highly complex organisation representing a number of different agencies, GC&CS did not rely on informal networking and university admission boards alone to supply its staffing needs. The three military services provided and paid for the majority of the Park's predominantly female workforce. With their own training programmes and aptitude tests, the forces were well placed to identify and select appropriate girls. No matter what job they were destined for in the Park, Bletchley wanted the best.

However a secret world hidden away in Buckinghamshire and a series of nondescript outposts were not the destinations that most young women anticipated when they signed up to wear a uniform. Nor was Bletchley necessarily their first posting. But as obedient girls and conscripted personnel, they were expected to do what they were told.

Exceptional WAAFs

Keen to have a hand in her own destiny, Gwen had pre-empted conscription and applied to the Women's Auxiliary Air Force before she left school. Enticed by her first boyfriend in his beautiful blue Air Force uniform, she thought, 'By God I am not going to join the ATS; I will look like a sodden ginger pudding! I am going to join the WAAF.' She wasn't alone; the WAAF was always a more popular choice than the dowdy ATS (Auxiliary Territorial Service) and at the height of recruitment 2,000 women were joining a week. In the wake of her Uncle Ralph's death, Kathleen was another early applicant. Poster-sized, groomed, mascaraed women led the charge; by 1941 government propaganda worked hard to convince women military life had a glamorous edge.

Kathleen soon discovered the reality did not live up to the image. 'We queued up for our uniforms which made no concession to our shapes as they were modelled exactly on the men's.' An Air Force belted jacket and straight skirt eliminated all curves and the blue cotton shirt came with a stiff, separate collar. The memory still propels Kathleen to touch her neck where the skin was once rubbed red raw.

Wearing uncomfortable black lace-up shoes she then proceeded to be 'knocked into shape' by a fearsome drill sergeant. 'Marching was the order of the day.' A bellowing male in an immense parade ground was a culture shock but at least Kathleen got paid. 'Fourteen shillings and sixpence. The first money I had ever earned.'

For Gwen, forced to bide her time in a dull Home Office job before she could sign up to the WAAFs, the first few weeks of military life in Morecambe remains an altogether more treasured memory. Trained by a guardsman, she 'soon recognised the fascination of moving in synchronised figures, like a corps de ballet . . .

by the end of six weeks we were marching gaily for ten miles, singing all the way'.

'Oh heavenly Morecambe! I still think of it as romantic when I see it on telly.' When Gwen talks of the past and her part in the war it is a performance, her voice ebbs and flows with enthusiasm. Occasionally she gets distracted (and amused) by a broader theme or thought. 'I think my mother was horrified and worried about me a lot. She expected me to write her this weekly letter, which was a chore because I was having this exciting wonderful life I couldn't tell her about.'

Gwen's mother wasn't alone; much of adult Britain was worried about the nation's daughters leaving home in a defeminising uniform, some parents resented mobilisation as an unwelcome 'intervention into the realm of private life'. But for girls like Gwen it was a new beginning.

> We were meeting people all the time and there were lectures about things you never knew anything about: the history of the Royal Air Force, Nazi philosophy and theories about what was going on in Germany. It was a complete revival, although I dearly loved Talbot Heath, you can't go on having school lessons forever.

Even Kathleen's more ambivalent account reveals a momentum and vigour that had previously been lacking in her life.

Part of the WAAF induction was a series of Trade Tests. In these Kathleen surpassed herself and was given an additional six weeks' training, this time in Shrewsbury where 'under a vow of secrecy we were told the astonishing facts about radar'. Early on the RAF made it very clear they had no intention of allowing girls to fly,[1] but there were seventy trades into which women might be selected.

WAAFs with a particular aptitude were assigned work in top-secret areas. Kathleen was soon sewing on the telltale lightning flash

---

1. Due to the demand for more trained pilots in secondary roles, that had changed by the end of the war.

that confirmed her new status as a radio operator. In the spring of 1941, there was an exciting first posting on the Isle of Wight, where she took orders from plotting stations, monitored cathode-ray screens and scanned the night skies for enemy aircraft. At last she felt fully engaged in the war. Admiral Godfrey dutifully drove down from London to visit his eldest daughter during her training.

He had never seen me in uniform before and I suppose that must have been quite a surprise.

'What are you doing with yourself, Kathleen?' he asked.

'I can't possibly tell you, Father. It's a secret,' I answered. He was of course delighted.

As head of Naval Intelligence, it is likely that Admiral Godfrey may have had a hand in his daughter's subsequent transfer. He knew she spoke German, after all. Either way, within a year Aircraft Woman Kathleen Godfrey was redeployed to Bletchley Park.

———— • ————

After her stint at Morecambe, Gwen did not enjoy such an auspicious start. She underperformed in her Trade Tests. Talbot Heath School for Girls had not equipped her with the knowledge of how to fit fan belts or change a fuse, she couldn't do mathematical progressions beyond the twenties and was unable to slot upside-down shapes into a dodecahedron. Her hearing was poor (and still is: 'this miraculous modern hearing aid has changed my life!'), so radio work was out of the question. 'The only thing I could do was write a short essay on why I wanted to join the WAAFs.'

Gwen was destined for 'dull old Innsworth' and work in the 'RAF Records Office'.

Sharp as a tack and impatient with the local part-time clerks (who she remembers as 'slow of comprehension'), Gwen was soon promoted to corporal and running the show. 'You can't live in a muddle, can you? But they could, the RAF, and I am sure they still do!' Gwen set about re-ordering the unworkable filing system. When she was only halfway through this mammoth task an 'immensely' senior Air Commodore made a surprise visit to the station. Gwen's half-filled 'bins' of record cards demanded an explanation, which in turn exposed the former chaos of the Records Office. The officer in charge was swift to shift the blame onto Gwen.

> As I went to the door to close it after the visitors, I heard our officer say, 'She has only very recently been promoted to corporal, and evidently hasn't got the hang of the work yet. We must put someone else in to take over.'

Gwen was livid. She had been undermined and to this day believes that her gender was part of the problem. 'Had I been a man then he would have spoken to me directly: "What is it you are trying to do, Watkins?" But because I was a girl – "Oh well, she doesn't really understand what needs to be done."'

Gwen pauses here to make a broader point. 'It was a trial being a girl. I always wanted to be a boy. I felt that being a girl one was at a disadvantage.' Gwen is the only woman in this book who is frank and unforgiving when it comes to the secondary status of women before, during (and after) the war.

Most of the others are resigned.

'That's how it was back then.'

'You just got on and accepted it.'

But not Gwen. The young corporal demanded a transfer. 'My reason was that it would be better if I were at a station where my languages could be useful to the war effort.' The Trade Tests had not discovered her linguistic talents, so carefully honed at Talbot Heath. When pushed, Gwen also risked admitting to her Commanding Officer, 'The flying officer in charge did not find my work satisfactory.' Anything to leave the Innsworth Records Office. Her timing was impeccable. Under new leadership in 1942 Bletchley Park was expanding fast but because of its extensive security requirements the use of native German speakers, (predominantly Jewish refugees) was problematic. British linguists were at a premium. Gwen was promptly summoned to an interview at the Air Ministry in London. It was the next vital step towards a posting 'which I would not have missed for worlds'.

'We're in the Army now!'

Dubbed 'Queen weed in the garden of the service girls' by the *New Statesman and Nation*, the ATS had an image problem. Hidebound by the anachronistic practices of the British Army and packaged in unflattering serge khaki tunics and brown shoes, the Auxiliary Territorial Service's recruitment levels lagged well behind the WAAFs and Wrens. With ATS girls seen 'as all peeling potatoes' and doing the 'dirty work for everybody else' (and according to Gwen looking like 'sodden ginger puddings'), by 1941 a strategic rethink was necessary. A massive propaganda campaign showed off the new-look Service. The feminine appeal of a modified uniform with tighter waists and padded shoulders was emphasised and the caption 'Adventure Through Service' aimed to highlight the wide range of occupations now available. It was during this rebranding process that Charlotte applied for the ATS. Needless to say, it wasn't her first choice (the Wrens were). But the prospect of 'Adventure Through Service' was surely preferable to being stuck on a domestic science course in Shrewsbury? And above all else Charlotte was eager to serve.

Bar a very brief stint as an exchange student in Germany, Charlotte had been educated at home in Herefordshire. By her own admission she'd led a sheltered life. Basic training in Wrexham came as an almighty culture shock. In her published memoir she writes: 'the biggest shock came from viewing the social behaviour displayed by the girls and in particular the varied standard of table manners. Until that point I had naively believed everyone had lived as I had.'

Over coffee in her sitting-room she supplements this description with a colourful anecdote.

At the barracks there were some rough diamonds. Gosh yes! The mess had tables for about ten people and the food was brought in – vats of scrambled egg. Well one or two of them didn't wait to start or sit down, they just dived in as soon as it was put on the table! They were like animals at the trough!

Well-brought-up Charlotte was horrified. 'I said, "Sit down! How dare you!"' Mid-story she laughs at the memory of her indignant younger self telling the others what to do. 'I think I was perfectly horrid. I hadn't been to the jungle of school and I was blissfully unaware there might have been a pecking order. I just instinctively came out with it.' Needless to say her outrage (and authority) did not go unnoticed. 'I have often wondered whether my explosion at the breakfast table was the reason why I was given a stripe rather smartly.'

By the end of Charlotte's training stint she had been promoted from private to lance corporal. Today Charlotte is still a woman of considerable presence with a direct blue-eyed gaze and an innate respect for order; it is not difficult to understand why she was singled out so early on. Those striking personality traits and a reference to spoken German on her CV were enough to ensure that while others were allotted more humdrum trades, Charlotte was ordered to attend an interview in London. She, like Gwen, was one step away from her ultimate destination – Bletchley Park, otherwise known as Station X.

Betty's entrance into the ATS came two years later, in 1943. At the start of the war her shoe factory had switched to making Army boots; it was hard work manipulating and machining pieces of tough black grain leather together and as a reservist occupation it might have been Betty's only job for the duration of the war. But then her mother died and that changed everything. 'I was shattered. I was rudderless and homeless.'

Unable to afford medical treatment, Gracie Quincey died prematurely from cancer. 'It spread everywhere before she told anyone.' Betty remembers, 'She was having difficulty getting dressed. I didn't see the tumour but her arm began to stick out at a funny angle and by then it was too late.' Without her mother, young Betty felt unwanted in her brother's house.

Joining the war effort suddenly seemed like an attractive option. 'I never considered the Wrens. They were more upper class. No. Not for girls like me. For my station in life it was either the Army or making munitions.' Betty was determined to avoid the latter. 'That would've involved living in someone else's house in Leicester and I just didn't want that, so I joined the Army.'

For Betty the ATS was a perfect fit. It offered her the chance to get away from the bleak confines of her factory job and 'be someone'. As a volunteer at her local fire service she already knew she loved wearing a uniform. To underline just how important this was to her former self, Betty retrieves a cut-out cardboard picture from a large box and lays it down on her swirled burgundy carpet. The girl looking back at us is alert and smiling, her wave of dark hair tucked beneath a jaunty hat and her buttons gleaming. The introduction of clothing coupons in 1941 had little impact on a girl brought up making do with garments her mother cobbled together. It never occurred to Betty to complain about her ATS uniform – quite the reverse. But it's the gusto with which she recounts her three-week training at Northampton's racecourse that really gives away just how important she considered Army life. Standing tall, swinging her arms, she forces home her point:

> I loved drilling and marching. It smartened you up and got you on edge. Get up and go – the Army gave you oomph!
>   Some of 'em that joined up were scruffy. They were slouched but my goodness they soon got their shoulders back!

Betty had found her calling. Years earlier her elementary council education had underlined the importance of Britain and its empire: 'We had a big atlas put up on the wall all marked in red, you were British and you were proud of it. You were not just an ordinary person!' and through service Betty was given a chance to prove just that. At the racecourse it wasn't just her marching skills that were being observed. Aptitude tests soon ascertained who was capable of what.

Some girls were destined for little more than the militarised housework (cooking, cleaning) the ATS was renowned for, but not Betty. 'I took my test. Reading, writing, checked your hearing and then I was given a choice.' Betty was offered a 'man-sized job': she was going to be a specialist wireless operator at 'Y' listening station – Bletchley's crucial sister service. 'I was told to get my kitbag packed and that was it.' Betty was sent off for extensive training on the Isle of Man. 'I thought, what 'ave I let myself in for?'

Both Charlotte and Betty were about to become part of Britain's vast enemy interception and code-breaking network. No matter that they started out in the less popular 'rougher' ATS, Bletchley Park and its outstations had a knack of finding quality and talent. Their rigorous multi-agency recruitment process explains Charlotte's parting comment after a long day talking about her past.

'Yes, at the Park generally there were people of quality.' She smiles. 'A few bad ones got through, but not many.'

Schoolgirl Wrens

'There is something deep in my heart, I know ought to be told you, and probably I am the best person to do it.'

The bombing of Buckingham Palace had a transformative effect on Queen Elizabeth's wartime popularity. Overnight the people learnt to love their resilient little Queen. And Elizabeth loved them back. It was her idea to address the women of the empire in April 1943.

'What have I done' you might ask, 'compared to what my boy has to put up with dodging submarines in the Atlantic or chasing Rommel across Africa? You have done all that he has done in different degrees, endured all that he has endured. For you like him have given all that is good in you regardless of yourself. No man nor woman can do more.

The broadcast was intended for every serving woman, but it was delivered by Her Majesty, the Commandant-in-Chief of the WRNS. Earlier that day the Queen had been in Westminster Abbey for the fourth anniversary of the inauguration of the Women's Royal Naval Service. She listened to the Archdeacon with tears in her eyes. 'You are the daughters of a seafaring nation. The salt of the sea is in the British blood. Be prepared to sacrifice yourselves for the cause in which you firmly believe.'

But most girls did not need to be told; unlike the other Services, the Wrens never required conscription to fill their ranks. They were invariably first choice. Of the fifteen women featured in this book, ten wanted to be Wrens. Just four were successful.

As the smallest service and with a surplus of applicants, the Wrens could afford to be discriminating. No wonder Bletchley Park's first director, Alastair Denniston, and his successor Edward Travis, both naval men themselves, recruited extensively from this select pool of women. Alan Turing's cumbersome Bombe machines were just some of the technological giants that the Park gave birth to. Increasing numbers of competent reliable girls were needed to operate this cutting-edge equipment. It is not a coincidence that by the end of the war in Europe over half of Bletchley's uniformed female staff were Wrens.

In the early 1940s Cora was just a teenager. She had a crush on a boy called Robin who cycled past the house and the nearest she'd got to the war was lessons in Talbot Heath's air raid shelter and practising her basic language skills on French soldiers who'd landed in Bournemouth from Dunkirk. 'I was crippled with shyness, all I could say was *bonjour.*' But Cora did have the nous to work out early on where she would best fit in the jigsaw puzzle of war. 'To my mind nothing looked smarter than a group of marching Wrens.' Aged seventeen she instructed her father (Cecil Pounds, the owner of Charlie's Cars) to write a letter to the naval recruiting office on her behalf.

Well into her eighties and still stylishly dressed, Cora is clear about what motivated her decision. 'They had the best uniform and I've always loved clothes.'

Appearances mattered, especially to teenage girls, and the Wrens trounced the competition when it came to looking good. Their Director Vera Laughton Mathews had the wherewithal to commission the elite fashion designer Edward Molyneux to come up with a sleek couture uniform and the effect was striking. For those promoted to officer rank the prize was a dark navy, double-breasted jacket, a svelte skirt and a tricorne hat. Cora was onto a winner, joining the Wrens was the most fashionable war work.

But before any uniforms were distributed there was hard labour in cumbersome overalls miles from home. For Cora and Ruth, both just out of school, and Joanna who had notched up a year in a domestic science college, even the journey to the remote Scottish training camp was a rite of passage. It was the first time Joanna had travelled by train on her own. 'Being a nice well-brought-up child I let people on the train first so by the time I got on there was no room left!' Amid the crush she befriended a good-looking naval nurse; they sat on their luggage and enjoyed attention and drinks from soldiers. This was Joanna's first big independent adventure. Her father, Group Captain Stradling, had chosen her two boarding schools and insisted on the domestic science college, but alone Joanna had walked into the Wren recruiting office in Gloucester. 'Yes, signing up was the first time I had taken control of my own life.'

Tullichewan Estate, tucked away to the west of Glasgow, had been requisitioned for the war effort; it was a Wren training camp between

July 1943 and late '44. Cora, Ruth and Joanna's applications had coincided with a recruitment drive designed to support the planned invasion of mainland Europe; thousands of girls were being put through their paces. Basic Nissen huts took over the walled garden. In a gesture to their naval affiliation, these accommodation blocks were referred to as cabins, but there was no boating action or reef knots. Nor were there any sailors, much to Cora's disappointment. The training was pretty menial. Ruth, having given up her university ambitions to join the Wrens, was indignant when asked to clean lavatory floors, but tolerated the chore more willingly when she discovered the girl scrubbing next to her had an Oxford degree.

The Spartan conditions and brusque military conduct were unsettling. 'One girl in the bunk beneath me couldn't take it. She started crying and didn't stop. Eventually she was taken away and put in confinement. We could all hear her. Screaming and screaming.' Joanna was relieved to find a companion, Maggie from St Mary's Hall, one of her old boarding schools. Cora's experience was similarly transformed by the presence of two former Talbot Heath pupils – evidence, if any were needed, that the Wrens generally attracted 'the right sort of girl'. Nonetheless little Cora, who had never been away from home, was shocked by the Wrens' loose-lipped behaviour. 'Some of them were older than me. I was prim; I didn't see the necessity for "bloody this" and a "bloody that".' Over seventy years later she neatly recalls that these 'raunchier' girls 'did not make the Bletchley cut'.

Ruth's recall is precise.

'You are going to P5. You are doing SDX, that is Special Duties X.'
    'What is X?'
    'We don't know.'

She remains certain that the Wren officers who selected her really didn't know what X was. However, having received a few dud

Wrens early on, Bletchley had instructed the Admiralty 'to impress upon the selectors the importance of the work on which these Wrens are employed and not to send us too many of the Cook and Messenger type'.

After two weeks of training, Ruth was deemed to be of sufficient calibre to work at HMS *Pembroke V* (the naval term for Bletchley Park). Like Joanna and Cora, she didn't take a written test but the officers in charge knew the girls came from reputable schools and had passed their School Certificates.

Cora, whose Talbot Heath friends were also selected, believes there was more to it than that. 'I think it was about how you conducted yourself and how you spoke.' And Cora, as we know, was not 'loose lipped'.

Nor was Joanna, who was keen to hold on to her new-found independence. She even managed to convince herself that marching up and down was purposeful. 'It does teach you to think of other people; you can't let someone else down.' And the end result of all that drill was worth it. 'Maggie and I were given a choice between two jobs – plotting or working with light electrical equipment in the country. Light electrical equipment! I thought that sounded fun!'

It was within a few months of each other in 1944 that this trio of middle-class, educated, teenage girls were given their orders. Now smartly attired in crisp white shirts, collars and ties, clutching their ditty boxes and kitbags, they headed south into the unknown.

Bletchley Park's naval recruiting network had chosen well: all three were diligent, enthusiastic and capable of keeping a secret.

6

Skills, Security and Secrets

Pamela was in a quandary. She knew that appearing in a West End play would transform her stage career. In an age before television, the cinema was the theatre's only rival and few venues were more prestigious than London's Aldwych Theatre with its three-tiered auditorium. But there was a war on.

Today Pamela is wary of romanticising the early 1940s, but of one thing she is sure. 'The common enemy draws people together like nothing else. There is no doubt that the spirit in England during the war was one of service.' Having sent her letter of application to Bletchley Park she was obliged to attend the subsequent interview. A Cambridge academic and a key recruiter of talented personnel at the Park, it was Frank Birch who interviewed Pamela. After a few German tests he was quick to inform the self-assured woman in front of him he'd like her at the Park. If the British could speak any language it tended to be French; Pam's German was a valuable and rare commodity.[1] But it just so happened that Frank Birch was also a keen actor (with *Aladdin*'s Widow Twankey his standout turn). So before she made her decision, Pam decided to take this theatrical don into her confidence. She said to him, 'You know about the stage. What should I do here? I am an actress and I've had my first West End offer?'

Frank Birch's response was swift and to the point. 'The stage can wait, but the war can't.'

So Pamela, still clueless as to what she would be doing there, dutifully agreed to go to Bletchley Park.

1. In 1938, 72,466 pupils entered for School Certificate French, compared with 9,935 for School Certificate German.

Interviews

Pam is at least three years older than all the other women interviewed in this book. At twenty-four, she had lived: the blue train
across France, a grand boyfriend in Germany, theatre school in
London and a professional career on the stage. Nonetheless the
Bletchley interview has remained with her to this day. It would
make an even greater impression on younger, more naive girls.

Many thousands of recruits were selected en masse for operational and administrative roles. Usually a general assessment,
such as the one Wrens Joanna, Ruth and Cora went through, was
sufficient, but for candidates singled out for more specific tasks
(in the case of women, often language based) a more thorough
interview was deemed necessary. Neither Gwen nor Rozanne ever
went to university but their anecdotes suggest these interviews
shared certain qualities with the Oxbridge entrance procedure.
For some, the 'collegiate' Bletchley experience started early.

Rozanne arrived in London for the interview feeling nervous. A
woman and then a man questioned her and there was a translation
test. This was no ordinary conversational Italian – the text in question focused on the inside of an aeroplane cockpit. Rozanne's knowledge of aviation terminology in Italian was non-existent. She botched
the test. But it didn't matter. The interviewer told the bright, attractive girl in front of him, 'You certainly don't know much about this
but you have a good imagination.' In Bletchley Park the 'power to
apply knowledge as a basis for guess work' when struggling with
snippets of intercepted information required a creative mind.

Rozanne had just that, so passed the interview. The technical
Italian would come with time.

Gwen was equally floored by technical vocabulary. Feeling
unwell with a crashing headache, mid-interview she panicked that
her opportunity to leave the wretched Records Office in Innsworth
was slipping through her fingers. 'I thought, bloody hell, I have
come up from Gloucestershire and I have to go back to
Gloucestershire and he is turning me down like a bedspread.'

The wing commander in question told her sharply, 'We are wasting each other's time' and that her 'vocabulary was insufficient for the purposes for which I should be needed'.

Livid, Gwen decided to take matters into her own hands (once again). 'I bet my vocabulary is better than yours,' she insisted. 'Have you read as much Schiller and Goethe as I have? Do you know a lot of the *Dichterliebe* by heart? How many German songs can you sing?"

Years later, in her sitting-room walled with Victorian literature, Gwen guffaws with laughter. 'Being a squadron leader he probably had never heard of a poem in his life!'

Exhausted from a long day in London, young Gwen ended the session by vomiting into his waste paper basket. As she stumbled away down the corridor she recalls hearing laughter. If nothing else, Gwen's had been a memorable interview.

Within weeks she was transferred to Bletchley Park.

For Charlotte the interview was a more civilised affair. It was conducted in German at Devonshire House in London's Piccadilly,

> with a very pleasant twinkly-eyed Army Major from the Intelligence Corp. I was asked how I would communicate with someone in Scotland to which I responded I would do so by telephone, in writing, by telegram or by courier.

Charlotte is certain he was testing her lateral thought and general intelligence. She passed his test 'but still did not know what was going on'.

Thanks to their Uncle Bill, it was again the head of BP's naval section, Frank Birch, who interviewed the Moller sisters, Doris and Georgette. They couldn't offer German or Italian so there was no test, and with no test there was no clue as to what they would be doing. 'Frank didn't tell us anything about the work. Just that it was secret.'

Indeed virtually all the girls left their interviews none the wiser about what their actual employment would be in the Park. This entry in Ann's diary is a case in point: '13 July 1943: Interviewed in hut near gate by Mr Saunders (staff officer) – mainly him telling me about conditions here.' She goes on to recount details of her pay (£150 a year until she is twenty-one), her shifts, her leave, and the cost of her billet accommodation. She is even told there is a good chance she will start with her friend Frances in September. However there is no mention of the work she will be involved in. The unknown didn't dampen Ann's spirits; after her twenty-minute interview she declared. 'All MOST hopeful.'

This generation of young girls had been brought up to do what they were told and ask no questions. According to Lady Jean, 'it was made clear to me once I had started work it would be very difficult to leave'. But the finality of the situation does not seem to have put her off. At the beginning of 1942 she simply collected her rail warrant and headed towards a 'terribly secret' place called Bletchley Park. It was wartime; the country was being governed on a 'need to know' basis and the Bletchley Girls, exhibiting a level of trust that would be considered extraordinary in today's world, made that job much easier.

Gwen's journey stands out. Having arrived from Gloucestershire at the wireless operating centre, Chicksands in Bedford, she was told, 'Don't put your kit down, Corporal. You're going on right away.'

The sergeant then made a glib remark about blindfolding her before she was put in the back of a blacked-out van. By this time young Gwen began to feel decidedly anxious and her eventual arrival at the Park provided little reassurance. Standing alone at the 'magnificent gates' she was told by the guards she'd arrived at 'the biggest lunatic asylum in Britain'. But to find that out for herself Gwen would have to wait – she wasn't allowed in without a pass.

When Gwen arrived she knew nothing about GC&CS but

GC&CS would soon know everything about her. Both she and Rozanne note that in the wake of their interviews several weeks passed before they were sent to Bletchley. Once there Gwen's wait still wasn't over: confused and hungry after her long journey from Gloucestershire via Chicksands, she was bumped from Bletchley to an old vicarage in a neighbouring village. Forbidden to leave the premises as no one knew when she would be 'collected', Gwen spent several days picking gooseberries and chatting to a couple of equally nonplussed girls under the supervision of a WAAF officer. Like everyone else in the Park, she was being 'vetted'. Extensive security checks on new recruits were standard procedure.

During her interview, Ann was told she would 'hear in a day or two if refused, in two weeks if accepted'. A fortnight later Bletchley had not managed to get in contact with one of her referees so Ann's place remained unconfirmed. It was over three weeks later that she finally received a positive confirmation from the Park. 'Hurrah!' Ann had been admitted to Britain's most secret organisation.

A Separate Secret Service

Unlike all the others, Pat and Betty weren't mysteriously bundled off to Bletchley Park nor to one of its outstations. But although Pat had successfully rebuffed her godmother's efforts to send her to Buckinghamshire, she still ended up serving in the secret codebreaking nexus. Both she and Betty were destined to spend the latter half of the war hard at work in listening stations across the country. Their pricked ears became part of the Y-service, without which there would have been no messages to decode, no secrets worth keeping.

'I have always said to myself – they couldn't have done it without us!' Betty repeats this point more than once: Bletchley was nothing without its sister Y-service, which sent thousands of intercepted enemy communications to Buckinghamshire every day. While others were summoned to the Park, these two women were hand-picked to work at the coal face of wartime espionage; their tools were boxy radio receivers and Bakelite headphones and their skill was a capacity to listen in secret, one in German, the other in Morse.

For a while it had looked as if Pat wouldn't have much of a war at all. A fellow country girl, she suffered from the same affliction as Lady Jean – bovine tuberculosis. Swollen lymph glands had forced her to abandon London and return to dreary Lancashire. Her dream of joining the over-subscribed Wrens was in jeopardy but unlike Lady Jean, Pat had a secret weapon – she could speak German. Lancashire was immeasurably cheered up for her by the continued presence of her family's Jewish Austrian maids and Pat's German was soon more than proficient. She was just what the Wrens had been told to look out for by the Y-service, desperate for linguists.

While Bletchley Park had begun earmarking 'the right type of recruit' as early as 1937, the listening stations found themselves ill prepared for war. Having anticipated that the Germans would impose a radio silence at the beginning of the conflict, they were astonished by the increasing number of enemy wireless communications they picked up as the Nazis swept through Western Europe. Bletchley Park had anticipated that the more mobile the war became, the more dependent on the radio the Germans would be, but their sister listening service misjudged the situation and was left playing catch-up. The armed forces were promptly instructed to find German speakers; with men required on the front line the focus quickly shifted to potential women. The situation was urgent. Every recruit not only had to be security cleared but needed competent German listening skills, which were not commensurate with the formal written study of languages taught in Britain's pre-war schools. Unlike the girls at Bletchley Park who worked with written German, Y-service listeners had to have a finely tuned ear. Pat stood out; she was from a trustworthy military family and possessed excellent German listening skills acquired from a bona fide source – domestic servants based in England. She was duly summoned by the Wrens for a language test in Liverpool's Royal Liver building.

> I met a young naval officer there and he asked me what I was going to be. I said, 'I don't know, they haven't told me what will happen if I pass.' We agreed that I would probably be a spy and I had a sinking fear of being dropped over Europe. I was nervous.

She passed the test, and in desperate need of linguists the Wrens saw fit to overlook her patchy medical history. 'I went for a check-up on a very hot day in Preston and they said they would accept me for service in the UK but not overseas.' So no parachuting across Europe then. Instead Pat's long-awaited military service began in London's Mill Hill, where she spent the heatwave of August 1942 'wearing a summer dress and marching around like an idiot'. But the square-bashing didn't last long.

Assigned as a Special Duties Linguist, Pat said goodbye to the tart in the bunk bed opposite ('she was the first I'd ever met, the Wrens weren't all posh'), took her little round hat and serge coat and set off for the opposite end of the capital. She had been given an address in Wimbledon and was told there she would undergo a very secretive training. She knew better than to ask any further questions.

———— ◆ ————

ATS girl Betty was also obediently heading for a destination miles from home. In the autumn of 1943, having been selected as a wireless operator, she was en route to the Isle of Man. Having spent her whole life in land-locked Northamptonshire, she had never been on a boat before. It was one of many firsts. Soon she was living in a seafront hotel in Douglas, the island's capital, but this was no holiday. In the dining-room of the boarding house Betty underwent three months of relentless Morse-code training. More easily transmitted over greater distances than the human voice, Morse was used extensively as a means of communication by both sides in the war; training new recruits was standard practice.

'We did what we were told. They said, "You're learning Morse code. Put your headphones on!" So we did and they didn't 'alf pinch! 'orrible old metal things. Made your ears sore.'

For weeks Betty sat listening to dits and dahs; now in her armchair she easily lapses into the Morse alphabet – it is her second language. 'It began very very slowly and then soon the Morse got faster and faster. In the end it got so fast the teachers couldn't do it quick enough so they used recordings. That was horrendous.' The girls who couldn't keep up were sent back to the beginning of the course but not Betty; at well over twenty-one words a minute she soon had one of the fastest Morse speeds. However, despite being a record 'Morser' she was still none the wiser as to what she was being trained for.

'Not a word was said about the nature of the work we would be doing. NOT A WORD.' Some of the girls Betty was training with did try and ask. 'But we was told: "You do NOT ask questions. You get on with the job you are training for. Do you 'ear? You get on with the job you are training for!"' Betty didn't need reminding, she had always done what she was told. A lifetime of hardship and low expectations left her ideally placed to cope in the Army. Finally in January 1944 Betty, with about a hundred other ATS girls, was transferred to Harrogate where she was informed she would be working on the Yorkshire Moors. In the bleak midwinter this was an invidious prospect, but still no explanations were given. It was too early for that; Betty had not yet signed the Official Secrets Act.

Highly Confidential

Angus is Ann's husband. Also a war veteran (and a nonagenarian), he supplements his wife's memories from an armchair.

There were a lot of posters in the war. If you were told not to talk, you didn't talk. I remember one: 'Be like Dad – keep Mum!' Yes and there was another with a woman on a sofa and a couple of officers chatting her up. 'Keep mum, she's not so dumb!'

Angus did not work at Bletchley but like everyone else during the war he couldn't fail to get the message: 'careless talk costs lives'. The Ministry of Information had gone into overdrive. Part of a massive extension in state activity, films and colourful posters bombarded the senses and the need to keep shtum was a central theme. But if propaganda and wartime confidentiality were one thing, the level of secrecy at Bletchley Park was quite another.

It is self-evident that Britain's code-breaking operation had to be walled off from public view. If the enemy got wind of the inroads being made into their most confidential encrypted messages they would crank up their security measures and block out the Allies' most valuable source of intelligence, thus nullifying Bletchley's existence. The Park took this need for total confidentiality very seriously. They went to extreme lengths to maintain secrecy at every level; no worker was immune. The fifteen Bletchley Girls in this book were not all from the same class, they did not do the same job, nor did they all work within the confines of the Park itself. But they did have one common cultural bond: they were part of a secret world about which they could not breathe a word.

Talking to them decades later the degree to which that need for confidentiality was drummed in remains startlingly apparent.

'It was just so hush hush. Unbelievable, incredible when you think about it.'

'It's hard to believe now but we knew we must not say a word.'

'You couldn't say anything. That's just how it was.'

Phrases like these reoccur throughout our conversations. Overnight, secrecy became a dominant feature in each of their young lives, and it all began with the signing of the Official Secrets Act. According to Pat, 'That was when everything changed.'

The Official Secrets Act (OSA) was first passed in 1911, justified as a necessary extension of national security in the face of an increasingly belligerent Germany. By the time war broke out in 1939 it had been strengthened twice. As a law, individuals were automatically bound by it; the signing or swearing-in process was a salutary reminder to the signatory that they were under an obligation not to breach state secrets. No woman featured here has forgotten her introduction to this Act.

Charlotte remembers a vast document that she was forced to read on the spot. There and then she had no choice but to swear she would abide by its awesome demands. Gwen was staggered by a diminutive wing commander's pronouncements on the subject of the OSA: 'It clearly states that if, by doing any of the things I have warned you against, you disclose the slightest information which could be of use to the enemy you will be committing TREASON.' Nervous (and impressed) she read through the 'piece of rather yellowish paper' but to this day remains none the wiser as to what it was she signed. Adrenalin had temporarily overtaken her considerable intellect.

Muriel was just fourteen, too young surely to be under oath?

'No! They weren't worried about how young you were because you couldn't blab. You were sworn to secrecy when you walked in.' Muriel is adamant. It is impossible for her to even contemplate that she might have breached Bletchley's confidentiality, no matter how young she was. From the outset, indiscretion was never an option.

For seventeen-year-old Cora the initiation procedure was so surreal (and intimidating) she got the giggles. 'We were all putting up our hands and swearing to King and country and I couldn't help myself.' A totally mystified Cora had been herded from the railway station, through the well-guarded perimeter of the Park and into the manor house. Before she knew it, she was in the oak-panelled ballroom being lectured to on the subject of secrecy.

'We were told we must not tell anybody anything, not even anyone in BP. You don't say what hut you are in, even.' No wonder

101

Cora got the giggles – she had no idea what they were talking about.

Fellow Wren Joanna was also herded into the Park with twenty other girls; her induction took place in a hut at the hands of a civilian. Aware that her job involved 'light electrical work' Joanna was more in the know than Cora, and with a military father (Group Captain Stradling), she insists she needed no reminding of the importance of state secrets. To this day she remains forthright on the subject.

> Now when the government says 'don't' we say 'why not?' But then we had much more common sense. We knew damn well what will happen if we blab. It will kill people. We didn't need help. We knew we couldn't talk for a reason.

Joanna may not have required help keeping secrets but Bletchley Park took no chances. Not prepared to rely solely on the Official Secrets Act, procedures were kept clandestine and there were a series of ominous lectures and warnings.

Air Commodore Charles Medhurst dropped his daughter Rozanne at her billet in the village of Fenny Stratford the night before she began work at Bletchley. She still had no clue what she was doing in Buckinghamshire. 'I had been told by my father that "the people at the Park" would tell me what to do. Until then I was to say nothing, ask nothing.'

Later that evening a man arrived and 'gave me a pass ticket' and said it was 'vital to look after it well, lend it to no one. Keep it safe.' The next morning Rozanne set off to the Park on her red bicycle. She was immediately ushered upstairs in the big house where a forty-five-year-old professor, Tom Boase, gave her a lecture. Rozanne writes in her private memoirs that it was a brilliant clear talk about what she would be doing at the Park but goes on to concede, 'My memory of it is: NEVER talk to anyone about what you do, even to your fellow workers, and if you, on purpose, do so you may be shot!'

Death threats like these were not uncommon. The wing commander who oversaw Gwen's induction made a lasting impression on the eighteen-year-old recruit when he finished his sermon on secrecy with a florid threat. If she disclosed any information she 'would be liable to the extremest penalties of the law, and I'm not sure whether, at the moment, that's hanging or shooting by firing squad'. Startled, Gwen's first response was to assume he was joking. He wasn't.

Meanwhile Georgette recalls that during their interview Frank Birch told the Moller sisters their work would be very secret. 'He said we couldn't say a word and if we did we would be shot at dawn. I suppose he meant it!' On the telephone, sitting in a hammock in Texas, Georgette now sees the funny side but back then, for two girls who had just escaped Occupied Europe, the world was a scary place.

Ruth, who was eventually posted to Eastcote, one of Bletchley Park's outstations, is unsure of her initial movements. But she can remember signing something. Having been warned she would be working anti-social hours with no promotion and that once she was 'in' she couldn't leave, Ruth was then told the work was very secret and that if she signed the OSA and subsequently broke her oath of secrecy she would go to prison 'at the very least'.

Ruth pauses, mid-mouthful (by now we are eating lunch in her north London home). She reflects on this dire job description and the threatening secrecy that came with it and remembers her response:

> I realised whatever we are doing, it is so secret that if you say anything you have to go to prison, 'at least'. I didn't know what 'at least' meant. I thought what could be worse – chop off your head, hang you or deport you? I suppose everyone else thought the same.

After three months of training and a second remote location, Betty's working life in the Army also began with a warning: 'If you break your oath you are committing treason. What you are doing is important. You speak nothing of what you are doing out of this camp.' Here Betty stops and allows herself a smile. 'But the thing was, we still didn't know what we was doing!'

This emphasis on secrecy was tantamount to indoctrination. Bletchley could not afford to compromise its work. Muriel remembers being shown a film reinforcing the subject of confidentiality and Charlotte has never forgotten her intimidating induction with an Army captain: 'the implications of breaking our silence remains with me today. There were degrees of punishment to fit the severity of any betrayal – the most serious being the death penalty.' The captain's warning was silently underlined by the presence of a gun on the table.

Meanwhile in Ann's diary is proof that the Park's obsession with secrecy has not been exaggerated with the passage of time. On her first day at Bletchley, 28 September 1943, she writes:

Had a very interesting talk by Mr Fletcher who is I believe head of our section! He is awfully nice and young for so important a position. Gosh! What secrets this place contains – terribly thrilling, important and vital. And the security –

Two days later Mr Fletcher's first lecture is supplemented with a 'talk by Mr de Grey (second in command) on secrecy.' Later that same night Ann had already lied to her landlady 'Mrs C' about the work she was doing at the Park. 'She told Mr C I did clerical work like their niece (heaven forbid!) and he said I must find letter writing easy when I did clerical work all day. Gosh! It's nice to smile to myself!'

In fact, Ann with her Oxford maths degree worked right at the heart of the code-breaking nexus, in Hut 6, the 'Bethlehem' of Bletchley Park, where German Enigma messages were decoded. But the family she lived with, like her own back in Oxford, had no clue what she was up to.

For others the adjustment was less easy. Selected for the Y-service, Pat had been sent to Southmead House in Wimbledon, but before she began her training she too was introduced to the Official Secrets Act 'and that made all the difference to everything'. Still garrulous at ninety-one, Pat is a very good storyteller. Later she would become a successful journalist, but in August 1942, under oath, she committed herself to secrecy. The implications weren't easy. As a cipher officer in Egypt, Jean, her younger sister, had also signed the Official Secrets Act. Two sisters who'd grown up together sharing everything, suddenly had secrets; huge blank spaces that they could not talk about. 'It was a very binding act. It did feel restrictive. You had to be aware of it.' Even now when discussing the subject Pat chooses her words carefully. 'I think it made me secretive for the rest of my life. Yes, it did.'

7

Secret Work

Once shrouded in secrecy, Bletchley Park is now a vast museum open to the public. On its website it promises visitors 'the largest and most comprehensive collection of Enigma machines in the world' – a clear indication of the vital role this machine played in Germany's wartime communications. By 1945 the Nazis had deployed over 100,000 of these electronic lookalike typewriters, which beneath their innocuous appearance housed an extremely sophisticated cipher system. Each Enigma machine used a series of rotors with numbered ring scales and electrical connections on a plugboard to encrypt and decrypt messages. The German military believed this system to be impenetrable. Certainly the possible number of settings (158.9 million million million on a standard three-rotor Enigma), the daily changing of those settings and the numerous different versions of the Enigma machine and message keys in use represented a challenge of enormous complexity for Bletchley's cryptanalysts. No wonder that in 1940 the first steps towards unravelling Germany's encoded communications were greeted with euphoria.

> I can remember most vividly the roars of excitement, the standing on chairs and the waving of order papers, which greeted the first breaking of Red [Enigma key] by hand in the middle of the battle of France.

These are the words of Stuart Milner-Barry, a cryptographer and later the head of Hut 6, and they are often recalled in history books. The immediate impression given is of a park heaving with excited geniuses, in the know and at the top of their game. But that impression is misleading.

'I wish I could remember if I knew I was working on Enigma messages. But I don't.'

Pat has since learnt she was intercepting German Enigma naval codes but back then she is not sure she was ever told about Enigma. She tuts; memory is an unreliable tool. Betty still doesn't know whether the Morse she was reading was Enigma-encrypted or not, and she had no idea the humming 500cc motorbikes that visited her remote location on the Yorkshire Moors were destined for Buckinghamshire. She didn't know of Bletchley Park's existence.

Gwen meanwhile is certain. 'I'd never heard of Enigma. Not in all the time I worked at the Park.' Gwen decoded the Luftwaffe's messages that didn't use Enigma, so it is perhaps more understandable that she was not informed about Bletchley's most iconic opponent. But her ignorance is also symptomatic of the compartmentalised reality endured by the vast majority of the code-breaking workforce. Cora still has no real clue as to what the sheets of 'noughts and crosses' she worked on day and night actually represented.

Explanations were supplied on a 'need to know' basis. The lower rungs of the pecking order were filled with women who worked in an information vacuum, clueless as to what was going on around them. So much for Enigma, some of them didn't even know they were involved in a code-breaking operation. They were small cogs in the Park's vast infrastructure, and there was only one thing they could all be sure of: that their work had to be kept absolutely confidential.

Rozanne recalls walking into the wrong room by accident. '"No no!" a man said, "You can't come in here!" He slammed the door shut in my face!' Everyday pleasantries were not guaranteed in a place where secrecy was paramount. With little else to go on, that secrecy nurtured a sense of expectation among its recipients. What they did necessitated sentries, oaths, threats, guns, high walls and passes, surely therefore it was worthwhile?

Doris nods her head. 'Yes, it did make me feel it must be very important work. Otherwise why the secrecy?'

The Information Age

In an era when girls did what they were told, Charlotte's testimony stands out. She didn't just abide by the rules, she enjoyed abiding by them. She was a very good soldier. It is easy to imagine her sitting upright at her desk in her khaki tunic and shirt, with her soft brown hair neatly tucked two inches above the collar, quietly confident, surrounded by older men in uniform.

> Yes, in the early days they were all older men. But that was okay, I was more used to men than women. Dad was a cricketer so the house was often full of his cricket friends. They didn't faze me. Not much fazes me – just a rough sea!

She looks up and laughs, remembering herself at nineteen walking past the sentries, diligently showing her pass, then on, via the sweeping path, around the emerald splash of grass and into the 'large ugly house'.

In September 1941, a month before the 'Wicked Uncles' sent the candid letter to Churchill that set so much change in motion, Charlotte became the first girl in this book to work at Station X. Through the vaulted gothic-style inner porch, past a gloomy panelled entrance and up the timber stairs into an extended southwest wing, Charlotte took her seat daily (or nightly) in one of the former guestrooms above the ballroom. It's possible she was even working in the nursery. She remembers a small room with an open fire, the embers of which were invariably insufficient to keep the four occupants warm.

Three men at desks and Charlotte – a small part of Major Ralph Tester's military section.

With the help of Charlotte's graceful descriptions, the image of a young girl working in secret in a now iconic building is powerful. It is also only half the story.

> Nothing was in clear language, it was all in groups of letters or figures on A4-sized sheets of paper – masses of them. All we were doing on the card index was putting things into date order and registering them under their call signs.

It didn't matter that Charlotte couldn't understand the code that she was tasked to sort. Her job was not to understand, it was to register every message that passed across her desk. Beyond her department and rank these traffic logs and indexes would be analysed for telltale patterns that might indicate enemy movement and intention, their coded contents would be unravelled, translated and evaluated, the final product would be filed for cross-reference purposes. But none of that was Charlotte's business. She did not even know what went on in the next-door room; her lot was to input data.

'Yes it was boring,' she admits. But seven decades later Charlotte remains sanguine. She had been given a very secret job to do and no matter how tedious it was she would do it to the best of her ability. 'All I was concerned with was recording everything. I didn't know enough to say anything and I had no wish to say anything.'

This self-contained girl, brought up in the middle of nowhere and home schooled, had a remarkable capacity to cope with one of the Park's most prevalent features – monotony.

For Betty, work took place in a purpose-built Army block.

> There was about a hundred of us. I was in set 2, my set number was 6. I always sat at the same desk and listened to the same frequency. It was German military codes I was taking down. That is all I can tell you.

Her job in an Army hut on the 'bloomin' cold' Yorkshire moor, miles away from Bletchley Park, was as compartmentalised as

Charlotte's. 'Oh I did wonder about the codes. Yeah. But if you asked you just got the same reply: "Get on with the job you are trained to do and don't ask questions!"'

Bundled up in khaki serge, ATS girl Betty knew better than to make a fuss.

> Every dot, every dash had to be listed. Every message logged, dated. There was a graph that you had to fill in every quarter of an hour. If you didn't know a letter you didn't guess, you just left a space and carried on. You did NOT guess 'cos you might have guessed the wrong letter.

Like Charlotte, Betty was hand-picked from the women's Army, and she too was an exemplary worker. Her ears, craning and twitching, picked up the enemy station's Morse communications through the atmospherics and her meticulously filled sheets of paper provided the undigested fodder that, at the opposite end of England, girls like Charlotte had to register. Neither knew of the other's existence. 'The messages were called traffic. A girl came and took the message, rolled it up and pushed it into a tube. Where it went I don't know.' But she remembers the motorbikes sitting, waiting, before careening through the night (and day) to reach their Buckinghamshire destination – an umbilical cord supplying the Park with its life blood.

Germans transmitted signals at volumes designed for their own purposes not for distant enemy ears; Betty had to strain for six hours at a time. 'Oh it was stressful! Catching every sound in time.' And then just as suddenly the same job was mindlessly dull.

> Sometimes there was no signal, then you would write NHR – Nothing Heard Required. You could sit for five or six hours and listen to nothing, just atmospherics. But you couldn't leave your seat. Ooh no.

In Bletchley Park's postwar review, under a section entitled 'medium or low grade labour' is the observation: 'It was astonishing what young women could be trained to do.' But given Betty's previous job, working day in day out at a shoe factory for a pittance, perhaps it is not so astonishing. She happily tolerated the tedium; for this young girl the Army had given her a purpose and an identity. 'I was someone!' And indeed she was, she was one of Britain's secret listeners upon whom Bletchley Park depended.

Charlotte began her working life at the Park registering freshly received Y-station traffic still wrapped in its encrypted packaging. However there were plenty of girls at the other end of the Bletchley equation who had similar jobs. But these women were indexing messages that had already been decoded; their job was to translate, order and file on a massive scale. Only by sorting the contents of thousands of messages into vast databases of technical and military terms, enemy sightings, locations and movements could the raw decoded material be marshalled and turned into useful intelligence – or Ultra (the cover name for the high-grade signals intelligence produced at Bletchley Park). The records were a treasure trove of extraordinary information. So sophisticated was the Park's indexing system that some academics have argued it undermines the idea that our current epoch is the 'information age'. But unlike today's world, in Bletchley's pre-computer era the information had to be filed by hand. And that was a very dull job.

Pamela now laughs at the memory, but back then it was a different matter. Head of the Naval Section, Frank Birch, had cajoled her into forgoing her first break on the West End stage. He convinced Pamela that her language skills must not be wasted. Her expectations were raised. And then there was the signing of the Official Secrets Act.

'I thought at first I was going to be dropped from an aeroplane into Germany. Goodness knows my German wasn't really good enough for that but one has exalted ideas when one is young.' She clears her throat and adds mischievously, 'And one had been selected for one's brilliance!'

Twenty-four years old, worldly, ambitious and attractive, for Pamela her job in the Indexing Section of Hut 4 came as a crushing blow. 'I was doing nothing but copying words onto cards. Anyone could have done it with School Certificate German.' There she was, stuck in a wooden hut, working as little more than a glorified admin assistant.

I met Adam, her seventy-six-year-old nephew in the kitchen, on a hunt for tea bags. 'Ah my aunt is amazing,' he said, 'but perhaps she is not as good at talking about Bletchley as other parts of her life.' That's not entirely surprising. The Park has an extraordinary legacy – some argue its intelligence shaved two years off the war – but such an achievement has encouraged hyperbole and distortion. Pamela is determined that no amount of retrospective glorification will disturb the memory of her own experience. Translating words onto cards from broken bits of German ('they were a bit like modern text messages, I suppose'), in an unremarkable part of England, was not what she'd imagined doing when she sacrificed the opportunity of a lifetime.

Small wonder her primary memory of the mansion is of a 'pretty hideous building'.

Unravelling Enigma

Ruth still takes her volunteering at Bletchley Park very seriously. She regularly gives up her Sundays and travels from north London to Buckinghamshire where she shows the assembled audience how to set up a Bombe machine. Once described as having the appearance of 'great big metal bookcases', it was Alan Turing's and Gordon Welchman's invention of this iconic electronic testing device in 1940 that radically increased the rate at which the Enigmas' settings were discovered, thereby ensuring the decoded messages were still operationally useful in the field. No wonder

Ruth is keen to remind her modern audience of this machine's starring role in Bletchley's history.

Immaculately turned out and precise in her use of code-breaking terminology, there is not much Ruth doesn't know about the Bombe and its capacity to crunch through Enigma's codes. But seventy years ago things could not have been more different.

A slight woman, Ruth recalls feeling weighed down by her unwieldy kitbag on the long walk from Eastcote tube station – after a brief induction at Bletchley Park she'd been transferred to this north London suburb. Here, for security reasons, 120 Bombe machines were housed in what had become Bletchley Park's largest outstation. Ruth eventually arrived at two purpose-built Ministry of Defence blocks; flanked by armed military police and surrounded by thick brick walls, one of these was to be her new workplace. It was here she met her mechanical destiny.

Explanations were kept to a bare minimum. '"We are breaking German codes." That's what we were told by the petty officer, who smiled at us and said this as if it was very exciting but I was unimpressed.'

Ruth, bright, competitive and well read, had grown up on a diet of Biggles and his fantastic flying adventures. From the age of ten she had read of stolen codes and spy work; at school there were secret circles and codes to crack in comics. Frankly, why would she be impressed? And to top it off she had been informed there could be no promotion – Bombe operators remained Bombe operators. 'That was particularly disappointing for me because I liked to win things'.

Small wonder then that the Bombe, a black brute of staggering proportions, strumming and rattling, blocking out the light, intimidated rather than excited its new operative. However Ruth's feelings were irrelevant; she knew that in war as in life, 'nice girls do what they are told'.

In the summer of 1944, Ruth joined an operation at its zenith. With 1,676 Wrens dutifully tending 211 Bombe machines, the black gold of Britain's code-breaking mission was more than ready for the Allies' push across Europe. Expectant Bombes throbbed with around a hundred rotating drums, twelve miles of wire, and one million soldered connections apiece. Every set of three coloured drums represented the rotors on the Enigma machine and each Bombe was capable of driving through all 17,576 possible rotor positions in approximately thirty minutes. Negotiating miles of snaking cable, the Wrens on duty plugged the machines up at the back and prayed for a positive 'stop' that would reveal the settings of the Enigma key in question.

After D-Day these Wren–Bombe teams helped harvest more than 18,000 Enigma messages daily. But that wasn't always the case. The first Bombe only arrived at the Park in March 1940. Both expensive and complex to make, two years later Bombe numbers remained low. The continuing shortage of these one-tonne machines created problems for Bletchley's Naval Section. Admiral Dönitz, the German military's most security-conscious leader, did not share the High Command's overblown faith in Enigma's unbreakable reputation. His machines were protected by 336 possible rotor (or wheel) Enigma configurations as opposed to the 60 available to the German Army and Air Force. This extra layer of encryption put a strain on the Bombes, which took more than five times as long to deliver a verdict on the naval settings. The handful of three-wheel Bombes available were unable to cope with the backlog. It was Bletchley girls, engaged in a Turing technique called Banburismus, who were employed to make up the difference. Their task was an invidious one.

In early 1942 Lady Jean arrived in Hut 8.

> It is little use asking where, what or why but for the next year I marked the letters in the German messages then perforated those same marks and then compared one message on top of the other that I had marked. If three holes were on the top of three other marked ones these were put through the hatch to the next room. Doing this for a year sent me nearly crazy.

How Lady Jean had longed to join the heroes of war. Her beloved Commando Johnny died in the line of fire, and he was not alone. Pilkington was another Commando Jean came close to; he died in Italy in 1941. Barred from the Wrens and stuck on Arran for the first two years of the war, Lady Jean had dreamt of a noble destiny in this bloody conflict. At last in late 1941 came the tip-off from Mountbatten and a command to be at a 'certain London office, a certain room at a certain time'. It boded well. This was, her smart girlfriends assured her, a truly secret mission. Imagine then the crushing disappointment of that first day.

'I was taken to Hut 8 where the head of the shift tapped the table and announced, 'This is a new recruit, Jean Graham, from Scotland; take her and show her what to do.' The technique didn't take long to learn, but it took mindless hours to execute. Lady Jean spent her shifts hunched over meaningless strips of 'lavatory paper, marking letters, punching holes, comparing papers'.

Years later she tries to describe what she did; the monotonous tone she slips into is as revealing as her words. 'I had no idea how boring it was going to be. It was excessively boring!' Arran's Lady had been reduced to little more than a drum in a Bombe machine. She loathed her job at the Park and talks of it with reluctance. Even Buckinghamshire does not escape her wrath.

'Bletchley was a terrible place for fog. Day after day we'd have thick pea soup fog.' The fact that she knew she couldn't leave compounded her misery. Secret missions are notoriously hard to wriggle out of.

———◆———

Lady Jean – an aristocrat – was never destined for university; Ruth on the other hand had matriculated but then war got in the way. With no degree, the chances of either getting a skilled job at the Park were slight. (There were already plenty of Bletchley Girls with degrees consigned to menial jobs.) Ann, however, was an exception. Having studied mathematics at Oxford for three years, upon arrival at the Park in 1943 she was handed a job commensurate with her intellectual capacity. If Ruth operated Bombes and Jean simulated the work of Bombes, it was Ann who helped create the operating instructions ('menus') for the Bombes. Right at the centre of Bletchley's code-breaking infrastructure, in the Machine Room in Hut 6 (home of German Army and Air Force Enigma-encrypted messages), Ann was given two weeks' training. Her main task was learning to compose these 'menus' for Bombes. Although forbidden to make reference in her diary to the nature of the work she was doing, it is clear she found it satisfying. By the second week Ann writes: 'Enjoyable day. Hard working and even asked for advice by the other three!' And it is with a note of triumph that on the 29 October 1943 she observes that her friend Martie, 'Has a job which does not require a degree.'

Ann remembers feeling challenged. 'If there was known to be something important you were harried. You could feel under a lot of pressure. I personally work better under pressure.' In the next room cryptanalysts were coming up with 'cribs' that would help provide a way in to the settings for the Enigma keys that day. (This process was possible thanks in part to the German habit of using stock phrases in their coded communications – *Heil Hitler* was not uncommon.) It was Ann's task to convert these guesses or cribs into specific 'menus' (diagrams) as quickly as she could. They were then placed into a wire tray with a shout – 'Menu's up!' The head of the watch (sometimes Ann) phoned through the menus to an outstation (invariably Eastcote or Stanmore) where they were used to set up a Bombe machine (cue Ruth). The daily race to package the cribs into tight workable menus that delivered Bombe 'stops' suited Ann's temperament. '29 December 1943: Worked like the devil all day. Good fun.'

Although Hut 6 now has iconic status, there was nothing romantic about Ann's place of work. By the time she arrived the wooden cabin had given way to a concrete block. She remembers a 'soulless' brick building with Crittall steel windows; 'more like a hospital with big rooms off corridors'. While her mathematical skills brought her cheek by jowl with 'an elite within an elite', like the other women featured in this book, Ann had no overall context for the work she was doing.

> I knew I was breaking German codes, but I didn't know where they came from and I didn't know or hear the word Enigma until decades later. I think I did once see a Bombe, though not at first. We were told so little.

But in Ann's case the building and the broader picture didn't matter. Even in her free time she was someone who enjoyed solving mathematical puzzles and a flippant comment made decades later says it all.

'There was a girl in our room who just wrote letters. She did hardly any work. I felt sorry for her. She really missed out.'

Job Satisfaction

Most of the 7.5 million female workers engaged in the British war effort found themselves doing fairly menial jobs. Ann was lucky. In her case the realities of a workplace she had deliberately targeted lived up to her expectations. German-speaking Pat was another lucky one. On her intensive radio telegraphy course in Wimbledon, Pat's brain tingled with a fresh challenge. Her instructor was none other than Lieutenant Freddie Marshall. At the outset of war Freddie was one of the few naval officers capable of understanding German. He spent the first months of the conflict trying to bridge the linguist gap single-handedly, frantically translating the plain language radio communications that proliferated as the Germans smashed through Western Europe. The job soon overwhelmed him but Freddie was a fighter. Rather than despair he set up a two-week training course. The aim was to give German speakers practice in handling wireless receivers and exposure to German communications and nautical terms. Accuracy and speed were essential; the listening service could not carry deadwood.

Pat found herself in a mocked-up Y-station. 'Freddie was in one room with a microphone and we sat in another with headphones and receivers. He broadcast the kind of German messages we'd have to listen to. There were the call signs and the code groups.' What Pat remembers as meaningless clumps of four letters 'Anton, Bertha, Cesar . . .' were in fact simulations of the scrambled naval Enigma messages that the Bletchley Park conveyor belt (made up of Jean, Ruth, Ann and thousands of others) would have to try and decode.

'It was in plain German, the letters went on and on,' Pat recalls. Then over his resonant voice Freddie would build in interference, fading and interruptions. Through all this aural clutter Pat had to write down 'EXACTLY' what she heard. There was no margin for error. At the end of a frantic two weeks the girls were tested; only then could Pat finally begin waging war against those Germans she'd so enjoyed 'bombing' in the local quarry as a child.

<hr>

Of course job satisfaction was about more than the mere task at hand. The country was at war, the enemy had to be beaten. The Ministry of Information was formed the day after Britain declared war, on 4 September 1939, and from May 1940 onwards Government propaganda was focused on a predominantly domestic campaign: everyone was encouraged to do their bit and each individual action mattered: keeping 'mum', swapping roses for cabbages, saving petrol and putting up with a mundane job to 'free a man for the fleet'. The message was clear: the home front would help win the war. Bletchley's code-breaking 'factory' benefited from the national emphasis on service, duty and sacrifice. Pam may have longed for the West End stage but that did not impact on her diligent indexing skills; Charlotte was capable of much more than registering traffic, but the quality of her work remained exemplary; and Ruth gave up the dream of promotion and mastered a machine that daunted her, in the sure knowledge she was finally hitting back at a regime she had known was evil from the age of nine.

But perhaps more than all the others, it was the Moller sisters who really appreciated the opportunity to join the war effort. Ejected from their Belgium home and forced to endure a tense waiting game in Continental Europe, bolshie Georgette had hardly been able to contain herself.

Neutral Portugal, full of German soldiers, had proved a particular trial. 'They were everywhere. I couldn't stand them. They spat on the floor.' The bigger sister, outraged by her own helplessness, wore a Union Jack emblazoned on her chest when out in the Portuguese capital. Her lack of fluent English didn't stop her feeling very British. On the phone line from Texas she reiterates this point, adding, 'I still am very proud to be a British citizen; I am not a US citizen,' before returning to her story.

> One day I met a German on the pavement in Lisbon. Now it is polite that a man should move if he meets a woman. But he wouldn't. He just stood there in his uniform. Well I didn't move either and eventually he had to step into the road.

Having lived side by side with the enemy, both girls were overjoyed to arrive in the Park. So what if initially their job only involved putting the cipher text printed on strips of gummed paper into a contraption that looked like a peculiar typewriter? Labouring under the dubious title of 'Hags', the nickname given to the girls working with messages from the Hagelin machine C-38m used by the Italians, Doris and Georgette were the latest additions to a team whose ultimate aim was to find breaks in the Italian Navy's communications. The simple tasks they were initially assigned were both repetitive and pressurised but the girls didn't care; long shifts in a dingy British hut were infinitely preferable to being rudderless and homeless on the Continent.

———◆•✦———

Some didn't even need the added incentive of fighting an enemy; the secret allure of the Park was enough. Muriel was fourteen years old and by her own admission 'not particularly interested in what was going on in the war'. But as an evacuee she had lived in the village of Bletchley for over three years and shared a room with a sister who enjoyed a secret life in the forbidden Park. Growing up, there was always a healthy dollop of sibling rivalry between her and Anita – when she was little, Muriel remembers telling tales on and arguing with her sister, who was always three and half infuriating years ahead of her. One incident saw Muriel exact revenge on Anita's pyjamas with a pair of scissors.

'Oh yes, I could get on her nerves!' Muriel admits.

And now that same sister was in the adult world of work, while Muriel was excluded from the Park by a well-guarded perimeter fence. No wonder she feels her life took on an extra dimension when she finally got beyond the sentries and started work at Bletchley Park. 'It felt like walking through the back of the wardrobe. I loved it. I really loved it.' At last Muriel was in her very own Narnia; a messenger girl picking her way between a scramble of blocks and huts, delivering envelopes of classified information and photographs to anonymous recipients or stuffing them into pigeonholes. Just out of school, with the most basic of educations, she was an unlikely link in the chain of interception, decryption and intelligence, connecting 'the ever so beautiful' main building and the surrounding sprawl of shelters.

Very young, petite and playful with a delightful smile, it is no surprise that cutie-pie Muriel received greetings and waves wherever she went. 'Everyone was ever so friendly. 'I took it all in my stride. I loved it from the beginning.'

For the first time Muriel was earning a wage. 'I remember I got 12/6 a week in old money. So yes pocket money, but still!'[1] Although invariably paid at least a third less than their male

1. In today's money (2014) that is the equivalent of earning £17.95 a week.

equivalents, for some women life at the Park began with a small financial fillip.

'BP was a promotion. Automatically.' And to a girl like Gwen, promotion (more than money) mattered.

Highly confidential, GC&CS needed some way of justifying the pay grades of individuals who lacked a job description: advancement through the military ranks was an easy means of doing just that.

Sergeant Gwen had a certain ring to it; she immediately recorded evidence of her success in a local photographic studio and sent the picture back to her proud parents in Bournemouth. The girl in the photograph has a wide intelligent face and fair hair that daringly skims her collar. (There are no sergeant stripes on show – she didn't wait for them to be issued.) Gwen was on a high; through her own ingenuity she had been promoted to a top-secret Park where petty military rules and uniforms were of little concern. She still had no idea what her job would involve, but that didn't matter. She was determined to make the most of this strange new world she found herself in.

In fact Gwen had been earmarked as a decoder working on low-grade Air Force encrypted messages. Far removed from the Enigma-orientated operation a couple of huts away, in a separate timber construction (possibly Hut 10) she was to unravel all the Luftwaffe's air-to-ground communications that did not involve a bulky Enigma machine. These messages built up patterns of enemy movements, supplemented other intelligence and on occasion could prove useful guides into Enigma encrypts.

On her first morning Gwen was introduced to the head of section, Lyndon Bennett; he proceeded to baffle her with his tortuous inability to explain her new duties. Gwen was left with no option but to dive head first into code books, key sheets and German-language guessing games.

Never one to shy away from a challenge, she attempts to re-enact her role at the kitchen table in Mumbles. 'Your job was to take the code book . . .' (Here she gets distracted. Apparently some of the code books were 'dirty', splattered in blood and brains – vital stolen property from downed German aircraft.)

> So you take the dirty book, and you follow it to convert the code into raw clumps of German that you give the translator. You would often see a German word coming out. I would say I've got an 'E'. Somebody else might get the 'B' and everybody would put their kracks [solutions] up on the board. *Bericht* (report) might be the word. You did have to use a bit of German and some intuition because there were gaps in the messages.

Here Gwen stops, clearly thinking. 'A lot of it was quite repetitive, but it didn't matter.'

Rozanne arrived in the park two months before Gwen; they both worked in Josh Cooper's compartmentalised Air Section although they never knew each other. While Gwen focused on low-grade Luftwaffe traffic, Rozanne with her valuable Italian background was unpicking the main Italian Air Force ciphers. Under orders from Hitler, in March 1941 General Erwin Rommel's Afrika Korps arrived in Libya to bolster the flailing Italians. The result was a series of brutal pushes across North Africa. This war in the desert was a protracted, bloody affair and the interception of high-grade Italian Air Ciphers that, on occasion, contained 'hot' information about the enemy's air cover and supplies was invaluable.

The work was at the sharp end of code-breaking and yet Rozanne describes a scene more reminiscent of a university study, chock-full of books and scholars. In a hut beyond the tennis courts, she stepped into 'a room full of people and full of tobacco smoke!' Amid the daunting fug and the who's who of male academics she grappled with her new role.

'There were reams of paper. Girls would bring in great bundles in haversacks.' In an effort to remember, Rozanne closes her eyes and motions one hand over the other. 'There was a technique you learnt to break the code, it was quite specialised. You tried out various numbers until bits of words started to make sense.' One of only two women in the room, Rozanne was told she was a 'deco-dist'. The higher-status 'decoders' were much older men. They found the groups of letters and numbers that Rozanne then applied to piles of messages in an attempt to decipher the Italian. Her furrowed brow suggests that the job was taxing and not entirely dissimilar to Gwen's: a repetitive version of hangman in a foreign language springs to mind. It is perhaps not surprising that Rozanne's memory doesn't dwell on the technicalities of this job. Like Gwen she loved the Park, but it wasn't the work that fired their imaginations, rather the erudite world that grew up around it.

Fish

Many of Gwen and Rozanne's memories feed off the idiosyncratic nature of their early working quarters – wooden and intimate, brimming with quick minds and the potential for further learning. However this cosy image is by no means shared by all the veterans.

When Gwen and Rozanne entered the Park during the first half of 1942, fewer than 1,600 staff worked there, but the process of rapid expansion was already fully under way. By the end of 1944, Bletchley boasted 8,743 military and civilian personnel (three-quarters of whom were women) and a clutch of larger two-storey blocks, purpose built with improved insulation. The speed at which Britain's code-breaking operation was growing meant the increased adoption of mass factory-style employment methods. Eastcote and Stanmore outstations, home to nearly all the 211 Bombes, claimed the vast majority of Wrens, but by 1944 buses of additional ratings were also deposited daily (and nightly) at the Park gates. Neatly starched in white collars and navy skirts, 250 of these young girls would be herded into the Newmanry (established in 1943 and named after the mathematician Professor Max Newman) where they became vital component parts of a ground-breaking operation.

The Newmanry section was tasked with reading the highly sophisticated 'Fish' encrypted communications between Hitler and his High Command in Berlin and their front-line military leaders. Up to a hundred times longer than Enigma messages, and revealing the game plans at the heart of the German regime, highly secure Fish communications were invaluable – so much so that a technological whopper was born to help analyse their contents: Colossus. Designed to source the words of one of the world's most notorious dictators, Colossus is widely hailed as the world's first electronic computer.

And for some, cracking 'Fish' codes was a 'far greater achievement' than the breaking of the Enigma ciphers. Certainly the Lorenz machine, which encrypted Fish traffic, was a more modern, sophisticated device than the Enigma. But in 1944 Cora Jarman, aged seventeen and a half, was decidedly underwhelmed.

> We sat at school desks. There was a leading Wren looking over us and we were given pieces of A4 paper on their side. Each one was named after a fish. But not cod or haddock. No. Never cod or haddock.

Cora is drinking diet cola out of a crystal glass; the ice cubes clink whenever she takes a sip. After much thought this stylish woman's most poignant memory of her job at Bletchley Park is the absence of ordinary fish names among the bleak, bream, turbot, grilse, tarpon . . .

Cora shakes her head. 'There were so many messages being sent in, when one didn't come good you were sent another one.' She was checking for a match, but she didn't know why or what it meant. 'Checking checking. It was very boring. There were no written messages.'

The different Fish were the individual names given to various links in the so-called Lorenz SZ encrypted Tunny network. By 1943, networks carrying these high-grade teleprinter-based ciphers spanned Europe, and new links would soon criss-cross the Western Front as the German High Command frantically communicated with its stretched war machine. Traffic from Jellyfish (Berlin to the West HQ at Paris) and Bream (Berlin to Rome) were prioritised at Bletchley Park – intelligence from both were vital for the campaign in Italy and the long-planned Allied landings in France. Searching for matches between encrypted messages, Cora was helping to work out the complex settings of the twelve-wheeled Lorenz machine which produced these high-grade ciphers. But she knew none of this. To her, the intercepted teleprinter code looked like noughts and crosses. Cora's boss was the legendary Professor Max Newman (Alan Turing's maths tutor and a key player behind the invention of machinery to break the Lorenz codes), but Cora is not sure she knew him.

'No, I don't know if I met him, I might have done, I just don't know.' Apparently Professor Newman thought that many of the Wrens under him wouldn't be interested in having their work explained to them, so he didn't bother. Yet Newman's cryptanalyst staff remember him as informal and engaging; someone who encouraged brainstorming tea parties and open books in which to share new ideas. In other words Professor Max Newman was a model employer – unless you were a low-status girl, that is.

In 2014 Cora still wasn't aware that all those years ago she was helping to identify the Lorenz machine's wheel settings. Wrens like her diligently looked for seven settings, while the other five and the wheel patterns were found by a giant machine.

'Oh yes!' Cora nods, finishing her diet cola, 'I do remember a Colossus at the end of the corridor. It was a noisy enormous thing. Only tall Wrens could work it so that ruled me out completely.'

Fellow Wren Joanna Chorley wasn't tall exactly, but she did have very long arms (and a fertile mind).

I met the Colossus just after I had signed the Official Secrets Act. I saw this astonishing machine the size of a room. It was ticking away, and the tapes were going around and all the valves, and I

thought, what an amazing machine. There were valves and tran-
sistors and flippy-flappy things. Like magic and science combined!

The Colossus had caught Joanna's eye, but her assignment was to
deliver tapes. 'Then I had to mend tapes. I hated it.' Next she had
to load tapes.

The Heath Robinson machine guzzled a lot of tapes. Colossus's
messy inelegant predecessor was a rapid counting machine which
required two teleprinter tapes running at high speed and in sync
to identify the code-wheels' patterns. Joanna was soon sporting a
paper cut.

> The Heath Robinson was a horrible machine, the tapes had to be
> put on wheels, and the wheels weren't sprung so you couldn't
> move them around and regulate the tension of the tape. It was
> always ripping or exploding.

Two hundred and fifty Wrens worked in the Newmanry and the
impressions remembered by two, Cora and Joanna, are very
different. But there are also similarities. Whether tending paper
cuts or checking noughts and crosses, neither relished their job
nor did they understand what they were doing. But unlike Cora,
Joanna had a clear goal: 'When I saw the Colossus, I thought this
is what I want to do.' Unbeknown to her, she had fallen in love
with the world's first electronic computer.

'That is what I was working towards – I wanted to operate
Colossus.'

Wrens like Ruth, at the Bombe outstations, were firmly told
there could be no promotion, but no two sections in the code-
breaking operation were the same. In the Newmanry the obsolete
Heath Robinson counting machine was soon overtaken by its
flash new competitor. The Colossus, equipped with high-tech
electronic valve pulses and complex circuits, read characters at
two and a half times the rate of the clunky old Robinson and a
second, even more sophisticated version was designed in response

to the Germans tightening the security of their Lorenz cipher machines. Five days before the planned invasion of Europe, on 1 June 1944, Colossus 2 was fully operational. By the end of the year another seven had been delivered to the Newmanry.

Arriving at Bletchley shortly after the D-Day landings, Joanna's timing was perfect – no Colossus could be turned off and each needed a diligent team of operatives working in shifts around the clock. Within a month she had landed her dream job tending one of these technological behemoths.

Today, a warm, comfortable person, she is mildly amused by her status as one of a handful of women still alive who can claim to have operated the world's first prototype computer. 'It's a bit silly really isn't it? But I did love the beast.'

Joanna vividly recollects her shifts in the Newmanry. It was here, inside the section's steel-reinforced walls, that she enjoyed her only real experience of the Park.

'You see, I didn't stay in Bletchley, oh no! My living quarters were something else entirely!' And she laughs. It turns out Colossus was just the beginning of an epic war story.

8

Billets, Bunk Beds and Big Houses

Lord Mountbatten had told the Duke of Montrose his daughter's health would stand a job at Bletchley Park if she had a good billet. Forewarned is forearmed – the Duchess took no chances.

Upon hearing her youngest daughter would be posted to Buckinghamshire, she wrote to a close friend who lived in the vicinity and asked for help. Lettice Bowlby, one of the Queen's ladies-in-waiting, was that friend. Lady Jean wasn't disappointed; her new home was the sixteenth-century Grange at Mursley, a small village five miles from Bletchley. Landlady Mrs Brazier-Craugh 'couldn't have been kinder' although hospitality was accompanied with rigid discipline: 'We all had to stand strictly to attention every night when the anthems of the Allies were played before the 6 o'clock news.' Having grown up in two Scottish castles Lady Jean was accustomed to endless domestic protocol; with a smile she concludes, 'but it really was a lovely billet'. Her mother had made sure of that.

Lady Jean neatly avoided the vagaries of humble Buckinghamshire life as experienced by so many Bletchley Park employees in their compulsory local billets. Most new recruits were told where to go on arrival, irrespective of their middle-class expectations. However, despite her plush living quarters, by 1943 Lady Jean could boast a staggering knowledge of available accommodation in the patchwork of local villages surrounding the Park. Her new job demanded it of her. She had lasted less than a year 'ticking those wretched pieces of paper' in Hut 8 when she went to Frank Birch (again) and begged for her release. The Park 'was like a prison, yes it really was'. Not an unsympathetic man, but bound by rules

128

that stipulated Bletchley employees could not leave of their own accord, Frank's solution was to transfer her out of the hut. Lady Jean's second job at Bletchley Park was in the billeting office, where she 'tapped on most doors of Buckingham, Newport Pagnell, Leighton Buzzard etc. etc.'

In an era when girls were expected to do what they were told, Jean had proved there was always room for an exception, even during a war. The daughter of two ducal houses, perhaps her upbringing, surrounded by numerous staff, left her less prepared to tolerate what she considered to be a futile task. All these years later, she won't be drawn, but does concede that in an otherwise deferential age she might have been 'a little bit different'. And, of course, it didn't help that her friends Sarah Baring and Baroness Trumpington had 'far more interesting jobs' courtesy of their German.

But Hut 8's loss quickly became the billeting office's gain. Perspicacious Frank Birch no doubt recognised that a woman he felt unable to say no to would be well placed recruiting rooms from Buckinghamshire's occasionally reluctant residents. After all, a tweed-clad Lady knocking on the door of a humble railway cottage was not an everyday occurrence.

'I found on the doorstep people were very nice and receptive. Yes, wonderful. It was a great experience.'

An aristocrat she may have been but small island life and the companionship of nannies, gamekeepers and gardeners ensured Lady Jean could chat to any social class and her manners were (and still are) first rate. She was instructed by the Billet Office to leave no stone unturned. The Park, whose employee numbers had doubled in a year, were desperate for accommodation. By 1944 over 4,000 staff were housed in the most unlikely nooks and crannies of Buckinghamshire and Bedfordshire (the military accommodated another 4,000). Lady Jean had to use all her charm. 'Most people had jobs themselves; it was marvellous really they were prepared to have a stranger in their house. But if they had a spare room they had to give it up, so yes I talked them into it.' Her charm was accompanied by compulsory guile. 'Obviously we couldn't say this was for code-cracking work. No no no! I told them the government is moving all the important files out of London.' And that was that. Very few said no to Lady Jean.

Home from Home

Bert Dickens was a garage mechanic and drove a lorry up and down to London while his wife Moll, a farmer's daughter, looked after their two boys and cooked wholesome meals with garden vegetables and astutely managed rations. It was a simple life in the small village of Fenny Stratford, a stone's throw from larger neighbouring Bletchley. Then, one spring day in 1942 (a year before Lady Jean was transferred to the Billet Office), her equivalent came to the Dickens' modest house and told them that a girl called Rozanne Medhurst was to arrive shortly and that they 'must' take her in to live with them as she 'was doing "war work" at "the Park". Nothing else was explained.' A week later an attractive nineteen-year-old girl, with lively brown eyes and a heart-shaped face, arrived at their 'tiny' house, accompanied by her father, Air Commodore Charles Medhurst. No wonder Moll Dickens looked 'both surprised and intrigued'.

Rozanne was feeling equally perplexed. At this point she still had no idea what life at the Park involved; everything was shrouded in secrecy. 'Then my Pa left me. It was a "stiff upper lip" emotional moment!' Rozanne was on her own. It was fortunate therefore that beneath her astonishment Moll also looked 'warm and welcoming'. That first evening was the beginning of a devoted friendship between Rozanne and the Dickens family. 'I knew no one, had never been near this part of England before, and this place was to be my home. With them [the Dickens] thank God it was to be a happy three years.'

From her gentle description of their house, with its 'tiny cold bathroom tacked on beyond the kitchen and one small "visitor's room" never used and always cold', it is clear that initially the

Dickens' 'council house' was something of a culture shock to Rozanne. The first to admit that her own voice is 'frightfully old fashioned . . . one can't help it, it is just the way one speaks', Rozanne is undeniably upper-middle class. However, just like her landlady Moll, she's also warm and accessible.

Born in her grandparents' Yorkshire vicarage, with a garden full of 'masses of flowers', Rozanne knew instinctively that despite the basic amenities, her new home in Fenny Stratford offered her the most important comfort – familial love. She is quick to point out that 'only a few well-off people had central heating in 1940. All our houses were freezing in the mornings and in the winter and we dressed accordingly.'

Today Bletchley and the surrounding villages have been gobbled up by the ambitious new postwar city Milton Keynes; with the area now well within London's commuter belt it is hard to imagine the modest parochial scene that existed between the wars. Back then Bletchley was little more than a junction town; a stone's throw from London on the North-Western rail line and a significant node on the Varsity route between Oxford and Cambridge, it was best known as a place to pass through. Railways were the area's main employers; neighbouring Wolverton had the biggest rail-carriage industry in the country. Workmen and their families lived in an assortment of railway cottages and interwar semis and it was predominantly within this local community that the Park housed its employees.

Rozanne's billet, a compact three-up, three-down with an outdoor loo, was pretty standard. Certainly by the time the majority of female workers were arriving in the 1940s the early male cryptanalysts and their assistants had already bagged the most proximate, agreeable accommodation.

Private hotels and pubs were particularly sought after (three of Hut 6's inner circle, Stuart Milner-Barry, Hugh Alexander and Gordon Welchman lodged at Bletchley's Shoulder of Mutton, a comfortable, thatched, two-storey pub with a gifted cook) while the men who brought their families often rented houses belonging to those serving on the front line. It wasn't long before most of Bletchley's prime accommodation was commandeered for Park purposes and billeting officers had to look further afield. For the new female recruits, many of whom had grown up in substantial houses with a clutch of domestic servants, the change required adjustment.

Charlotte remembers her last billet with fondness – she helped her landlady with the shopping, there was a large garden and orchard and jolly meals with two other ATS girls and the Foxleys' three children – but she is also refreshingly honest.

> It was the first time I had seen how another home functioned. It was very different. To be thoroughly snobbish, they were working class, I suppose. But I got on very well with them. I made a point of it; I didn't want it to be awkward. They were very nice.

Back in Herefordshire, Charlotte's parents had gradually improved their lot; by the 1930s the family's smallholding had running water and a bathroom. A strip-down in front of the fire at the Foxleys in the small parish of Loughton was like going back in time. It was a humbling experience but not an unpleasant one.

Meanwhile Gwen is adamant, she was unfazed by her simple billet. 'I was used to a working-class way of being – a lavatory in the garden with torn-up newspaper, no bathroom, a sink with cold water.' Her billet in the small village of Stony Stratford posed no problem for a girl born in West Bromwich. But beyond the basic amenities it was the emotional connection she enjoyed with her landlady Mrs Gladys Henson that transformed Gwen's lodging experience. Seventy-two years on, her words resonate with emotion.

> I was billeted with a saint . . . she had no idea she was a saint; indeed I don't think she thought very much about herself at all. She thought she was a very lucky woman, although she had left school at twelve to become a 'weeding woman' and then a milkmaid, and had been widowed when her only child was quite young. She told

me that it had been a struggle to pay the rent and feed and clothe her small daughter, 'but the dear Lord helped me wonderful'.

Many see the Second World War as a melting pot, a time when the distinctions between Britain's classes finally began to dissolve. But if a common enemy and big government briefly masked social divides, most remained within their own milieu. Bletchley Park – a predominantly middle-class berth – was a case in point. However billets were a different matter. Here in the privacy of the home, privileged girls lived cheek by jowl with working families and vice versa. A really successful match such as Rozanne or Gwen's was life affirming. Rozanne and Mr and Mrs Dickens stayed in contact with each other for the rest of their lives; still when she talks about them Rozanne's eyes shine. 'Bert died in a car crash but dear Moll lived on for another ten or fifteen years.'

Meanwhile Mrs Henson was so proud of her bright young lodger she gifted Gwen the use of her 'cherished parlour' for writing purposes. Before that it was 'never lived in, never used except for weddings and funerals, and always kept dusted and polished'. A slow reader, Mrs Henson greatly admired Gwen's literary pretensions (courtesy of Talbot Heath she loved poetry and frequently indulged in 'adolescent scribblings'). Her admiration was reciprocated. In fact such was Gwen's devotion to Mrs Henson it provoked a literary volte-face; in the war novel she dreamt of writing the heroine was no longer a brave, perky service girl, it was a 'little old woman who would have made any sacrifice to save a child from suffering'.

False Starts

Rozanne and Gwen were lucky. Their landladies and families provided more than just food and shelter. But for many locals the obligation to house and feed a complete stranger was regarded primarily as a business transaction. By taking in three service girls, Charlotte's host family, the Foxleys, heavily supplemented their modest income from the railways. As well as additional ration books, billets were given about £2 a week per lodger (paid for by the Government, the majority of which was deducted at source from the employee's wage). In her diary it is clear that before Ann even arrived at Bletchley Park, she was well aware what her accommodation would cost. '13 July 1943: Billets officially £1-1-0 a week but actually more.' £1-1-0 would come out of her weekly salary (which was £3 a week) and the state paid an additional 19 shillings to the landlord and provided the bed linen. In other words people were not being asked to open their homes from the goodness of their hearts and billetees were within their rights to expect certain standards.

Kathleen, as the daughter of Admiral John Godfrey, Head of Naval Intelligence and related to 'cousin' Neville Chamberlain[2], was the product of a privileged but dutiful upbringing. Early on she had learnt to rough it as a member of the WAAFs. During training she stayed in a Spartan boys' school in Yorkshire where they slept forty to a room with one basin and one tap. 'Everyone smelt and snored, and snow came in through the windows into our narrow beds.' (Sleeping with the window open was a WAAF regulation.) But if the conviviality of a shared experience made those early hardships bearable, the same could not be said of her solitary billet down a dark lane near Bletchley. 'It was a gardener's cottage, but not attractive at all. The food was ghastly. I don't ever remember having a decent meal during all that time.' Kathleen was less forgiving of domestic accommodation she had to pay for.

For Ann, as an Oxford girl, moving to Bletchley was not a wrench. The trains home were numerous and she knew several people at the Park before she'd even arrived. But like Kathleen and many of the other girls, she'd grown up enjoying a life of comparative luxury. Home was a handsome Victorian house in Oxford's suburbs. Herbaceous borders and rose beds adorned the property,

2. Kathleen was first cousin twice removed of the former British Prime Minister but the family referred to Neville Chamberlain as 'cousin'.

a kitchen garden and orchard guaranteed ample supplies of fruit and vegetables, and a lawn tennis court and a grand piano ensured there was never a dull moment. Even her university quarters at Lady Margaret Hall had included a shared bathroom and a private bed-sitting-room. However Ann was no fool, she knew that war meant compromise. Her mother had learnt to manage a large home minus two of her three domestic staff and every year Ann loved mucking in and cooking for a camp of Rugby school boys 'digging for victory'. So when, on arrival at Bletchley, she was posted to a red-brick terrace house in the drab railway town of Wolverton she remained upbeat. '27 September 1943: *Anything new is fun.*' Nonetheless she couldn't help but notice: 'Bath but no hot water. WC in garden . . . Not one drawer for my clothes! . . . after a bit I imagine I will tire of sharing a living-room like this.'

By day two the novelty of lodging with Mr and Mrs Clarke had definitely begun to wear off. 'Tea when got in – nothing cooked. When do I get my meat ration etc.?? Can't exist without hot water ever. Possible billet next to Frances. This is OK for a bit, but not for good.' Reading between the lines, Mrs C lacked the charm of Rozanne's Moll or Gwen's Mrs Henson and (strictly against the rules) she was a bit of a nosy parker. 'Mrs C asked what I did since I didn't wear uniform.' Ann was unimpressed. 'Told her Foreign Office – after all, it's on the billeting form I gave her.'

However, decades later, sitting in her homely apartment in Edinburgh's Inverleith, Ann is clear that it was not the lack of amenities nor Mrs C's personal idiosyncrasies that ultimately proved intolerable. (In fact she remembers the Clarkes as a kindly couple.) It was the filth. A neat clean woman, she brushes a hand down her wool skirt and grimaces at the memory of living in a very grubby house. During her fourth week in Wolverton, Ann risked a bath.

In other words, took buckets of water from the copper to the bath, but water quite filthy and couldn't even look at it. Washed in basin of cold water. How I loathe the dirtiness of this house. For the first time felt unhappy.

It transpired that Mr C had cleaned his work overalls in the water offered for Ann's bath. She began to keep an eye out for alternative lodgings and in the meantime tackled the house herself. '11 Nov 1943: Started cleaning my room as well as the bathroom and landing as Mrs C no time (talking to the poppy lady).'

Ann was within her rights to look elsewhere. Acute pressure on accommodation due to the Park's rapid expansion eventually led to the building of a civilian hostel outside the gates and a variety of military camps for service personnel, but in the meantime many girls took matters into their own hands. Ann was not alone. The amenable Foxleys were Charlotte's second billet – the domestic set-up that had greeted her upon arrival in Bletchley had proved 'totally unsuitable'. During her first nerve-wracking train journey to the Park she had got chatting to fellow ATS girl Wynn and later that same night they were billeted together in Bradwell.

> It was a council house with three bedrooms already housing a family of four. Tired and hungry Wynn and I were directed to the room which would be ours, only to find we had to share a bed! Despite our embarrassment, sheer exhaustion won over and we slept!

Charlotte, home schooled with one much younger sibling, was not used to such intimate communal living. She promptly swapped her billet.

Courtesy of its grander employees, throughout the war Bletchley was a place where connections mattered. With a large magnifying glass, Pam is examining a photograph of her one-time indexing colleague Osla Henniker-Major (née Benning). Pictured in a fur-trimmed cape in a plush coffee-table book celebrating *The Lost World of Bletchley Park*, Osla, we both agree, was a very good-looking girl. Famous for dating Prince Philip of Greece and Denmark (later to become the Duke of Edinburgh) she, like Pam, was also a debutante. According to the blurb in the book, when it came to housing Bletchley's grander girls

> perhaps there were some allowances made to class sensibilities, for many ended up in agreeably upmarket surroundings – local rectories and manor houses – where they might be expected to find 'their' sort of people.

But while some (for instance, Lady Jean) had family or friends who could pull strings in the local area, Pam was not a typical debutante. Indeed, sitting in her living-room in central London she laughs about her one-time 'deb' status. By the time she arrived at Bletchley in 1942, her 'coming out' in 1936 was already a distant memory. Unlike many of the teenage girls working at the Park, Pam had been living as an independent woman for six years. But if father and mother were no longer required to assist their daughter, that didn't make billet life any more palatable. Quite the reverse. Coming to terms with the tedium of indexing for the sake of the war effort was one thing, but being expected to share a stuffy room in someone else's house was an ask too far. Pam is matter-of-fact about the subject. No one, deb or otherwise, should be expected to live in an unaired room. Not prepared to wait for the billeting office to find her alternative accommodation, Pam looked in the local paper. Within weeks she had moved into a caravan.

Equally unimpressed with her set-up at the Clarkes', Ann was working hard to find a new place to stay. A visit to the post office in Wolverton town centre three months after her arrival yielded a hopeful advertisement: 'half-house to let, furnished, comfortable apartments, no attendance'. She dithered. Her billet wasn't great, but Ann knew there were much worse. (On 10 October 1943 she noted of some Park newcomers in Wolverton, 'three of them share a bedroom and are not allowed to go upstairs except at bedtime to save electricity!!') However her hesitation didn't last long. She took the address and had a peek at the accommodation from the outside. 'Looks quite nice.' The landlady in question was keen to cut a deal. On a prospective visit Ann was wooed by a Mrs Smart who talked 'twenty to the dozen', provided excellent cake and lent her 'some magazines'. It seemed almost too good to be true. Ann accepted the offer and handed her notice in with Mrs Clarke; only then was she warned by the billeting office that 'lots of people have been to Mrs Smart and immediately asked to be moved out'. Ann was no exception. Years later she explains how her new landlady 'stole some of my precious rations until I locked them in my wardrobe. She then got a locksmith to open the wardrobe in my absence.' Mrs Smart was clearly unmoved by the communal war effort. Ann was living with a thief.

Meanwhile Pam in her caravan had to rely on friends for warm water and washing facilities. She couldn't cook, but made do boiling the odd egg and visiting the Park's canteen. As a woman who already knew her own mind, she preferred living alone in a field to putting up with unsavoury shared accommodation. It is only when pushed she concedes that even as a young girl she enjoyed a

certain chutzpah . . . I don't think I was pleased with myself but I quite liked myself. I was certainly not apologetic in any way. I remember at times it was quite frightening imagining oneself being captured by Hitler. But I used to say to myself whatever happens I've always got me. I do remember thinking that was quite a comfort.

However when the male proprietor of her solitary mobile home knocked on the door once too often at an inappropriate hour, self-assured Pam decided that a caravan 'had not perhaps been the most judicious option'.

Like Ann, once again she was forced to look for alternative accommodation. It is no wonder that after the war Bletchley Park's second-in-command Nigel de Grey summed up the billeting process with the lament: 'the whole process is unpleasant and unpopular even to the patriot'. After all, there is no place like home, as Muriel testifies: 'I was living with my parents in Bletchley so it was all right for me, wasn't it?'

Barracks

When the guards told Gwen she had arrived at the 'biggest lunatic asylum in Britain', they were teasing her, but their joke was not without substance. The Park's curious hybrid of uniforms, casual attire, young women and older men busying in and out all hours of the day and night raised local eyebrows. Even the workers themselves were taken aback by the hotchpotch of military and civilian standards; having come from a conventional RAF barrack, Gwen had to adjust to a section where she was given the option of wearing her uniform but did not have to salute seniors – indeed 'it would have seemed ridiculous to salute them'. And in the evenings she could wander through Stony Stratford's High Street, peppered with pubs, stop to eat beans on toast and listen to the piano, before returning to her saintly landlady, no military drill required. However this 'part-time' military experience, although not uncommon in the earlier years of the Park, wasn't the norm for most service girls. Far from it.

A staggering 2,963 Wrens were recruited to work for GC&CS between 1940–5. Predominantly operating Bombe and Colossi machines these girls were posted to 'HMS *Pembroke V*' (the naval reference for Bletchley Park), and despite a distinct lack of maritime activity, naval protocol was ever present. Between shifts Wrens were not free to wear mufti and hang out in civilian billets. They were stationed in barracks, slept in 'cabins' and saluted the quarterdeck as they had been trained to do. There could be no haggling with a landlady; what the petty officer said, they did. However even these orderly Bletchley Park Wrens couldn't claim a uniformity of experience. Finding accommodation for nearly three thousand girls in and around the Park and its outstations was a challenge. No one naval barrack at HMS *Pembroke V* was the same as the next.

At the end of Eastcote's Lime Grove, across a public footpath and sitting opposite Block B, with its armed guards on the outside and an enormous Bombe collection on the inside, was Block A. This was Ruth's new home. As she had been taught in Scotland, the Wren rating saluted the quarterdeck with a national ensign fluttering overhead and was duly introduced to her sleeping quarters. Leading off a long dark corridor were a series of 'cabins', each of which housed thirty-six pairs of bunk beds in small alcoves separated by breezeblock walls. A year earlier the site's first Wrens, equipped with spanners and metal rods, had built a bed each and hogged the top spots. Ruth, arriving in 1944, had no choice: 'all the girls seemed to have got there before me and took the top bunks; if you got a bed with a big girl on top you were in for a stormy night!'

Fortunately, like many of Bletchley's recruits, even at eighteen years old Ruth was accustomed to managing on her own.

> At the beginning of the war Birmingham was a target area so Mum, my sister and I had gone to stay near my grandparents in Colwyn Bay. It was just a few weeks later when we heard father had had a stroke. Mother burst into tears and jumped on a train.

Evacuee Ruth, aged thirteen, was left behind in Wales. It was a watershed moment in her life; the Henry family never lived together again. Dr Isaac Henry survived for six more years, but he didn't regain his health.

Mrs Henry stayed with him in Birmingham and kept the surgery afloat while Ruth toughed it out in wartime Wales. No wonder years later she was able to write of her 'wrennery' in north London:

> the whole set-up of dormitories, school food, noise, lack of privacy and endless rules seemed to me no different from the days I had spent at boarding school in Colwyn Bay where I had been temporarily dumped at the outset of war.

It would take more than seventy-one new roommates and a bottom bunk to knock Ruth off her stride. Barrack life in a purpose-built block was not glamorous but it was eminently doable.

Some Wrens did, however, find themselves in more glamorous digs. By the time Stanmore and Eastcote outstations were opened, many of Buckinghamshire's Establishment had already been forced to relinquish their stately homes. Astonished Wrens were sent to Gayhurst Manor, Wavendon House, Wilton Hall and Crawley Grange, although these billets were often less luxurious than they appeared. Gayhurst and Wavendon were notoriously cold – the latter's outhouses offered Victorian working conditions and the former had to be shared with nesting swallows and greedy mice. The country house was invariably less comfortable than a utilitarian military block on the outskirts of London. But neither could compete with the scale and splendour of Woburn Abbey.

'No bats, no broken windows, no mice in the soup. Hardly!' Joanna laughs at the very suggestion. With Colossus arriving on the scene, the accommodation conundrum had again been revisited and the solution was an epic one. Joanna and Cora and hundreds of other Newmanry Wrens were quartered in Bedfordshire's most extraordinary home. Joanna shifts in her chair, her memories still vivid. Once home to Cistercian monks, by the 1700s Woburn Abbey had been transformed into an exquisite Palladian mansion. Even today, to look out beyond its Repton-inspired parklands is to witness Bedfordshire in a sea of dazzling greens. The girls had one of the finest views in England.

'It really was jolly cold.' Although struck by the memory of all that splendour, Joanna concedes there were drawbacks. 'We were eight in a room in bunk beds, there were glorious painted ceilings but you had to keep putting on more clothes to keep warm.' Joanna huddled under the eaves on the top floor of this awesome building, the back of which looked onto a majestic cedar, around which fanned a riding school, stable-quartering and courthouses.

Inside, most of the valuables had been stored underground and the pictures put away, but there was still plenty to get excited about. The swell in Joanna's voice says it all. 'Oh yes, and I can still see the huge marvellous bathroom with mahogany baths with brass taps and steps up and down. There was an ordinary bathroom too but we all queued for the glamorous one.' However old-school glamour could not overcome wartime frugality. 'The bath had a black line on it at 5", even though there was masses of water. We just accepted the rule, because if we went over the line then boring things might happen.'

Having never left home before, seventeen-year-old Cora's memories hang less on the exquisite vistas and architecture and more on the absence of creature comforts. 'After we had been signed in at the Bletchley mansion we were told where we were quartered, not billeted!' Reassuringly flanked by her two Talbot Heath friends, Cora recalls

> the servants quarters, up stone flagged stairs. We had a tiny little maid's room, with three bunk beds, three hard chairs and six Wrens. It was only when we got really cold we discovered that the wardrobe was hiding a gas fire. We would sit in front of it and dry our hair.

Dwarfed by their enormous surroundings and in the company of hundreds of other Wren ratings and Petty Officers, it is not surprising Cora and Joanna never knew each other. Nor did the Wrens have the exclusive run of the mansion. Cora thinks the better rooms were occupied by the Foreign Office but she is not sure; they were forbidden to ask questions. Joanna corroborates part of her story but reckons they were SOEs (Special Operations Executives). 'They were in the back half and we were in the front half. They were completely separate. We only met them in the grounds.' And then conversations didn't get very far. 'I met a man and we both agreed that we couldn't tell each other what we were doing.'

In fact the men in question worked for the Political Warfare

Executive. Based in Woburn since 1941, they focused on the dissemination of black propaganda in Axis countries. While Joanna and Cora helped facilitate the covert reading of Hitler's messages, these men (often with journalistic backgrounds) flooded Germany with false information – their aim was to undermine morale among the Third Reich's citizens. Pamphlets, ration coupons and leaflets were disseminated through enemy territory and 'black radio stations' broadcast into Germany from Bedfordshire. Key to the success of these operations was their total anonymity. The source had to remain unidentified for psychological warfare to gain the upper hand. Joanna and Cora and all of Germany were in the dark when it came to what was going on in the other half of the Abbey.

But as far as Woburn Abbey's proprietor, Hastings Russell, the Duke of Bedford, was concerned, any war work in the Abbey was undesirable. Under M15 surveillance for suspected Nazi sympathies the Duke made no secret of his pacifist ideology. Cora, who occasionally saw him wandering disconsolately around his grounds, wasn't entirely sure whether her landlord was 'all there'. She wasn't alone. The Duke's association with a pro-Nazi, anti-Semitic fringe in Britain left him isolated. In 1940 he returned from Dublin with peace proposals from the German legation, which the British press mercilessly ridiculed; it was the same year that his father died and Hastings became the twelfth duke of a vast estate already integral to the war effort.

But Joanna was unperturbed by the oddball aristocrat. She had grown up near the notorious Mitfords' Cotswold village where daughter Unity saluted the local postmistress with a saucy 'Heil Hitler!' and father Baron Redesdale strode around proclaiming the virtues of the Führer. She is very clear. 'There were plenty of right-wing people who were very pro-Hitler. We forget that now.' With a flourish she recalls the surreal sign the Duke hung at the entrance of Woburn's grounds for the benefit of his wartime guests: 'I know I have unpopular views but please do not take it out on the animals.'

9

Keep Calm and Carry On

Of the four Wrens featured in this book, Pat was the only one who ended up living by the sea. She enjoyed access to a beach and a requisitioned seaside hotel. Along with eleven other girls, Pat had been posted to Withernsea as a special duties linguist. A small town perched near the mouth of the Humber, perishing in winter and bracing in summer, it was the ideal location to pick up German naval communications across the Baltic and the North Sea.

Looking back makes Pat happy. 'We enjoyed ourselves very much.' She pores over an old album full of photographs: black and white snapshots of the beach, the sea's unbroken expanse pictured from the hotel and a couple of Pat beaming alongside a friend called Joan. Her dark hair has a slight wave and the light picks out the three shiny new buttons on her naval uniform. Having passed her training course in Wimbledon, Pat had waved goodbye to her little round hat and been promoted to Petty Officer.

But the levity captured in the pictures belies a much more serious mission. Pat and her colleagues were tasked with intercepting live radio communications sent to German vessels. The transmissions were found in the 4, 8 and 12 MHz bands; in the 30 to 50 MHz band there were ship-to-ship communications. 'We knew the frequencies that the Navy used within a certain bandwidth. So you sat and twiddled your knob on this thing up and down the length of the band.' Pat smiles, her voice animated.

As soon as one of their ships came up, if the officer in charge of our watch room wasn't there, she had to be fetched. It might be something significant. So you are writing down – bonk bonk bonk – and the other girl would tell the officer, 'We've got a German ship up!' The whole thing would be written down on a naval message pad and then one of us would call Station X and tell them, 'We've got a message to put through on the teleprinter.'

Station X was Bletchley Park. Pat is not sure if she made the connection between the Bletchley her godmother had recommended two years earlier and the destination X where she sent her messages. It didn't matter; what mattered was accuracy, efficiency and a twenty-four-hour listening presence.

A closer look in Pat's album and the severe face of Judy Fiddian glowers back. 'She was our officer. And there was the technician Mr Mason – he would have rather been on a ship. And sometimes people came and inspected.' Judy Fiddian carried the weight of responsibility for her girls. Germans didn't make a habit of repeating their radio transmissions. Pat worked in shifts (watches) around the clock. 'If we started at 8am one morning, then the next we would start at 4am. No one knew when the enemy would communicate with its fleet, or at what hour ships would signal.' The proximity of Pat's workplace helped ease her gruelling schedule. Like many of the Y-listening stations the Withernsea service was tiny; the girls slept, ate and worked in the same little seafront hotel.

Whatever hour of the day or night she was starting work, Pat simply had to walk up the stairs to the watch room. It was a privilege the girls in congested Station X did not share.

The Commute

Getting over 8,000 men and women into and out of Bletchley on a twenty-four-hour rota required extraordinary levels of organisation. The BP transport system was labyrinthine in its complexity. Only a few well-placed girls escaped its reach.

'I hadn't many clothes with me but I had my red-painted

bike!' Rozanne remembers. 'This was taken to the garden hut by Bert.' Sure enough, that first evening when a man from the Park came to see her, he explained 'where the Park was and said I could bike there'. The next morning she cycled the one and a half miles from Fenny Stratford to Bletchley. In fact her scarlet bike saw far more action than her 'funny little Austin with a dicky seat at the back'. She laughs, recalling the hood that went down on a car that had to be wound up. Within a year Rozanne had sold her Austin to a Pole; petrol rations ruled out all but the most essential car journeys and living near the Park meant cycling was the easiest option.

Even girls who didn't stay in the immediate vicinity occasionally resorted to pedal power. Within two weeks of starting at Bletchley, Ann cycled all the way back to her billet in Wolverton. The proud mathematician noted: 'Cycled home in 50 minutes – (12 miles an hour which is good going).' Ann and Rozanne's exploits conjure up the image of healthy, hearty wartime girls; in functional clothes and exercising daily, they certainly contrasted sharply in their energetic lifestyles with previous generations, when women's attire and societal attitudes encouraged little physical activity.

Looking back now, some aspects of her active life puzzle Ann. 'I just wish I could remember. I can't imagine how I did it.' We are standing in her kitchen waiting for the kettle to boil. Over lunch she has talked me through the maze of different Enigma permutations and tried her hardest to articulate the formulation of a menu for a Bombe machine, but now she is stumped. 'I just can't think how I found my way in a dark street on my bicycle.' Ann shakes her head in frustration. Before Bletchley she was an Oxford girl, and cycling across the city in a blackout back to her Headington home was almost a daily occurrence. She ought to be able to remember how she found her way at night.

Ann's diary goes some way to filling in the blanks. Shortly after she arrived at the Park, she caught the late 10.30pm transport back to her billet. Upon arrival in Wolverton she promptly got lost in the blackout and a local man had to show her where the Clarkes lived. It turns out Ann didn't always find her way in the dark.

Stumbling around in the inky black was a common wartime problem, exacerbated by shift work. The Ministry of Information went into overdrive: posters advised that care should be taken crossing roads, passengers should check train doors opened on to a platform and people should 'pause when you go out into the dark to let your eyes get used to the blackout'. For those cycling and driving on night-time roads, basic lighting remained compulsory.

Bletchley Girls were not allowed to bike around Buckinghamshire's country lanes without lights. Kathleen, another hearty lass who 'resurrected' her old bike for Park life, got a nasty shock. 'One dark night I was sailing merrily along, no lights of course, when I realised that someone was following me. I pedalled furiously as I was living at the end of a long dark lane, there was no escape.'

Much to her embarrassment she was being chased by the local policeman, who eventually caught his culprit, fined her a hefty ten shillings and forbade her to cycle without lights again: 'My first encounter with the law.'

The iconic image of girls on bikes cycling through Bletchley's green glades has become so intrinsically linked with the Park that today the code-breaking museum sports a rack of vintage cycles (no red ones, though). Sepia photos of service girls on bicycles in numerous books reinforce a cosy 1940s idyll.

But the reality was less romantic. Shift work was gruelling, the weather often dismal and cycling through the rain back to a cold billet, hard work. For those who weren't housed in Bletchley itself, the most practical option was to use the transport provided by the Park. The execution of 34,000 miles of passenger journeys a week required over a hundred drivers to run forty buses per shift. Although a cyclist herself, the arrival of dozens of buses before every shift remains one of Rozanne's most prominent 'Bletchley' memories. They would:

drop and pick up their human load, and disappear in a roar of noise and glimmer of partially blacked-out headlights. These noisy phantoms of the night (and day) would then drive away and vanish until the time of the next shift. In the night, the appearance of the buses would be followed by the patter of thousands of footsteps as the workers made their way to their huts, invisible in the dark, save for patches of torchlight in the otherwise total 'black-out'.

Kathleen also remembers the transport phenomenon, writing of how both day and night 'a fleet of buses and vans fanned out into the countryside'. Both she and Rozanne almost manage to make bus-use sound poetic, but the daily reality was a more laborious affair, as Ann's diary testifies. Based as she was, ten miles away in Wolverton, her work and social life were soon in sync with the bus timetable, although new drivers occasionally forgot to collect all their clients and Ann once missed the bus and had to hitchhike. The 'era of service' duly provided: she was only fifteen minutes late for her shift.

Charlotte meanwhile recalls a comical incident when she slept in and ran down the stairs half dressed, her Army-issue khaki knickers on full display. So numerous were the bus's stops she had time to pull on a skirt and walk down Watling Street to catch the same bus en route out of the village.

Lady Jean's relationship with the buses did not begin well:

> At Bletchley when I first got there somebody asked one of the bus drivers, 'Who's that tall girl there?'
> 'I don't know. She's the daughter of God knows who!'
> My nickname was 'the daughter of God knows who!' for a long time after that. Well I hated it!

Chippy bus drivers aside, the slow (uncomfortable) journeys into Bletchley did offer a great way of making friends. Frequent notices reminded staff that they could not talk about their work on BP transport (or anywhere else for that matter). Instead Ann organised cinema dates and enjoyed spotting colleagues from Oxford, while Cora, a latecomer stuck out at Woburn, 'only knew the people I came with on the bus', such was the segregated world of Bletchley Park. She refuses to romanticise the nine-mile slog to and fro. 'You tried very hard not to come on the bus with the food. It smelt to high heaven.'

Joanna concurs: 'By early 1945 there were so many Wrens, they cooked our food at Woburn and on the way to BP you smelt the food in the bus. It was horrible.'

Eating it wasn't much fun either.

The ATS girls who worked at the Forest Moor listening station stayed at St Ethelburga's – a requisitioned school in Harrogate. They travelled to the moor in troop carriers. For some the memories are so fond that during reunions they sing the songs they once sang in the trucks.

According to veteran Jay McDonald, 'Everyone sang those wartime songs.' But her story doesn't resonate for Betty, who stayed in a wooden hut in the school's grounds and did the same commute.

'Well I suppose they did sing, yes. "Roll Out the Barrel", "Pack up Your Troubles", "Kiss Me Good Night Sergeant Major". Yes they made a heck of a row. But I didn't have a voice. I never could sing.' Betty just wanted the journey to end and her work on the moor to begin. 'You see you were shivering in them carriers with flaps. Proper cold.'

Whether in Buckinghamshire or Yorkshire, suspension-free, unheated vehicles to and from blocks and camps had to be tolerated, but it is difficult to see how they made monotonous shift work any easier.

Shift Work

Pam is sitting in her London garden, listening to an extract from an academic article which analyses the achievements of Bletchley Park's indexing system. Linguists like her were tasked with producing order out of chaos, they were 'vital as intermediaries in the retrieval of information', providing access to a 'a vast corpus of knowledge beyond even the most retentive human memory'.

'Well yes,' she agrees, 'that goes without saying.' But Pam will not be induced to exaggerate her role in Hut 4's naval index. 'Every single reference to every single thing of any note at all was put on a card and cross referenced.' Day and night. 'Today of course it would all be done by hitting a button on a computer.' Only when pressed will she concede that certain skills were required.

'Assiduousness, I suppose, and attention to detail and memory. There were some very bright girls with first-class degrees working with me. But the job did not involve any imagination.' Here she smiles. 'My favourite bit was the shop window. Someone would come to the hatch wanting to know about, say, the *Scharnhorst* on a certain date, and you would go to the index and access the information.' It is not hard to imagine Pam, bright eyed and intelligent, efficiently finding her way through reams of cards and delivering the requested nugget of knowledge. Nor is it hard to understand why this human interaction stood out as a highlight in a job that was otherwise silent, meticulous and repetitive – qualities rendered all the more challenging in the middle of the night.

It is worth reiterating that in Bletchley Park's postwar review, filed under 'medium or low grade labour', is the observation that '[I]t was astonishing what young women could be trained to do.' But what is perhaps more astonishing is that girls did the jobs assigned to them under the punishing rigours of a twenty-four-hour shift system. And while much of the work did not require imagination, the pressure was exacting.

Beyond the haze of smoke in her hut, Rozanne was surrounded

by much older accomplished men: intelligence officer Joe Hooper (later head of GCHQ), Hugh Last, Oxford's Camden Professor of Ancient History and (in the adjoining room) Josh Cooper, one of Bletchley Park's leading cryptanalysts and head of the Air Section. It was an intimidating line-up for any nineteen-year-old to face. (Made worse when Josh Cooper lightly informed Rozanne he knew her father Air Commodore Charles Medhurst.) Although a mere 'decodist', Rozanne with her Italian language skills was now a member of this impressive team. She recalls: 'when we began to work there was silence and total concentration'. A tea break of ten minutes after two hours was followed by 'work and a concentrated silence again'. It was relentless. The shifts were generally eight-hour stretches, with swap-overs at 8am, 4pm and 12am, and the working week was often forty-eight hours long, occasionally rising to fifty-one hours. No let-up was tolerated.

Betty was accustomed to working long hours in a shoe factory. She was also used to being monitored for her productivity levels (and paid accordingly), so it might not have surprised her to discover that on the Yorkshire moors, while listening to the enemy's Morse imprint, she was being closely observed. 'Detailed breakdowns of rates of successful interception between group shifts and stations' were recorded. Betty had swapped one factory for another – although this time the stakes were high and she knew it. She didn't even like to take a loo break.

'Your set must not be left uncovered so you had to put your hand up and ask the set room sergeant, "Can I go to the toilet?" I only went to the loo if I was absolutely desperate.'

Even the shifts that yielded no sound from the enemy camp offered little respite. 'You just sat and listened. No! You would have been shot if you read a book!'

But when they did pick a signal up, Y-station listeners Betty and Pat were suddenly directly connected with the enemy through their headsets. The impact was not lost on Pat: 'I always thought it odd hearing the war all the time from the German side.'

Betty, although unable to speak German, built up a mental image of the Morse operators at the other end of the radio waves. 'I often wondered, "Well, what are you like?" I pictured them as great big bull-headed Gomorrahs, I would say they were all men. Yes definitely.'

That invisible line of noise kept Pat and Betty linked into the live dialogue of war at any hour of the day or night – they couldn't forget an enemy who jangled in their ears. But for the girls at Bletchley, isolated in the cordoned-off Park, the war was a more remote affair.

Staying motivated (and awake) was hard work. Throughout the night Georgette, equipped with meaningless encoded characters, painstakingly entered one letter into the keyboard and then turned the handle. And then another letter. And another. And another. One at a time. If the settings were correct, Italian text came out on strips of paper that were passed through a hatch into the Z Watch. Doris, the younger of the two Moller sisters, recalls nudging Georgette's elbow through the gloom. 'She would keep falling asleep at the Hagelin machine.'

Georgette now laughs about her errant ways. 'Yes, very often I put my head down on my hands and had a kip.'

Meanwhile her alert, ambitious little sister Doris progressed onto rodding – a technique perfected by Dillwyn Knox in the Cottage. She spent her nights running wooden alphabet blocks across code to recognise patterns and thereby uncover the Italian Hagelin's rotor settings. 'It was very interesting, I loved it. The translators would get very impatient. One of them, George Toplas, always whistled the Brandenburg Concerto at me while he was waiting.'

Enemy communications were an unpredictable twenty-four-hour affair and Bletchley Park had to co-ordinate its staff rotas accordingly. One night Rozanne was working late in the Italian air section. It was 1.30am and with the exception of Joe Hooper on duty at the far end of the room, she was alone.

'I was decoding a message freshly arrived on the teleprinter. After many trials and errors . . . the "groups" of numbers began to make sense, and I found myself faced with a message that made sense.'

The next few hours in Rozanne's life are the stuff of movies. In a small room in Buckinghamshire in the middle of the night, Rozanne was reading something no one else in the Allied Forces knew: in three and a half hours' time, at 4am, Italy's SM.79 torpedo bombers and SM.82 transport carriers were due to leave Tripoli and head across the Mediterranean.

'Imagine the thrill. I rushed to Joe Hooper with the message and he LEAPT from his desk in wild excitement. He tore along the passage to Josh Cooper's room.' This 'hot' information was radioed to the RAF in North Africa. 'Very soon our aeroplanes were in the air and ALL the Italian aircraft were shot down!' With the Desert War over in early 1943, the crippled Italians were heading for Sicily – thanks to Rozanne they never reached their final destination.

'It was the only time I did something useful in all the years I was at war. The whole place was alive with excitement. I got a pat on the back!' And then suddenly, towards the end of her story Rozanne's face crumples; she looks sad, almost scared.

It was awful. Terrible to think of all those people being shot down. I discovered later lots of the casualties were women and children coming back from service stations in Africa. I'd lived in Italy, the Italians were my friends.

She strokes the faded arm of her chair and sighs. Over seven decades later and there is a palpable tension in the room as Rozanne revisits the confusion of war and her own small part in it.

———•———

Rozanne's adventure took place in the middle of the night – it was a rare island in a sea of exhausting monotony. Gruelling shift work, like the obsessive secrecy, was an indelible aspect of Bletchley life.

In her memoir Charlotte writes, 'We worked a shift pattern 8am–4pm, 4pm–midnight, midnight–8am. It sounds easy but it was tiring!'

Today there is plenty of research to back up Charlotte. Shift work has an adverse impact on both mental and physical health. Immune systems, menstrual cycles, sleep patterns, mood swings and energy levels are all affected. The Park tacitly acknowledged the pitfalls of a twenty-four-hour schedule; Muriel aged fourteen was exempt from working nights and only after Ann had done a stint on days and evenings was she finally given a week of night shifts. She tried to sleep between 6pm and 10pm before her first midnight start but only managed to rest: 'Boiled an egg, had Oxo, went on my first night shift.' The next day there was more evidence Bletchley knew it had to look after its midnight workers. 'Excellent breakfast at BP after night shift including ½oz of real butter!' Ann noted that after her second shift she still 'felt fine'.

Working as she did in the Machine Room of Hut 6 at the centre of the Enigma code-breaking operation, an ability to perform at night was especially important. Every midnight the Germans changed the settings of their different Enigma networks. It was expected that by the morning the late team would have at least found their way back into the main keys such as Red (an important Luftwaffe network). Ann found working under pressure agreeable and the difficult hours seem to have had a bonding effect. 'Such fun on night shift when you are on with these people.' However the team effort involved more than just Hut 6. The 'menus' Ann formulated only delivered possible Enigma key settings once they had been run through a Bombe. At Eastcote's outstation those giant machines clattering through the night had to be perfectly programmed before any 'stops' could deliver positive results.

Ruth remembers the intensity as if it were yesterday.

Plugging up the back of these enormous Bombe machines was so exacting it had to be done in twos. All we knew was one of the most difficult things was to manage the sets of plugs. They had to go straight in the socket, not this way or that way, you must not bend them or you get a dreaded short circuit. You had to be 125 per cent accurate.

The machines were treated with the utmost care. 'At midnight the RAF would come in with trolleys and service the Bombes. They were very reliable machines; if they went wrong the RAF technicians always blamed us.' Ruth talks on; her minute, specific descriptions all these years later are a testimony to the perfect standards that were expected from the young Wrens. 'The wheels on the Bombe had rows of little wires like toothbrushes; they were spiky, all on a slant but one wire must not touch another wire.' The girls were given tweezers – crossed wires had dire mechanical implications. Smelly, oily and tiring, the Bombe didn't always yield a stop that delivered that day's key settings. At the other end of a scrambler phone back at Bletchley Park, Ann or her equivalent would run the provisional settings through an Enigma-adapted Typex machine.[1] Only if German words spilt out was the code broken. The girls had no clue what the messages said; that didn't matter. What mattered was that they'd played their part proficiently.

The words 'the job's up' were music to Ruth's ears. Once that message had got through to Eastcote she could strip her Bombe and begin the process all over again.

> You knew you had to be quick, especially at midnight when the codes changed. We knew if we didn't get a 'job's up' someone might not live. They made us aware it was important. You were so bushed as a Bombe operator at the end of the first night shift that on the second shift they had you sitting down doing the checking.

It was a relentless schedule and, as a perfectionist, Ruth soon discovered that the work took its toll.

1. During the Second World War the British used Typex machines to encipher their wartime communications. These machines used five wheels instead of the Enigma's three or four wheels and were therefore more secure than their German equivalents. It is believed Typex machine messages were never broken by the enemy.

Sickness

The sick rate at the Park fluctuated between 3 per cent and 4 per cent and by 1944 it was running at over 4 per cent; nearly one in every twenty-five workers was ill. It had been a long war, some were beginning to wonder if it would ever end. Miles from home, working topsy-turvy shifts and forced to focus for hours on end, Bletchley's young girls were not immune to the deleterious mental and physical effects of Park life. In his postwar review, Nigel de Grey recognised the benefits of youth (easier to train, more prepared to accept direction, more mentally flexible) but he also noted 'cases of mental breakdown occurred equally among young and old' and that 'both men and women are often tougher in middle age than youth'. In other words, being young was no barrier against illness. Quite the reverse.

> I went to the sick bay and I said, 'I don't feel very well.'
> The doctor said, 'What's the matter with you?'
> I said, 'I don't know,' and I started to cry and I cried and cried and my face was swollen and my eyes were swollen.

Ruth refers to her illness as 'burn out'. It is not surprising this young girl crashed.

By the time she arrived at Bletchley, the middle-class world Ruth took for granted as a child had already been shattered. Her father's stroke in 1939 left the family in dire straits. 'Mother had a crippled husband and there was a war on; it was the bitter aloes in the pudding.' Money was very tight and a landmine blew out the doors and windows in the Henrys' Birmingham residence. The family home was ransacked. 'Everything was taken, all the things you value as a child, knick-knacks, souvenirs, books. The house was a real mess until after the war.' For the petite eighteen-year-old arriving at Eastcote outstation with her kitbag, life had prematurely lost its sheen. And then there were the barbed-wired blocks, the bunk beds, the military drill and the Bombes – night and day. Within months she succumbed to exhaustion.

'The petty officer came to see me and she said, "Oh dear, oh dear."' Ruth was promptly put to bed with a huge jug of water. 'When I woke up they said "drink" and I would drink and then sleep. I was asleep for four days. All I did was drink my water, go to the loo and get back into bed.' After four days Ruth still felt unable to eat anything, so the doctor administered a large dose of castor oil. 'For goodness sake! Then I really couldn't eat anything.' Concerned about their vulnerable Wren, they summoned Ruth's mother from Birmingham.

'Well, being a good Jewish mother she brought me half a cooked chicken. Of course I ate that!' Off ration and very hard to come by, the succulent bird went down a treat. Wren rating Ruth was granted two weeks' leave. She returned refreshed and Bombe-proof.

Mental breakdown or 'burn out' was sufficiently prevalent in the Park for comparisons between age groups to be made in the postwar review. Ruth is convinced that they were familiar with the symptoms she exhibited; it was clear from the assured way they treated her. 'The trouble was we changed our shifts each week. All of a sudden you had had it.' Beyond the bleak backdrop of war, Ruth blames her exhaustion on the punitive shift patterns.

Even energetic Ann, who thought nothing of cycling ten miles to work, struggled. Having declared she 'felt fine' after her second shift on night duty, things quickly went downhill. By day three she noted: 'Felt pretty bad when I got up. Got through my egg with an effort because couldn't very well throw away such a thing as an egg. Developed a cough.' Day four: 'Slept for three hours, then only dozed for rest of the time. Couldn't eat anything when I got up, either, in spite of no lunch. Developed a streaming cold overnight.' She struggled through the rest of the week on Oxo, toast, apples and aspirin. News that other girls couldn't sleep was reassuring, but her landlady's efforts to remove a big chest of drawers from the room when she was trying to sleep went down like a lead balloon. Ann sounded a triumphant note when the week was finally over. 'Finished night shift . . . off on leave for a whole five days.'

Some did not escape so lightly. 'It was terrible really.' Doris's French accent is prominent as she moves quickly over her most traumatic Park memory. 'We were all staying in a hostel and a girl committed suicide. I knew her, it was very shocking.' She doesn't remember the girl's name and there is no record of her death, but the hostel, built in 1942 to accommodate female civilian staff, was temporarily closed.

Georgette confirms the story. 'It was kept very secret, they never said why or what hut she worked in.' Neither sister can be sure what exactly motivated the young girl to take her life but both cite shift work as a contributing factor.

Georgette recalls, 'You couldn't sleep in the hostel. Especially in the day you couldn't sleep. You could hear people walking in the corridor all the time. It was very unsettling. She couldn't handle it.'

The Moller sisters were lucky; their English father was posted to Bedford. They never had to return to the hostel on Wilton Avenue.

———————◆·◆———————

In his biography, Bletchley Intelligence officer Peter Calvocoressi identified 'Chiefs' and 'Indians' among the BP workers. The 'Chiefs' were preponderantly male and had better jobs, while the 'Indians' (often women) were the support staff with less responsibility and less access to 'the brush of real events'. Perhaps inevitably, affection for Park life was by no means unanimous among the 'Indians'. One veteran remembers 'Nissen huts, beastly concrete paths, ablutions with rows of lavatories and basins set side by side in a drafty concrete hut . . . I loathed Bletchley Park.'

She wasn't alone. So strong was Lady Jean's antipathy towards the Park that within a year of her arrival she was on the verge of a breakdown.

Asked to explain how she felt, Lady Jean pauses. Only after some thought does she confide in me, her long fingers twitching with old anxiety: 'I was nervy, not sleeping, miserable.' Confronted with a broken woman, her boss Frank Birch realised he couldn't let his young charge go crazy. Her sideways move to the billeting office was his temporary solution. Lady Jean is adamant it wasn't the shift work that unnerved her, rather the unadulterated monotony of a seemingly never-ending job. 'If you can call it a job, ticking boxes. I would get up every morning with dread. It went on and on, ticking ticking.'

The state of despair Lady Jean describes was not uncommon. There were hairline cracks beneath the celebrated facade of Park life that couldn't always be ignored.

Burn-out aside, hard work and close quarters made the Bletchley Girls susceptible to the broad sweep of infections that thrived in wartime Britain. Vaccinations were still in their infancy.

'I felt rotten one day and went to the doctor. He poked around and said, "I don't think there is anything wrong with you. You're fat anyway, aren't you?"'

In fact the brusque doctor got it wrong: swollen Charlotte had the mumps. When the diagnosis was finally made she was swiftly removed from the Park in a military ambulance and taken to hospital in Northampton.

'I was feeling so sick on the way I asked the driver to stop. I got out and found myself face to face with two guard officers who were pretending to be Germans.' Charlotte had landed slap bang in the middle of a military exercise prior to the D-Day landings. 'Planes were hopping over hedges at very low levels and vehicles were everywhere.' The two 'pretend Germans' asked for a lift. 'If you want mumps,' came the reply. The men, who were about to hurl themselves into Occupied Europe, decided the risk was worth taking. Charlotte sighs. 'What happened to them, I will never know.'

Rozanne went to hospital with eye strain ('I got terrible head-aches night and day, it was the awful bar of lighting above one's head') and Lady Jean did a stint in one with appendicitis ('It was okay, it didn't burst and I got to go back to Scotland'). Pat mean-while had a very interesting stay in a Beverley hospital; she had contracted TB again.

> I don't remember the gland being very painful. In fact it was rather fun as there was a young man there having his legs patched up. He was training to be a pilot and every time he put the plane into a dive the veins in his legs split.

With time on their hands, Pat and her anonymous airman explored the delights of Beverley. Together they pottered around the town; Pat remembers the exquisite blue ceiling in St Mary's church peppered with gold stars and a daring promise from her airman. 'He said that when he was better he would fly his plane down low over the hospital so I knew he was thinking about me.'

She wasn't disappointed. 'Sure enough he did and found himself back in hospital because the veins in his legs burst again!'

'I got jaundice and was confined to the san. It may have been caught from a boyfriend at the time.'

Jaundice (or viral hepatitis) was the scourge of the Army in the Middle East and Mediterranean, and it just so happened it could also flourish in a draughty hut in Buckinghamshire. Pamela was properly ill for the first time in her life.

> Well because everything you do at that age is quite fun, to begin with I thought, 'Oooh good, I will lose some weight!' but it really was quite nasty. I went off everything I liked. There wasn't much wine around but even if there was I couldn't have drunk it and I couldn't touch an egg.

Pam's eyes went yellow and her skin went yellow. She was down in the dumps and liverish with an infection that could wipe out its victims for at least a month. Then, joy of joys, she met an old friend. Eileen Rhodes, with whom Pamela had acted in *Playboy of the Western World* in 1939, stumbled into the san, sick. Hurrah! Freed from their work booths, thrown together in the sanatorium, the two actresses quickly hatched a plan. 'We decided to put on a play together. *Candida!* She would act in it and I would direct it!' The seed was sown, Pam couldn't wait to get better.

10

There's Nowt so Queer as Folk

Actress Pamela was (and still is) a woman who makes an impression. But it was not on the stage (nor in a sanatorium) that Rozanne first met her most significant Park friend.

'I was standing waiting for Pamela on the lawn outside the mansion. Yes. We were both looking for each other and then we met and we got on like a house on fire! We've never looked back.'

We are sitting in Rozanne's living room; spring is pushing up around the window of her Oxfordshire home. There are daffodils and birdsong and the distant strum of a far-off mower but Rozanne does not notice, she is fully focused on a very different England in a very different time. 'I remember it like it was yesterday.'

Meeting bohemian, thespian Pamela was a huge deal for young impressionable Rozanne. 'Pam was on the verge of being a rebel. She was more than stylish, she had her own style. She wore trousers and tunics and never wore a hat. And she was terribly brainy and very quick at picking up languages.'

Rozanne was smitten from the outset. Pam, in her London sitting-room, smiles at the details of her friend's description. 'Zan is a wonderful romantic, she loves a good story. I don't remember wearing tunics! But I suppose I did have a few more clothes than some of the other girls.' And then she laughs her full throaty laugh.

There is no disguising the deep affection that exists between these two remarkable women and has done ever since their friendship began seventy-two years ago on a nondescript patch of grass outside a manor house in Buckinghamshire. The meeting was not a coincidence.

Tom Boase was head of admin in my hut and he had taught Pamela's brother at Oxford. He said, 'The sister of an undergraduate I know well is here and I would like you to meet her because you don't know many people and she is nearer your age.'

It turned out that Tom Boase was not only a Professor of History of Art and Director of the Courtauld Institute, he was also an astute manager of people. Here was an example of Bletchley Park's leadership at its best, looking out for the welfare of their isolated workforce. Tom recognised that Rozanne, confined to her small Italian section stuffed full of much older academic males, needed friends nearer her own age, and was able to suggest the ideal match. From a similar class (although Rozanne wasn't a deb – 'No, I was definitely one rung down!') and both harbouring creative ambitions, the girls had much in common.

Rozanne was duly impressed by the elegant woman who greeted her on the lawn. 'Pam had a presence. I admired her and was rather swept up by her. She is still my closest friend. Yes, I regard her as my best friend.'

Work Colleagues

In fact Tom Boase had no need to worry about Rozanne. 'You see, everything is terribly exciting when you are young and away from home,' she explains, and life in her hut proved no exception. Warm, open-minded and spontaneous, this gamine dark-haired girl was much taken with the huddle of academics and older men in the Italian air section. She remembers them as 'friendly, polite and easy to get on with'. There was one man in particular who transformed her working life. Rozanne had noticed him that first morning when she entered the foggy hut: 'Inside this room opposite the door sat Professor Last (Hugh) seated at the table with a large bookcase of books perched on the end, almost cutting him off from the others.' Rozanne's designated work station 'looked towards Hugh Last's

163

bookcase . . . He had, I noticed from the first, wise dark eyes, a solemn manner but also a delightful smile.'

For Rozanne, Hugh was:

> observant, polite in an old-fashioned way, he seemed to belong entirely to an academic world, referred to Oxford as his 'Alma Mater' (Brasenose College particularly), was shy of women and lived, or had lived until coming to Bletchley PK, a bachelor Don's college existence, with little idea of how the real world lived.

This gauche professor was immediately taken with Rozanne (one can only imagine the breath of fresh air she must have been in an otherwise stuffy male room). 'From my work place I could see his dark eyes observing me.' Eventually Hugh summoned up the courage to ask her to lunch. Rozanne was stunned. She still remembers the invitation as an 'extraordinary thing'. The nineteen-year-old politely accepted and they set off to the canteen together. This one o'clock rendezvous became a regular fixture, as did the Latin lesson that followed in the coffee hut near the mansion. No matter that Rozanne 'had never had a proper education', she was now being taught an ancient language by the Camden Professor of Roman History.

Through Hugh, Rozanne's working life was transformed; a kaleidoscope of experiences presented themselves to her. 'I was soon invited to the manor in Newton Longville where he was billeted with Tom Boase and Rhoda Welsford at old Lady Welsford's house.' Rozanne would get on her scarlet bicycle and join these three esteemed Bletchley employees (all more than twenty years her senior) for a slap-up meal. She laughs now at the vivid recollections: Old Lady Welsford so grand and puffy, forcing her elderly academic charges to sit at the table like polite schoolboys, the ancient 1916 car that brought the trio into work ('there was a huge bonnet well ahead of the car and at the back it was built up like an old coach') and the lessons that Rozanne learnt. 'It was a fascinating time for me, I had always loved history, Roman history in particular, though I was a complete amateur in all such things.' For both Hugh and Rozanne this was no ordinary friendship.

> Soon I was inextricably involved with Hugh Last, who began to be in love with me, though very conscious of his age. (He was forty-six but behaved more like a man of sixty-six!) and I just nineteen. I became very fond of him and he remained a friend for life.

But there was no physical contact, not even a kiss. Rozanne smiles at the very suggestion and then tries to explain the world she grew up in:

> He was just a wonderful person and a typical product of those times. It is rather unbelievable to hear but there were several professors then who were not married. No, they were not gay, but they probably never had relations with women. It was taken for granted they were bachelors, that's who they were. They went straight from being brilliant sixth-formers into the very masculine world of academia.

War and, with it, Rozanne's arrival, turned Hugh's ordered world upside down, but he was far too much of a gentleman to step outside the lines with this vivacious, much younger woman. For her part, Rozanne was equally moved. 'The memory of those early days are very vivid to me still. I shall never forget his devotion to me and mine to him.' At the very end of her unpublished notes on Bletchley, Rozanne adds a touching anecdote that underlines her earlier sentiment: these were very different times.

> One funny old-fashioned thing was that for 6 months after starting work at Bletchley Hugh Last always called me 'Miss Medhurst' when talking to me; and it was a great moment when he announced to me, 'Might I address you from now on as

165

Rozanne?' This is not as unusual as it seems today for people were much more FORMAL in those days.

———◆———

By her own admission Charlotte had grown up with very few friends, having been home-educated in remote Herefordshire. Beyond the secrecy and long shifts she therefore took great comfort from the companionship Bletchley offered. Working upstairs in the mansion she was in the prime position to enjoy her coffee breaks downstairs in the Recreation Room.

> We would get chatting with different people. Because of the nature of the Official Secrets Act you couldn't talk about work, never. It was always social chit chat. I think that helped you facilitate friendships because you couldn't talk 'shop'.

It was over coffee that Charlotte had her first taste of America. Although never numbering more than a couple of hundred, a spattering of American cryptanalysts had been piloted into most huts from 1942. If much of Britain swooned when the GIs arrived, Bletchley bristled. Charlotte recalls an atmosphere of 'we will show 'em how it is done!' But any sense of 'them and us' didn't stop this self-possessed young woman breaking the ice with a man called Walter Sharp. She couldn't get over his accent, nor his Americanisms. A little taste of Hollywood had landed in Buckinghamshire!

'Sidewalk, garters, pants, the accent can sound pretty awful!' Charlotte smiles; she had found a new friend.

But socialising wasn't always so straightforward. 'It is not easy to express, it was not well regarded for you to make friends in other sections. The head of the section might check on what you were up to, who you were mixing with and warn you off indirectly.' Gwen is trying to explain the conundrum that was Bletchley Park – now widely regarded as a place full of fascinating people – and why access to those people was restricted. The concentric circles of secrecy, guarded more closely in some huts and sections than others, meant there was no 'one size fits all' social template. With no one to make connections for her, and no sociable coffee breaks in the mansion, Gwen had to make her own way. Having spent the first nine years of her life as an only child she was used to that. Gwen, like Rozanne, worked in a small department in Josh Cooper's Air Section, where the recruits were disproportionately male, older and erudite. Precocious scholarship girl Gwen was in her element.

Tellingly, the chapter in her memoir where she explains her initiation into the secret world of deciphering Luftwaffe traffic is entitled 'Making Friends'. In her most recent email to me she writes: 'I do hope you will come again. I should like to tell you more about some of the remarkable people at BP.'

What left a lasting impression on Gwen was not the work itself but rather the colourful collection of individuals she worked with. This young girl, who had only just waved goodbye to a routine life of school, Mother and Father and a ploddish clerical post in Gloucestershire, was immediately impressed by her outlandish colleagues. There was Denys Webster, an avid Arsenal supporter who loved Italian opera ('I can still hum arias from one of his [Bellini's] operas, which instantly brings back Denys' absorbed and blissful face'), Maurice Zarb, a banker of Maltese, Arabic and Greek descent who quoted Eastern love poems and believed there was no more amorous music than Mozart's ('conversation with Maurice was like being fed delicious and fascinating food') and just one other woman. Wrapped in voluminous kaftans and scarves, this exotic older lady would 'pour out to me a long lament about her lost happiness, and her yearning to go back to the Cambridge Ladies College where she had been a professor of Eastern Languages'. Gwen had found her own little piece of paradise. Even better was the assurance that there was more excitement to come.

'A poet!' Here Gwen almost squeaks on a quest to recall her excitement. A real-life poet was due to return shortly to the department. Welshman Vernon Watkins – affectionately regarded as the joke of the section – had been much talked of in his absence and young Gwen was all ears. It is impossible to underestimate her mounting sense of anticipation. By the age of six she was already reading Rudyard Kipling's *Kim* and formative memories include her impoverished grandmother's great bookcase bulging with Victorian prose. Gwen was a natural wordsmith ('poetry was always my greatest interest'), so the prospect of meeting a man who had recently been published by Faber and Faber and knew T. S. Eliot was a very big deal.

> It is difficult now to remember or imagine the enormous cachet derived from being a Faber Poet (and even more difficult to envisage, without actually looking at old newspapers and magazines, the really colossal amount of space devoted to reviews).

Gwen was star-struck before Vernon had even returned from his (failed) commission. Indeed, before she had even read one of his poems. ('I couldn't understand them when I did!')

His grinning gentle Welsh face pushed its way around the door and everybody in the room gasped.

Vernon Watkins had not only failed to become an officer (he'd marched his squad into a brick wall and forgotten to take his rifle with him for the passing-out parade) but he'd also returned to Bletchley with a shaven head. He looked like a slightly surprised convict, but that didn't stop him from riffing with the head of section about his disastrous RAF commission interview. The Air Commodore had not thought poetry a suitable pastime in war:

> He said he hoped I wasn't writing any more while I was serving in the RAF. I replied that as a matter of fact I wrote poems all the time, because what poets wrote about war was far more important than what historians wrote.

Gwen was agog. She hurried to her seat and scribbled down as much of the conversation as she could remember. German tuning messages would have to wait; Vernon had just given her a perfect nugget for 'the great comic novel I was going to write after the war about life in the air force'. That particular book was never written but Gwen had not misjudged the 'massive initial impact' of meeting Vernon. What began as another unlikely Bletchley friendship would go on to change her life forever.

Seniors and Eccentrics

Not only did Bletchley cryptanalyst and historian Asa Briggs observe of the Park, 'I had never seen so many women in my life!' he also emphasised the importance of good relations between 'the younger and older members of the BP community.' Inevitably perhaps, with so much time spent locked in gruelling shifts, harmony across these gender and age divides was paramount.

Although few expected genuine friendship to blossom, many young girls, some in their first paid job, were struck by the warm, easy-going individuals who managed Bletchley's vast workforce. No matter that they got paid significantly less than their male equivalents, both Pamela and Rozanne are adamant that they never felt talked down to as women at the Park. Name-checking chess master Hugh Alexander and Harry Hinsley, who she worked alongside in the Naval Section, as examples of friendly cryptanalysts, Pamela emphatically adds, 'it never felt like there was a divide between us, unlike in that film [*Enigma*] which suggested that all the women did was carry coffee trays'. Ann remembers Stuart Milner-Barry (latterly the head of Hut 6) as a big bear of a man who would come and stand over the radiator and casually chat with his staff. Likewise, Pamela and the Moller sisters all remember Frank Birch, the theatrical don in charge of the Naval section, as a fair 'jovial' fellow.

Even stooped bespectacled professors were apparently able to let their hair down. Joanna, by this time an efficient Colossus operator, recalls Professor Max Newman as 'an absolute darling, a very very nice man. Very considerate of others.' Perhaps her affection was reinforced when she saw his 'terrific jitterbugging' in Woburn's village hall. Either way, Cora, a more junior member of the Newmanry team, was not even graced with an introduction to the mighty mathematician, proving personal recollections are just that: personal.

Josh Cooper, one of Bletchley's most renowned code-breakers, was Rozanne's top boss in the Air Section but she was unperturbed by his razor-sharp mind and her description is more reminiscent of a bumbling uncle. 'He was tall, polite, shambolically dressed and he continually ran his hands through his floppy brown hair.' She did, however, recognise his brilliance (or at least the more curious manifestations of it). 'He would go down to the lake with a cup of tea, deep in thought with the codes, and at the end would throw the cup into the lake. Yes, I actually saw him do that. He had a photographic mind.' Through her intriguing work colleagues she even got to know Alan Turing. 'He was polite, kind and intelligent but preferred the company of men.'

Alan Turing, now widely credited as being the father of the modern computer, was with his 'brilliant mechanisation of subtle logical deductions' the main man behind Bletchley's Bombes. His machines had transformed the decoding process, delivering tangible results for Montgomery in North Africa and turning the Battle of the Atlantic towards Allied advantage. Despite the Park's compartmentalised systems, many had a pretty good idea that this 'prof' was the *genius loci* at BP. But of the thousands who worked there, few met him, and fewer still actually knew him. (Even Baroness Trumpington, who was at the Park from 1940, only met him once when delivering a message, and then she can't recall if he said 'thank you'.) Lady Jean Graham, however, worked directly for him in Hut 8. Alan Turing was responsible for the Banburismus process which saw her frantically ticking paper all day. However she bore no grudge. 'He was an awfully nice man.' She smiles at the list of personal idiosyncrasies: 'shabby, knitting, nail bitten, tieless, sometimes halting in speech and awkward of manner', a man famous for his gas masks and curious cycling habits.

Yes he had lots of eccentric behaviour. I talked to him often and saw him every day. We were in a big room at one end of the build-ing and he came in and would say, 'Now where is the Norwegian stuff?' or 'Have you got today's letters from Norway or Italy?'

And you would say, 'Sir I have them here.'

'Oh that's all right. Thank you.'

Lady Jean worked in Hut 8 in 1942. The fact that she remembers Turing as an 'awfully nice' accessible man is particularly striking given the pressure his hut was under that year. In February 1942 a fourth Enigma wheel was introduced by the German Navy for cipher machines being used on the Atlantic U-boats' net – the result was catastrophic: Bletchley Park's naval code-breakers were thrown back into the dark. The Shark key wreaked havoc; 'during the first eight months of 1942, over 4 million tonnes of shipping were sunk by U-boats at the rate of more than 500,000 tonnes per month. Between 60 and 108 ships were sunk during each month.' Minus the necessary cribs and without high-speed four-wheel Bombes, Hut 8 was in dire straits. The message settings produced by the four-wheeled Enigmas meant that even Banburismus was rendered ineffective. When it came to Shark, Lady Jean was ticking in vain. Despite the air of failure, however, she only has good things to say about Alan. 'They worked jolly hard. There were beds on the floor; some of them slept there.' Joan Clarke, one of Bletchley's rare female cryptanalysts, worked with Alan upstairs, and was at one time his fiancée. Lady Jean remembers her well: 'She was a very bright woman. She really loved him, I think.'

There has been much speculation about this relationship between Alan Turing and his female colleague, Joan Clarke; the story had just been reincarnated again, this time by Hollywood in *The Imitation Game*, with Keira Knightley as Turing's unlikely leading lady. Jean recalls that even back then, in the thick of war, gossip was rife.

Everybody talked about their engagement. They thought it was fantastic that Joan should be going around with him. She didn't know [he was homosexual] to begin with and when she found out she said, 'You knew what he was and you never told me!' She didn't know and she felt a fool.

Lady Jean's story contradicts the suggestion made by Turing's main biographer, Andrew Hodges, that Joan was aware of and unfazed by her fiancé's homosexuality. Maybe, as Hodges suggests, on Joan's part there was a misunderstanding over the word 'tendencies' in relation to Turing's homosexuality. Or perhaps once the engagement had been called off and Joan felt hurt, the story was conflated.

In wartime Britain homosexuality was illegal, but in some circles the Park fostered a more tolerant attitude. For Rozanne, with Church of England vicars on both sides of her family, it was 'a real eye-opener'.

Most of the people I met before BP got engaged and were married. It didn't occur to me that life could be different. But at Bletchley it was less clear-cut. I was aware of homosexuality and I knew that Alan Turing was a homosexual, and others. But BP was avant-garde and I was young and picked up on the feeling amongst people that this was perfectly normal.

Aristocratic Jean, no doubt aware of Establishment Britain's revulsion towards homosexuality, was deeply touched by this 'sweet handsome' man and his predicament.

I had an idea when I was there. I wish I had carried it out. I would like to have written to Winston Churchill and told him, 'this man saved the country', you know, that sort of thing. 'I feel that Britain should give him something in return.'

What she had in mind was the idea that Britain should gift Alan Turing a large house in a town with a big college, 'somewhere like

Canada where there is no law against homosexuals'. It is unlikely that Turing, never particularly secretive about his homosexuality and fully engaged at the forefront of British technical innovation, would have accepted the offer of a house on the fringes of the English-speaking world, especially as Canadian laws were no more tolerant towards homosexuals than Britain's. However, the fact that Lady Jean even had such an idea ('I remember having that thought in the Park') reveals the supreme confidence afforded by her noble birth. 'My family knew Winston Churchill because father was in the House of Lords. He could have spoken to him.' It is also indicative of the deep loyalty and affection she felt towards Turing.

'I didn't do it and I wish I had. Alan . . .' She stops briefly before articulating what came next. 'Ten years later they went and operated on him and then he committed suicide.'

Birds of a Feather

Pamela is circumspect. 'I suppose some of the girls working in my section were more conservative than I was. They were quite "debby", I think you would call them Sloane Rangers now.' And while the common assumption of 'ever present pearls' among Bletchley's indexers doesn't resonate, she concedes this may have meant she wore them too. 'People did wear a lot of pearls.'

Pamela never confined her friendship circle to Bletchley's high-society set. But when she advanced from her indexing role to run the administration of the whole index she missed their chat. Managing them was much less fun. Their antics have subsequently acquired legendary status. Jean Campbell-Harris (now better known as Baroness Trumpington) recalls, 'we girls did everything we could to think of to lighten our lives and I am afraid that I often behaved very badly indeed'. What follows is a list of high jinks: false notices telling staff what to wear to work, irreverent ditties saved for long night shifts and a farcical incident involving three debs and a careering laundry basket. Needless to say Sarah

Norton, Osla Benning and Jean Barker were duly punished and didn't work together for another three weeks.

While Pamela, at least three or four years their senior, was duly promoted to head of the naval index and given the invidious task of drawing up shift rotas for this social set, Lady Jean simply wished she was in the same section as them (Hut 4, by then in Block A).

'Ha yes!' she hoots, 'Baroness Trumpington! We still phone each other from time to time. Yes she definitely had more fun in her section. I didn't speak German. I could speak French but not German.' (All these years later the lack of German still niggles.) 'Yes we were good friends, we still are. There aren't many of us left now.'

Although never destined to work together, Lady Jean and Jean Campbell-Harris did find each other. From the same aristocratic world and standing at six foot tall apiece, they would have been hard pressed not to.

'The Baroness speaks her mind! She always has done.' Lady Jean is referring to *Coming Up Trumps*, Jean Trumpington's recent memoir in which she gives her old friend a fulsome mention: she was 'born blue-blooded and everybody in her family was a duke (she was related to the whole damn lot of them, mainly through her mother), but she never had any money'.

Lady Jean is suitably amused. 'No, but neither did she; Sarah Norton and Osla had much more!' No wonder the two tall Jeans resorted to swapping clothes.

A conversation that starts with the Baroness, soon fans out to other girls.

I shared my billet with Mary Rouse Broughton, her father was Master of the Hounds in peacetime. She came from Downton Hall, Ludlow; she was crazy about riding. Then there was Elspeth Davidson, her father was badly bombed, they moved out of London to Aberdeenshire. She married the factor of Balmoral Estate, he later became the deputy ranger at Windsor Park. And Lady Margaret Stirling-Aird, I knew her before I went to the Park.

Within the BP community Lady Jean quickly found her own set: smart girls who spoke the 'language' of the landed gentry. This was partly the result of Bletchley's recruitment and management methods, the impact of which was not lost on Peter Calvocoressi, an intelligence officer in Hut 3:

> As a consequence of the recruitment . . . nearly all of us had had the same sort of education and shared a common social background. We made, unwittingly for the most part, the same assumptions about life and work and discipline and values. Although we had never met before . . . we half-knew each other already. We fell easily into comradeship and collaboration.

Undoubtedly like-minded friends with familiar views and life experiences were a comfort when working away from home. Oxford graduate Ann remembers being surrounded by equally talented young women in the Machine Room of Hut 6. 'Most of us had degrees in economics, law or maths.' No wonder Asa Briggs, a cryptanalyst in the neighbouring watch room was struck by the numbers of well-educated women. Ann soon became his friend. In more ways than one Bletchley Park was a home away from home for her. She often bumped into kindred spirits.

Ann's second full day at the Park was 28 September 1943: 'met Diana Taverner after lunch (LMH)[1] and she looked after me until I walked into Mabel Senior!' Although not all the girls in Hut 6 were Oxford Alumni, their backgrounds were not unfamiliar. 'Daphne has two brothers at Eton, she never took School Certificate, was going abroad at fifteen when war broke out.' Ann's brothers went to Rugby and it was with Rugby schoolboys that Ann enjoyed her wartime summer camps. The connections she made there weren't wasted at BP. '4 Nov 1943: RAF man in hut from Rugby. Lots of Rugbians here. He was a school master

1. Lady Margaret Hall, the Ladies College at Oxford that Ann attended.

and said, "It's bad luck on the boys who come here at seventeen and see no more of the war."'

The gender division was clear. Men were the combatants and women the non-combatants. If claustrophobic 'safe' Bletchley was not deemed gallant wartime service for a boy, the reverse was true for a girl. Indeed, locally BP girls were considered a 'race apart, distinctive for their air of elegance and education' and were the envy of those engaged in more menial war work.

Doris Scorer and her friends repaired aircraft in the local Wolverton Works; Ann and many of her colleagues were billeted in the same town. The factory girls could only speculate as to what the 'immaculate and very stand-offish' BP girls did 'over there at the Park'. Doris, the teenage daughter of a charlady, was blunt in her appraisal: 'We could see that they came from good backgrounds while we were what was termed "born on the wrong doorstep".' Bound by secrecy and class, the BP girls 'didn't mix much'. They didn't need to; they had each other.

———◆———

Rozanne has never forgotten the day Kathleen appeared in her block.

> About two months after arriving in the Park I met a WAAF called Kate Godfrey, the nineteen-year-old daughter of Admiral Godrey RN (he was then Chief of Intelligence in the RN and my father was Chief of Intelligence in the RAF – an odd coincidence!).

But given both men's links with the Park it wasn't such an odd coincidence. The girls had more than their father's professions in common; both endured limited educations (much to Kathleen's later chagrin), had been imbued with a love of music and dance, were equipped with at least one foreign language and almost shared the same birth date (bar a day or two). Needless to say, 'Kate and I became lifelong friends.'

Meanwhile from within her hut Pamela managed to find a fist-ful of bright, like-minded girls to share her third billet. Still not content to rely on the whims of the billeting officer (despite the caravan debacle) she rented her own self-catering accommodation. The result was a roaring success. 'We lived as five girls. There was Anne, Naomi, Juliet . . . some had been to university, none of them were really debs.' A stint at domestic science college for at least two of the girls kept food on the table, while Pamela ('hope-less in the kitchen') tackled the garden. 'I remember growing vegetables. I grew broad beans and they got black fly. I wasn't very good at it but I rather liked the idea.'

With her own house Pamela was at last able to play hostess. 'We gave what we thought were splendid parties!' Impromptu get-togethers were social highlights in an otherwise fairly mundane existence. Pamela recalls: 'There was a girl called Maxine Birley, the Comtesse de la Falaise as she became; she was a great beauty and mad about France and I remember her giving a party at which we all had to be very French.' New friends Pamela and Rozanne decided to share their November birthday celebrations and Maxine (accord-ing to Cecil Beaton, the only truly chic English woman of her generation and a must-have party accessory) was duly invited.

We had terrible difficulty getting any sort of alcohol, in the end we got some fairly revolting Algerian wine. Maxine decided to pick lots of flowers and she put one in everybody's glass. It completely ruined the drink but she thought it looked so romantic!

Few mixed in the rarefied social circles through which Maxine moved. But an accommodation rethink in 1943 due to rapidly expanding numbers at the Park forced service girls (including WAAFs Maxine and Gwen) to give up their billets and live together in purpose-built military quarters.

Although sad about leaving saintly Mrs Henson, at the unpop-ular RAF camp Gwen did at least meet girls who had 'been unknown' to her 'among the thousands in the Park'. Maxine was particularly memorable.[2] Gwen vividly recalls an elegant girl with a slight French accent who never ate in the sergeant's mess, was swept away by Americans in Jeeps waiting outside the gates, and only ever got in just before the 23.59 deadline. She was also quite unable to do her own laundry – or even brush her own hair. Vera, a fellow WAAF and former factory girl, took to washing the stacks of underwear she found beneath Maxine's bed ('lovely delicate things of apricot or almond-blossom pink or primrose silk, trimmed with lace'). When Maxine eventually left, for Gwen 'all the glamour left the hut, too'.

With good friends almost anything is tolerable. Cora was part of a trio from Talbot Heath and Joanna had her old school friend Margaret and soon made many more among the Colossus Wrens.

Even little Muriel didn't feel left out. Promoted to Hut 4, where Phoebe Senyard, a well-heeled middle-aged woman, was head of section, Muriel was treated so nicely she wonders if Phoebe wasn't also Jewish. Lunchtimes involved her older sister Anita and kosher sandwiches by the lake and in the evenings the Bogush's house at 27 Duncan Street welcomed respected members of BP's Jewish community. Hut 4 linguist Walter Eytan had established a Zionist Society and with his brother Ernest and mathematician Joe Gillis they discussed weighty matters: the future of an independent Israeli state and prospective Jewish immigration to the Holy Land after the war. Many of these meetings took place at Joe's apartment but come Friday the men would often enjoy a Shabbat meal with Muriel's parents Rebecca and Phillip.

'Yes, they came home with my sister. We were never short, there would be chicken soup or fried fish or something.' For teenage Muriel political discussion about a future Israeli state carried little weight but she sensed this was something important, that

2. With the passage of time Gwen remembers 'the French comtesse' as Francine, not Maxine, in her memoir.

these men mattered. Her intuition proved right. Walter Eytan later became the director of Israel's Foreign Ministry. At Bletchley Park he is remembered as part of the team who 'intercepted a signal from a small German-commissioned vessel in the Aegean, reporting that it was transporting Jews . . . en route for Piraeus *zur Endlösung* ("for the final solution")'. Walter instinctively knew what it meant.

Bletchley workers were predominantly middle class and English, but Jews and Americans were not the Park's only cultural exceptions. With blonde braided hair piled on her head, white socks and sandals and broken English, more than once Doris Moller was asked if she was German. It didn't help her confidence, nor did the landlord of her first billet. Captain Burly in Milton Keynes told the Moller sisters, '"If you don't speak the Queen's English, don't speak at all!" After that we dared not speak a word.' Having felt so keenly British on the occupied Continent, the two half-Belgian sisters found that Bletchley took some getting used to. Doris couldn't understand all the English colloquialisms and never went anywhere without her dictionary and her sister. Georgette did her best to steer them along an English path. In the canteen just outside the Park gates the two girls would take elevenses facing the wall. 'We were so shy but because we were from Belgium we liked to dunk our toast into our coffee. We didn't want people to see this.'

Clinging to each other like limpets, initially the two sisters didn't find Park life easy. Doris, who now loves returning to the Park, is frank about the early years. 'I loved the work but no, I don't remember having fun. No.'

Everybody's Bletchley was different.

11

Downtime

'The social side, the gay side was essential. It was a wonderful way of letting off steam. And a lot of people there were actors and actresses.'

For young Rozanne, whose own stint at the Webber Douglas theatrical school had been cut short by the Blitz, Bletchley provided an opportunity to tap in to a rich cultural seam. Seventy-two years later she remains wide-eyed at the memory of the creative world she found herself in aged nineteen.

> I was a dancer at BP, I had done a lot of dancing when I was young. I was so lucky to be in the chorus. Lots of people were involved, there was a large theatrical quota. Pamela was a professional actress. She had done all these things already and she was in lots of the Bletchley Revues.

Then suddenly, mid-story and quite without warning, Rozanne bursts into song.

> At the age of sixteen I was kicked by a mule
> Seduced a school master before I left school
> But I longed to experience life in the raw
> That's why I came here . . . whatever it's for?!

Throwing in an artistic shrug to underline the last line, Rozanne ends Pamela's ditty with a flourish. 'She was a very good actress,' she adds. 'We had such fun and we danced as well.'

Cast aside what mothers knit us
Put on clothes that really fit us
Sophisticate black is de rigueur
A hat that leaves your hair free to curl
Peacetime glamour only more so
Once a week roll out the torso
Dab away the wrinkle and the frown
Throw your cares away and go to town!

Rozanne remembers the songs – word (and pitch) perfect – as if it were yesterday. An accolade indeed for Bletchley's artistic legacy.

Life's a Stage

In his book *The Secret Life of Bletchley Park*, Sinclair McKay emphasises the 'markedly more highbrow' nature of BP's cultural life in comparison with the artistic fare served to the troops, which he claims was deliberately 'pitched at a certain emotional level that could be enjoyed by all – popular culture at its best'. But Pamela doesn't agree; troop entertainment wasn't always popular culture at its best. If nostalgic Britain holds on to the high notes of George Formby and Vera Lynn, much of what ENSA rolled out for the Services was distinctly second rate. Having done her share of treading the boards in front of the troops she recalls: 'I think they would have liked something more intelligent. I remember a terrible one, *Grandpa Sees it Through*. It was a second-rate farce.'

However if peripatetic servicemen got what they were given, McKay is right: it was very different at Bletchley Park. In situ for the whole war, blessed with the run of a mansion, sizeable grounds and later a purpose-built assembly hall, educated Park employees were well placed to create their own entertainment. Indeed, from the outset they were actively encouraged to do so. Initially fearful that drab little Bletchley would undermine the fettle of smart young recruits, BP management showed a forward-thinking 'concern with staff morale'. Early on they understood that 'operational efficiency was affected by the provision of recreational facilities'. Bletchley Park's Recreation Club was born, and notes promoting Highland dancing, drama groups, chess clubs and gramophone recitals were pinned on a board. Pamela concedes that despite its rapid growth, even in 1942 the place retained 'a collegiate air'.

For young girls like Rozanne and her new friend Kathleen, the dramatic and musical opportunities were unforgettable. Primed throughout their youth to embrace the arts, both girls leapt at the opportunity to perform. Kathleen smiles when her daughter pulls out a Xerox of the original programme for 'A Concert of English Music by the BP Musical Society'. The performance advertised was *Dido and Aeneas*, an ambitious, full-throttle three-act English opera. Fortunately the Park could field a conductor among its intelligence officers. Herbert Murrill was Professor of Composition at the Royal Academy of Music and would later become the head of music at the BBC, but for the time being he was stuck in Buckinghamshire. His efforts with amateurs Kathleen (in the chorus of Courtiers, Witches, Sailors, etc.) and Rozanne (a dancing Fury) were not wasted.

'The performance was a very big thing. It was a nice episode.' This analysis from Kathleen is particularly poignant. That she, like Pamela, was once a valued indexer using her schoolgirl German to sort and make sense of broken codes is no longer so memorable.[1] ('No, I'm not sure what I did. I think on the whole you could call the whole thing dull'.) But her bit part in this Trojan love story remains unforgettable. So too is a one-off visit from a tenor with a heavenly voice – Peter Pears. Fresh back from America with his lover and musical partner Benjamin Britten, the singer was successfully enticed to Buckinghamshire by Bletchley's network, and despite his official status as a conscientious

---

1. While Kathleen worked for Air Index in Hut 3 (Block D), Pamela headed up a separate Naval Index in Hut 4.

objector, 'Peter sang with our musical society in Handel's *Acis and Galatea.*' Another memorable moment.

Inevitably what proved head-turning for nineteen-year-olds Rozanne and Kathleen was less so for Pamela, who'd clocked up several years as a professional actress. Tellingly it is Rozanne who can recite Pamela's comic ditty 'At the age of sixteen I was kicked by a mule', not Pamela herself. Memory is selective.

What Pamela can remember is that during her first year at Bletchley, the West End play she should've been in – *The Watch on the Rhine* – had opened to respectable reviews (according to *The Times* it was 'a play rich in emotional undercurrents') and enjoyed a long run. But never one for self-pity Pam made the best of Park life. Her stint in the sanatorium with fellow actress Eileen Rhodes bore fruit. On the back of a programme for a Bletchley Christmas Revue is a promotion for the next production: 'CANDIDA by George Bernard Shaw, February 21st to 25th produced by Pamela Gibson'.

'Nowadays you'd call it directing of course. I thought I'd try my hand at something new, I had never produced before and I love Shaw. He is very much my period.' Pamela then gives a full summary of this classic drama; there is the clergyman Morell, 'a muscular Christian', his wife Candida (played by Eileen) and Eugene, the attractive poet who is madly in love with Candida.

> I suppose it is slightly old fashioned now but I rather liked it. She ends up staying with her husband, there is a famous speech at the end and she explains to the poet that he doesn't need her as much as her husband does.

Masculine weakness, feminine strength and emotional compromise are prevalent themes, although the reasons behind Pamela's choice of play were more practical. 'I didn't want anything too experimental for the audience and we had to bear in mind the ability of the actors.'

Bletchley's thespian attributes have been much lauded in recent literature. But the impression given is misleading. BP was a code-breaking factory not a drama school. Pamela is candid.

> This was not professional acting. It was a totally different feel. Amateur dramatics was a release; you were keen to remember your lines and put on a good performance but it couldn't be compared to the professional world. The Park was what it was, ultimately we were there to serve.

Of course everything is relative – for some of the young girls (including Rozanne and Kathleen) the theatricals were very impressive, but others found them less so. Ann grew up and studied in Oxford where she was an avid consumer of culture. In the months before she moved to Bletchley, she enjoyed *Gaslight*, *George and Margaret* ('terribly funny and extremely well done') and *Rebecca* at Oxford's Playhouse, so the first BP play she watched, *Much Ado About Nothing*, had a lot to live up to. Thanks to her diary we have a first-hand review. '28 Oct 1943: Gorgeous costumes and lighting. Benedict and Beatrice were excellent but rest could have been better.'

But even if the production wasn't flawless, at least it was entertainment. That same day Ann had worked extra hours, 'partly because there was nothing else to do'.

By no means everyone even went to Bletchley's thespian offerings. 'I didn't, it wouldn't have occurred to me to do so.' Gwen is matter-of-fact. 'The theatre set were different. They were nice but quite separate. There were some people who seemed to know everyone, that gave them a supreme confidence. To me they were high class.' Gwen makes sure she isn't misunderstood.

> They weren't snobbish, very few people were openly snobbish. I only remember one girl called Pauline who was very conscious of where people came from and where they went to school. But there was this dancing, acting set whose fathers were Air

The secret team code-named 'Captain Ridley's shooting party', on the lawn outside the mansion in Bletchley Park, during the Munich Crisis 1938.

Wrens operating one of the world's first electronic computers – a Colossus machine – in Bletchley Park's Newmanry.

Women using Typex machines probably in Bletchley Park's Block D towards the end of the war.

18-year-old Bombe operator Ruth in her Wren uniform.

Working veteran Ruth standing in front of a replica Bombe machine in Bletchley Park.

Sergeant Gwen Davies on arrival at Bletchley Park in 1942 aged 19. (Her sergeant's stripes have yet to be issued!)

Actress Pamela as featured in *Spotlight* directory, 1939.

Bletchley Park civilian Rozanne (Italian Airforce Section) in 1942.

Pamela (left) and Rozanne (right) in Rozanne's Oxfordshire garden, 72 years after they first met at Bletchley Park. Today aged 96 and 91 respectively they are still the very best of friends.

ATS girl Charlotte with her head of section Captain
John Burrows, in Washington DC, 1945.

Lady Jean on her 21st birthday, November
1941 just before she went to Bletchley Park.

Lady Jean aged 93 at home on the Isle of
Arran, April 2014.

The photograph rediscovered by Joanna in 2014, featuring 38 C Watch Wrens who operated the Colossus machines. Joanna is on the far right, second row from the back.

Veteran Joanna as featured in the *Daily Mail* , February 2014, standing in front of a replica Colossus machine in the National Museum of Computing.

Y-station listener Betty proudly wearing her ATS uniform, 1943.

Betty today outside her Northamptonshire home. She moved in when it was brand new in 1948.

On leave from Bletchley Park, mathematician Ann at her wartime graduation from Oxford University in 1944.

Pat (in white trousers) dancing with her fellow Y-station listeners outside their requisitioned seaside hotel in Withernsea 1943.

A recent picture of Pat taken by her late husband Ray Davies.

Muriel aged 16 in her favourite suede wedge heeled shoes.

Cora (bottom right) enjoying a well-earned day off in London's Trafalgar Square with fellow Wrens , 1944.

WAAF Kathleen in 1941 shortly before she was posted to Bletchley Park.

Sisters Georgette (left) and Doris (right) reunited with their father, John Moller in England in 1942.

Sisters Georgette (left) aged 94 and Doris (right) aged 92 in Northampton, September 2014.

Marshalls and Generals and that sort of thing and they were incredibly confident. Maxine was one of them.

At Bletchley Park (and everywhere else in 1940s Britain), the unspoken affinities that existed within society mattered. It wasn't that Gwen failed to join the thespian group – she didn't even try. Like so much of life at Bletchley, the acting world was one reality among many. But by virtue of its flamboyant credentials (and players) its place in Park life has retrospectively been exaggerated. Cora recalls no theatricals, nor does Muriel or Joanna. And proof that amateur dramatics was not strictly a class-bound activity, Lady Jean didn't buy into them either. 'No absolutely not. I didn't act.'

Confident, cultured and from Hut 6, Ann enjoyed Bletchley's dramatic fare but music was her first love. Having run the Oxford University Musicians' Club and sung in the Oxford Bach Choir she quickly capitalised on all the Park had to offer. Within a fortnight of her arrival she enjoyed a classical concert at the Assembly Hall, despite 'chairs too uncomfortable to appreciate' Beethoven. By the end of her second month she had sung with BP's Bach choir, played her records at the Bletchley club on their 'super radiogram-cum-television', and even attended a lunchtime concert where she thought the vocalist 'could have been better' but was much impressed by the 'excellent pianist accompanying him'. It was Bill Marchant, a big personality in the Park who later became a Professor of Music. Ann had a discerning ear.

So had Charlotte. Her destiny at BP was the Madrigal Club. 'I was rung up by one of the military chaps. We had phones between some of the offices and he said, "Are you interested in singing in a field tonight?" So we all went out in a field somewhere one evening.' Charlotte laughs and shakes her head of snow-white hair. 'Crazy! I don't know!'

Even a girl brought up in the middle of nowhere by a musical mother managed to find her milieu at the Park.

This smorgasbord of cultural offerings had an annual highlight. Above all else the famous Bletchley Revues have stuck in the

Park's collective memory. They were designed to celebrate and gently ridicule Park life, and senior cryptanalysts were not above joining in the seasonal programme of comic sketches and satirical songs. The ditties Rozanne remembers were written specifically for revues, which for her were an 'absolutely essential' release. 'There were a lot of people capable of producing revues; there were some very clever take-offs of the place.' This sentiment is reiterated in Ann's diary. '4 Jan 1944: Revue at 7.30. It really was excellent. Lasted nearly three hours with only one break – otherwise was continuous.'

With her exquisite comic timing and bohemian cool, Pamela featured prominently in Bletchley's revues. Together we look at a picture of an old programme in which she is cited as a performer in two sketches: 'Murder in the Cafeteria' and 'Rat-A-Plan, Rat-A-Plan'. It is then I read her a citation from a Bletchley history book.

> We had a brilliant chap called Bill Marchant who was deputy head of Hut 3 who was a minor C. B. Cochran and created a revue every Christmas. A lot of very bright people were there and wrote music and lyrics. I wrote a sketch and Pam was acting in it. No one was allowed to go to rehearsals but at that time I was going to Washington just before Christmas so I was allowed in and this glorious vision of loveliness stepped down from the stage and said 'your sketch isn't bad'.

The man quoted is the late Jim Rose. A well-connected (and fiercely good-looking) intelligence officer in Hut 3, he had just caught sight of actress Pamela Gibson.

The Flicks

By 1943 cinema admissions in Britain rose to over 1.5 billion; during the war watching a movie had become the nation's prime leisure activity and Bletchley village, with its two small cinemas, proved no exception. For many the sheer ordinariness of going to see a film explains why it doesn't always stand out as a noteworthy memory seven decades later, but Ann's diary fills in the gaps. '26 December 1943: Went to see "Foreign Correspondent", seen it before.'

Of course she had seen it before. *Foreign Correspondent* was only the second film Hitchcock had ever made in America and when it was released at the beginning of the war it was deemed unmissable.

'Hitchcock at his Best' roared *The Times* before going on to remind its readers that the solemn appeal of the final speech, 'America! Hang on to your lights, they are the only lights left in the world!' was in fact a postscript '(and frankly America the lights over here are holding out better than you had ventured to hope)'. Above all else this film was 'genuine Hitchcock', a spy thriller that aimed to provide escapism and entertainment. Stuck for things to do and reluctant to return to her mean digs, Ann chose to watch it a second time. In her first four months at the Park she also saw *More the Merrier*, an American comedy focusing on Washington's wartime growing pains; *Five Graves to Cairo*, an American spy story featuring a fictional Rommel in a North African setting; and *Two Tickets to London*, another American film about a US naval officer. Again, she sat through *More the Merrier* twice, 'as nothing else to do'.

Many working at Bletchley had the same idea; on 2 October 1943 Ann decided against the cinema because the queues were so long. Two small venues couldn't always cope with the demands of a young, eager 8,000-plus influx of cinema-goers. Tickets were cheap and at a time of rationed goods there was little else to spend their money on.

Tellingly the only movie experience Ann was genuinely impressed with was back in Oxford where she watched 'very good cinema'; *Dear Octopus* was the British drama Ann saw after she'd enjoyed a 'good tea in the Electric Cinema Cafe'. Bletchley's venues were drab in comparison and their cinematic offerings more generic.

For Ann, the quintessentially British *Dear Octopus* stood out, but it is no coincidence that the majority of films she saw in Bletchley (and Wolverton) were made in America. The early 1940s are celebrated as a period when Britain's 'national' cinema made some ground against Hollywood, with films like *In Which We Serve* (1942) and *Fires Were Started* (1943) boosting morale and conveying powerful wartime imagery. But having sat through the obligatory newsreels (Cora recalls, 'it was always the same man talking about the troops. There never seemed to be many casualties. I think it was to rally us'), most movie-goers were simply looking to escape, and invariably American films provided that escapism with more gloss and star power. (When the British magazine *Picturegoer* polled its readers in 1942 asking them to name the ten best films ever made, all the smash hits were Hollywood productions; none were British.) Even with the might of the Ministry of Information and its Film Divisions, British cinema couldn't compete.

For Betty, miles away in Harrogate, the cultural highlight of her war was *Gone with the Wind* in Technicolor.

'Ooh I thought it was lovely. I remember the whole of the film. It was Clark Gable and Vivien Leigh during the American civil war. Other films I can't remember but that one I can!' The same film played in Leicester Square for four solid years. At the height of the Blitz, audiences queued from first thing in the morning, while fires from the previous night's bombing were still burning nearby. Britain's love affair with America began long before the GIs came over.

Making Do

Technicolor cinema was about as good as it got for Morse-listener Betty in Yorkshire. What she goes on to cite is a detailed list of duties and ATS obligations that clogged her free time.

'In the evenings when you got back to camp, you had your food and then you had to clean your buttons. We used tins of wadding and Duraglit.' Betty took solace in this small reassuring task, one she mastered to perfection. There was a button stick which she neatly slid over the lapels of her jacket to protect the serge before buffing hard. And then she cleaned her shoes. 'You didn't have dirty shoes. No way! It didn't matter that you were on the Yorkshire moor, your uniform was pressed and polished.' Betty enjoyed being a soldier; nothing else mattered very much.

> There was a concrete area inside the school ground where we stayed. Imagine Horse Guards Parade – something like that. That is where we did our drill and you were never allowed to march across it, always around the side of it. There were men in the other part of the grounds but us women we marched without a weapon. Women were not allowed to operate weapons. That was not part of the service. I don't like to see women carrying rifles even now. That is not a woman's job.

The Great British patriarch had felt profoundly uncomfortable putting women in uniform – so firing a weapon was certainly never on the cards. The fairer sex could be victims of war but they couldn't fight back – not literally. That didn't bother Betty. A model service girl, she spent her free time walking the fine line between military pride and femininity, just as the Government had hoped she (and thousands of others) would.

'Half of you was in the military and the other half still proud to be a woman. It's hard to explain. I was proud to do something as a woman.' Even leaving her bed behind in the morning was a meticulous affair. 'Sheets and blankets had to be folded in a certain way. It was called barracked. You couldn't just get out of bed, you had to do it properly!' These routines consumed Betty's waking hours between shifts. There was little else on offer.

Betty didn't even dance. ('No, I just sat on the edge, I couldn't dance.') A committed Methodist, she had to make do with the Church of England inside St Ethelburga's grounds as a place of worship and never once did she complain about the long runs across the moors all the girls were sent on. 'We had streaming colds, but never mind.' Army life was what it was; Betty handled it off-duty and on-duty, no questions asked.

Although Y-stations were a key component of the code-breaking operation, the lives of their listeners dotted all over Britain, working in unlikely locations at the mercy of individual staff officers, had little in common with the girls who inhabited Bletchley's southern orbit. Outside their listening stints they didn't even have much in common with each other. A Wren linguist, Pat was also an outside listener but the tales of her off-duty seaside antics have a distinct *joie de vivre* that Betty's austere Army life in Yorkshire lacked. Even her first posting at Withernsea, by all accounts 'a dismal little resort', offered Pat and fellow Wrens bright moments of fun.

> We used to bicycle out to the mouth of the Humber and visit the lighthouse. Commander Casson would let us go to the top. He had been shot in the rear and had a metal plate in his behind and we thought that this was very interesting.

The lack of able-bodied men didn't get in their way. 'Oh no, we had our own tap-dancing troupe.'

More in keeping with Bletchley's mishmash of uniform and mufti, Pat wasn't obliged to wear her naval uniform all the time (attractive as it was). 'We were secret stations and supposed to draw as little attention to ourselves as possible. That meant we could wear our civilian clothes more than other Wrens.' Pat and her colleagues went to the cinema and on country walks in their own attire, rather enjoying the ruse. Even uniforms acquired their own wartime quirks. When Italy surrendered in 1943, the girls dressed up as ancient mariners in their duffle coats; a picture holds the moment for posterity. And Chief Petty Officer Pat (possibly inspired by Montgomery's iconic overcoat) devised her own battle dress. She still has a studio snapshot of herself in this voluminous trench coat, dyed navy and smothered in badges. 'No one objected,' she observes, a hint of surprise evident in her voice. There is even a picture of the listening Wrens dancing all in a row outside their seaside hotel in Yorkshire. Pat is sporting white cotton slacks, an abundant smile pushes up her cherry cheeks.

But it was her final posting to Abbot's Cliff in Kent that stood out as the most memorable. Perched up high overlooking the Channel, this is where daring Pat felt suitably connected to the war.

> We were so close to the Continent you could see the sun on the windscreens of the cars across the water in France. And the Germans carried on shelling Dover, there were doodlebugs and all sorts. If they started shelling and you were on the surface you had to get back to your station, but if you were in a restaurant called the Crypt you were allowed to stay as it was underground. So this restaurant was extremely popular!

Christened Hellfire Corner early on in the war, coastal Kent was notorious as a target for bombing raids. 'I remember an anti-aircraft shell falling into our watch room but luckily it didn't explode. Abbot's Cliff was the only station I worked at where there were military police.' Pat and her friends decided to take the initiative and ask if they too could learn to use a Sten gun. Fifteen enthusiastic Wrens proved irresistible. 'We took the gun apart and put it together again and fired at a target. Unofficially of course.' Pat looks up and grins. It wasn't the first time she had used a gun. Her stalwart military grandfather was determined he would defend the family home if the Germans invaded. ('He was sure they would land up on the quarry and come down disguised as nuns on motorcycles.') 'So me, my mother and the Austrian cook all had to take turns firing a gun at a target in the azaleas.'

Pat used every one of her three postings to really live the war. 'I am still sure I was quite right to turn down Bletchley Park.'

Even the majority of girls whose work took them daily past BP sentries often have very different tales to tell. Joanna and Cora didn't sleep in Buckinghamshire; their story started and stopped in Bedfordshire. About life in off-duty 'collegiate' Bletchley they remember very little because they didn't live it. The most fun Cora remembers having in the Park was midway through her nightshift. It was a dark winter's night, Cora and a couple of other Wrens were outside on a break standing by the lake and suddenly an urge took them. 'Yes! Let's do something mad!' It was too cold to swim but there was a small boat tied to the bank. 'Well, we had a row in the middle of the night. We didn't undo the rope, it was just a little sploosh.' For Cora, aged seventeen, this 'sploosh' helped to relieve the boredom of checking those interminable noughts and crosses and made a change from walking around the park in the pitch dark.

Anything else that stood out in Cora's young mind took place not at Bletchley but in Woburn Abbey.

Part of a little trio from Talbot Heath, the girls were left to entertain themselves in the vast mansion. The novelty of being a Wren rating in new 'quarters' helped. 'Because it was all so new to us we practised squad drill outside in the courtyard on our own. Attention! Turn Right!' And there were ballet moves across the upstairs 'cabin' in thick black tights and clumping black shoes. 'Three little girls from school are we!' When Cora thinks back, she is not remembering herself as an adult but as a child. Needless to say being plonked into England's most exquisite parkland had its advantages. 'The lake at Woburn was a great big one, much nicer than at BP.' Cora bought a pair of second-hand skates from a London lost property office and made the most of 1944's icy winter.

'The Duke of Bedford hated us skating. He said it disturbed the fish. Well I thought sod the fish!'

For Joanna it was the Duke's collection of exotic animals, not his fish, that caught her imagination.

> In the parkland there were Père David deer that had been saved from extinction. They had overlapping front feet; in the dark you could hear them click-clicking. And there was a herd of bison and wallabies.

Joanna spent hours exploring the exquisite grounds and their unusual inhabitants. And if her very own safari park wasn't enough, on days off with fellow Wrens she would bicycle the four miles down to Woburn Sands. 'We'd take a picnic with us and swim in the brick pit reservoir and then cycle back up the hill.' Wartime shortages saw America introduce the bikini but Joanna didn't partake. 'I think I wore an old black swimming costume from school. I wasn't particularly interested in allure. But I did have a Yardley's lipstick.' The off-duty picture Joanna paints – much like Cora's – is of a vibrant mix of snatched moments; modest exploits that vigorously countered long shifts and wartime privation. She pauses to remember her distant youth and then concludes: 'You see, Woburn Abbey featured far more for us than Bletchley Park because that is where we stayed and made friends.'

Refreshments

Among Rozanne's favourite memories is 'drinking tea and chatting in the big front room before or after one's shift'. A spritely girl, with cropped curled hair, a string of pearls and a simple jersey and skirt combination, she sat side by side with Professor Hugh Last; the quest was to learn Latin before the end of the war. No matter that tea was rationed and sugar scarce. In the summer the other option was to sit under the trees – sycamore, copper beech, willow – on the lawn 'quaffing cups of coffee or glasses of beer'. Heavily taxed and invariably watered down, beer was intermittently available from Hut 2. But for Rozanne the quality of the beverage was not important; these companionable interludes provided a frisson of the unexpected after all the repetitive work in smoky huts.

A young girl drinking beer with a professor twenty-five years her senior did not turn heads at Bletchley Park. Charlotte, who thought nothing of striking up a conversation with an American stranger, is convinced the complexion of the Park's personnel nurtured a laissez-faire attitude. 'BP was a unique set-up: the numbers, the mixed bag and the atmosphere of the place.' And of course there was a war on. Often for the first time in their lives, young women were away from home, independent and earning a wage. Beer on the lawn was just the beginning. Change was afoot; suddenly pubs were no longer an all-male preserve, although for the Bletchley Girls a lounge bar was a more likely choice. Ann's regular haunt was the Park Hotel. Still extant today a short walk from BP, this sturdy three-storey building (almost) retains the atmosphere of an old-school drinking establishment. Push through its double doors, peer beyond the wooden beams towards the bar and you can imagine Ann, with her dimpled cheeks and wavy dark hair, sitting at a table waiting to be served – her drink of choice was a gin and French. Sometimes even two.

Not everyone drank, however. Ruth's father was uncompromising.

> He would tell me, 'We've got a drinks cupboard. If you feel you want to try a drink you ask me, but there is nothing more disgusting than a woman who is drunk. It's only whores who go to pubs and get drunk!' He used the word 'whore' and for me that was the end of the story.

Ruth only risked one wartime tipple and that was in the company of her mother: 'I wasn't sure what it was, so I ordered a Drambuie. She was most amused!'

In this brave new world it was sometimes difficult to know exactly what one should order. Rozanne, although familiar with the Park's watery beer, was hardly a drinker. 'I was brought up not to drink. My mother was very fierce about it. She was terrified of drunks!' To get around the problem when out, Rozanne always asked for a shandy – 'that was considered terribly dashing'. At least she thought so until she went to a dance with some American soldiers and was asked what she wanted to drink:

'A shandy please.'
  'A what?'
  'A shandy.'
  'Eh?'
  'A shandy.'
  'Oh, give the girl a coke.'

Rozanne was left feeling young and rather foolish. 'It was a comedown to be given a coke.'

Food might have been less fraught socially, but was equally hit and miss in terms of quality. In the early days of the Park a chef came up from London's Savoy and cooked for the small staff, but that could never have persisted in the long term. The collegiate-style gathering in the mansion soon gave way to a purpose-built canteen. While much of the original Park has undergone an extraordinary (multi-million pound) face-lift in recent years, the cafeteria on Wilton Road, just outside the original entrance, wears a dark cloak of ivy. It is hard to imagine this was once Bletchley's dining hub, serving 30,000 meals each week and operating an almost twenty-four-hour shift system. Sheer volume conspired with wartime rations to ensure the food was unremarkable at best. Workers often anticipated the break a mealtime offered more than the food itself. In her diary Ann mentions who she goes to lunch with, but the content of the meals merits little attention. Rozanne has few complaints, 'I gobbled up whatever I was given', but she thinks opinions differed depending on the lives people had led before the Park.

For many Bletchley Girls wartime boarding school had provided the perfect training.

'No matter how much it made us retch we had to eat it.'

Ruth loathed school food. Her eyes filled with tears when she was forced to swallow a mouthful of porridge ('slimy like frog-spawn') and then another. 'They had as much idea about bringing up children as a pickled herring!' At least in her naval quarters she could leave what she didn't like.

Bletchley didn't escape its own horror stories. Lady Jean is forthright: 'The food in the canteen was indescribable!' As if boiled cabbage in vast cauldrons wasn't enough, one day she discovered two cockroaches in her stew.

The catering manager was unmoved. 'Well, it's protein isn't it?'

But unlike her good friend Baroness Trumpington, at least Lady Jean's innards didn't play host to a tapeworm.

———•———

By 1944 pressure on Park numbers ensured some of the catering was outsourced. Cora and Joanna were all too familiar with the re-heated vats of food that accompanied them on the bus from Woburn, an experience made much worse for Cora by the Americans who shared her mess hut in the Park.

'Oh,' she sighs longingly, 'the food they were allowed to eat!' Early on Roosevelt had declared 'Americans cannot live on British rations', but to watch well-fed Yanks chew their way through a meat ration twice the size of her own was painful. Petite Cora made do with fried bread and hot sardines. 'I can't tell you how nauseating it was in the middle of the night.' No special relationship was fostered in that particular Nissen hut. Small pleasures had to be found elsewhere.

One option was eating out. Food in restaurants was unrationed, although supplies were limited according to the number of customers and the cost was capped from 1942 to prevent accusations that the policy favoured the better-off middle classes (which it did). Needless to say in Withernsea, where Y-listener Pat was posted, there were very few restaurants, and certainly none were open on a Sunday. That is until a local entrepreneur had a bright idea. 'There was a cafe where you popped a shilling into a slot, ordered breakfast and waited. Then the slot would open and a grimy hand would pop out holding a plate with bacon and eggs.' In wartime England you took sustenance wherever you found it – Pat was a regular customer. 'I think it was the first take-away in Yorkshire!'

Bletchley, by comparison, was much better served. Presented with canteen food or recurring herrings, prunes and Oxo at her first billet, Ann regularly ate out. Snacks and sandwiches were available at the Station Buffet, as were cakes and coffee in a little shop near the Park. But her two favourite venues were the Garden Cafe and the Park Hotel – occasionally she visited both in one day.

Every time, these meals were worthy of a mention. Occasionally the food was 'excellent', other times there was a queue and the food was 'rotten'. With cash in their pockets and little to spend it on, many BP employees had the same idea. Little Bletchley was stretched to capacity, as was the rest of the country. Cheap 'British restaurants'[2] popped up across the board and eating out more than doubled in three years.

---

2. Bletchley also had a British restaurant but it was never a very popular choice among workers.

12

A Long Road

Even in our newfangled 'egalitarian' age, Lady Jean has a commanding presence. Quite how she must have come across in full flow as a young woman one can only imagine. However it is safe to assume that she was hard to ignore. Bletchley's rules stipulated 'once in, never out' but Lady Jean was hell bent on becoming the exception.

Already transferred out of Hut 8, after three months of chatting up prospective landlords across Buckinghamshire, Lady Jean was moved again, this time to the outer perimeter of Bletchley's support staff – the Motor Transport Corps. That was more like it! Motoring was still an elite occupation; only one in five families owned a car in 1939. She might not be able to speak German but Lady Jean was one of a few women who could drive a car. She was given a uniform (finally) and sent to London to take a test that would allow her to carry members of the public. The exam took place 'in a left-hand drive American ambulance going around Hyde Park Corner. I was quite terrified about that.' At last her adrenalin was pumping. Lady Jean duly passed the test 'and thereafter my licence said I could drive a bus; I could drive anything'. Equipped with an old Ford, up and down the country she travelled, chauffeuring Bletchley's VIPs and delivering important papers. London, Scotland, Oxford, Cambridge – nowhere was too far. On one occasion she even ferried her old boss, Hugh Alexander, who had subsequently replaced Alan Turing as head of Hut 8. She was driving him to London via Stanmore, one of Bletchley's outstations, when he suddenly volunteered: 'You were in the office, would you like to see a new invention?' Rather! Lady Jean got to meet the robot (a new four-wheeled Bombe) that had replaced the painstaking Banburismus process she had so resented.

'It was the size of that wall.' She gesticulates with an arm across the width of her amber-coloured drawing-room. 'It put through all the letters in a matter of minutes! Yes, seeing that was exciting.'

But technology, as Lady Jean was shortly to discover, had its drawbacks. In her new job whenever she was tasked with delivering Ultra intelligence or other important documents to a designated address she was always accompanied by a second person for security reasons. On one particular occasion 'the girl with me said, "Do you mind stopping at this little cafe?' I want to buy some cigarettes."' Lady Jean knew she should have said no, but what the heck? It was only a packet of cigarettes. So she said, 'Yes, all right.' The girl got out and bought her cigarettes, while Lady Jean locked herself in the car with her precious cargo. Upon her return to Bletchley Park she was immediately called in for questioning.

'Where did you stop?'

'You stopped on your way to London. Why?'

'The Oxford Circus traffic light only stops for three minutes, and you stopped for four?'

I explained to them that this other girl had wanted me to stop for cigarettes, but that I had locked myself in the car and there was no danger to the papers.

They were unimpressed. 'You know perfectly well you shouldn't stop!'

Unbeknown to Lady Jean her car had been fitted with a tachograph, a device invented twenty years earlier that records a vehicle's activities. Lady Jean shakes her head at the memory. 'I didn't even know what one was! No wonder lorry drivers strike these days.'

Whether inside or outside the Park, Bletchley took its security measures extremely seriously. Once more Lady Jean felt the noose tightening. 'I was being monitored all the time. It was very claustrophobic.'

Shuffling the Pack

Lady Jean was pushing to leave Bletchley; her sequence of moves from Hut 8 to the billeting office, then on to the Motor Transport Corps was not standard procedure. Most girls did the same job for the duration of their time in the Park or its outstations. There was little jockeying for position among women brought up to view work as a temporary expedient, employed in a temporary wartime environment, in a job which even had 'temporary' in the title.[1] Christopher Grey in his book *Decoding Organization* notes that at the Park there were 'very few examples of women being promoted from humdrum roles'. But if it was a challenge to stand out in a tedious job, it was not impossible.

Pamela's age (and considerable presence) singled her out for promotion. Here was a woman clearly capable of making management decisions. Frank Birch had done well to persuade her away from the stage. It wasn't long before she was sharing meetings with other heads of sections and running the Naval Index in Hut 4.

'Yes I suppose sometimes I was the only woman in those meetings.' Pam is modest about her achievements; she is of the opinion that someone had to do the job, and jokes, 'I think I was promoted because I couldn't type.' But as the Temporary Senior Administrative Officer she was head of a section that has subsequently been hailed as a precursor of the information age. Pamela was co-ordinating vital fact-finding forays long before the advent of the microchip.

'I was given my own room, I had some responsibility but it wasn't as much fun. I did miss the girls' chatter.'

Age and stage were also factors in Muriel's promotion. Just

1. Girls recruited by the Foreign Office had 'temporary' in their job title.

fourteen when she entered the Park, as a messenger Muriel had been given a less draining alternative to hut work, which required long stints of concentration. However, within months this spirited little girl proved herself. Soon she was sitting, pleased as punch, at a high table beside real Wrens sorting and ordering decoded material for the linguists in Hut 4.

'No it wasn't a problem, I found it easy. I just did what I was told.' As Nigel de Grey, the deputy head of Bletchley, commented in his end-of-war review, after six years people grow older, and Muriel was no exception.

———•———

Charlotte came of age tucked away on the first floor of the mansion logging traffic. Part of a small team, her assiduous approach to what was an undeniably dull task had not gone unnoticed. Major Ralph Tester (a prominent German linguist who established the Testery for Fish decodes) worked at a lectern in the same room. Aware of the Park's pressing need for more German speakers, in 1942 this 'nice fatherly' man approached the sole female worker in his office about her German. After all, Charlotte had gone on an exchange to Saxony three years earlier. 'He gave me a little test to see if my German was good enough to help with translations – he gently told me it was NOT!!'

But Charlotte wasn't crestfallen. 'Oh no, no. At least I tried. I take things as they come. There is no point in fighting against things that you can't do anything about.' She just put her head down and went back to work.

Charlotte might well have spent the next two years, like the first two, in that same small room in the mansion. However, war is an unpredictable master and Germany was not the only enemy. In late 1941, early 1942, Japan's sudden smash-and-grab through South East Asia was a bitter blow for imperial Britain. Hong Kong, Malaya and Singapore were quickly overrun, and Burma was next. The mother country's inability to look after her colonies had been cruelly exposed on the world's stage.

Britain's military focus remained the European war, but now our forces were fighting and dying in the Far East as well. Thankfully this ignominious imperial unravelling did not occur in isolation. A simultaneous Japanese attack on Pearl Harbor in December 1941 finally brought America into the war.

At last the green giant juddered into military action. 'Consider the tide turned,' proclaimed Churchill. 'The accession of the United States makes amends for all, and with time and patience will give certain victory.'

He was right, of course, and over the next three years the Atlantic alliance transformed every aspect of Britain's war machine, including code-breaking and intelligence. From Bletchley Park's point of view, America's progress in cracking Japanese ciphers was a vital resource and by March 1942 chief cryptanalyst Colonel John Tiltman had flown to the States to 'urge a division of labour', with the US concentrating on Japanese traffic and the British on the German and Italian. Information sharing and co-operation between the Allies improved but it wasn't always straightforward. Bletchley Park complained that the States paid scant attention to British interests in South East Asia and failed to prioritise Japanese traffic in the Indian Ocean where our fleets were patrolling. Not prepared to compromise British intelligence, BP's director Edward Travis ordered a major expansion of the Park's Japanese code-breaking organisation. What had been a small department under John Tiltman grew rapidly in 1943 and soon the volume of messages necessitated the pooling of all the Japanese subsections in a giant new structure, Block F. It was into this intimidating space – numerous spurs jutting off a long corridor dubbed 'the Burma road' – that swarms of predominantly young female workers were transferred. Among them was ATS girl Charlotte Vine-Stevens.

'I don't know who recognised I was reasonably good at paraphrasing.' Charlotte is still slightly bemused as to why she was hand-picked from her small corner in the mansion and moved into Block F to get her 'teeth into more "meaty" work within the Japanese section', but she is very glad she was.

'Oh yes, time passed much more quickly.'

An obsession with secrecy demanded that every decoded message passed back to the British forces fighting in Burma had to be paraphrased. Japan, like Germany, must never know we had broken their codes. Charlotte, once at the start point of the code-breaking process, was now at the output end of the Bletchley factory. She re-jigged messages to say the same thing, in a different way. It was the perfect job for a meticulous woman keen to prove her worth.

'Troops of 3rd Battalion will be moved to attack Kohima in three days' time' became 'Expect Kohima to be attacked 3 days from now by battalion strength.' And 'Division stationed Meiktila will attack from East – Mon May 1st' was rephrased to read 'Expect attack early May, to west, probably Jap division 10.'

'The paraphrased messages were sent in an inner and outer envelope, each with a coded address. I believe they were taken by dispatch riders but I do not know by whom.' Charlotte's explanation is peppered with pleas of ignorance.

'At my level we had no idea whether anything was successful.'

'Once I had paraphrased and sent it off I never heard anything more.'

'It is very difficult for people to understand . . . we were in a hermetically sealed room, in the sense that we couldn't talk, it wasn't discussed so I don't know the end of the story.'

No matter that her track record was exemplary, Charlotte was still left in the dark; Bletchley never breached its own secrecy protocol. But Charlotte didn't mind. 'No, I was very fortunate to have been asked to do the paraphrasing.' She was one of the lucky ones – a step up is always easier than a step down.

In the summer of 1943, just as BP was looking for additional womanpower in its Japanese section, the Italians abandoned their disastrous war and Rozanne's work as an Italian speaker in Josh Cooper's niche Air Section came to an abrupt halt. Instead she had to acclimatise to Block F, not as a paraphraser, but as one among hundreds of girls who endured the repetitive task of preparing endless Japanese codes and ciphers for a team of cryptanalysts. Rozanne gives the memory short shrift. Waving a hand vaguely she explains, 'I can hardly call it a job, it was just in the Park. Very very very dull. There were not actual things happening.' Her memoir underlines the deadening move: the 'Japanese section grew to be vast, and the whole place became different – much more bureaucratic'.

This is in stark contrast to Charlotte's recollection that 'there was a lighter feeling in the Park by 1944'. That was not Rozanne's experience, whose changed work environment was cruelly underscored with a personal loss. At the end of 1943 Professor Hugh Last, her confident and dear friend, left Bletchley suffering from a duodenal ulcer. One small handwritten sentence sums up her feelings. 'For me a light went out.' But the war went grinding on.

Was Rozanne's friend Kathleen also moved to Block F? The Park's Roll of Honour suggests so, but now Kathleen can't remember and the building was demolished in the 1980s so there is nothing left to trigger her memory. Whatever she was doing, it was so dull and the secrecy so binding by the time she wrote her memoirs decades later that detail was hazy. But Kathleen wasn't Admiral John Godfrey's daughter for nothing; she clearly did something right because she does remember being promoted. After two and half years in the WAAFs she (like Gwen) was a proud sergeant with three stripes on her arm. 'I was sent off with some of my friends to Lake Windermere . . . for an officers' training course' where she obediently marched up and down and promptly became an Assistant Section Officer. Somewhat confusingly this 'newly fledged' officer returned to Bletchley Park and 'carried on at the same tasks'. Still, at least a tailor in London had made her a swanky new uniform with a 'red silk lining' and a 'thin stripe on the cuff' (evidence of her new status for those in the know). Officer Kathleen could now also be paid more – few questioned the salary increase of a newly commissioned officer. At Bletchley Park there tended to be a discrepancy between the higher-paid uniformed staff and lower-paid civilian employees, with female Foreign Office workers at the bottom of the pile. But the spirit of national service did not encourage protests over pay.

'We were paid a pittance,' concedes Rozanne without any hint of resentment. Parliament's Woman Power Committee had demanded wage parity for equal work in return for their support of female conscription, but the 1941 National Service Bill made no reference to equal pay; the War Cabinet had blocked it. With the exception of a few highly skilled jobs that had previously been the exclusive preserve of men, on average women earned 47 per cent less than men doing the same job during the war. The fairer sex had long since learnt to put up with their lot; few complained about the pay gap and a group of largely middle-class girls trapped in the secretive world of Bletchley were never going to buck the trend. Money talk was vulgar and complaining unpatriotic.

Anyway war work was stimulating, at least according to Chief Petty Officer Pat. She had been promoted twice for her listening skills but further advancement eluded her. Pat thinks she knows why. 'I had a friendship with a naval officer.' ('It was very innocent in those days,' she adds quickly.) 'He was going to take me out in his motor torpedo boat.' Having already been on a patrol down the Channel in a single-engine amphibious bi-plane aptly named a Walrus ('it was absolutely wonderful') Pat was not going to turn down the offer of a second adventure. She was a Wren, surely the sea was her destiny? 'But our telephone call was intercepted and taking a Wren out in a torpedo boat was not supposed to happen. The matter went to a very high level.' The 'innocent' pair were reported and Pat didn't qualify for a commission at her subsequent board – the officer's training course never materialised. 'I think they thought I wasn't the ticket after that.'

Possibly not, but by the time Pat arrived at her final listening station, Abbot's Cliff in Kent, she could boast an impressive array of supplementary skills. To complement her plain language German, she learnt Morse code in a smoky room in Withernsea, and in a golf clubhouse in Lyme Regis she mastered direction-finding. Pat quickly became proficient at locating enemy vessels; even today the description trips off her tongue.

> You twirl an aerial around to where the signal is and let the watch room know the reading. They would tell the nearest intelligence centre. Other stations were alerted to get the same reading so the vessel could be pinpointed.

It was one May morning in Kent, having spent the night in the Abbot's Cliff direction-finding tower, that Pat stumbled out into the cow field and was confronted by the most extraordinary sight.

'I saw some heads coming up over the cliff top. I couldn't believe my eyes, it was Churchill's Homburg hat and Monty's beret, I'm sure it was. Oh my Goodness! I didn't know what to do.' The young Wren was rooted to the spot, gripped by terrifying indecision. 'You see I wasn't wearing my uniform. You are only allowed to salute if you are wearing a hat and I wasn't wearing a hat. But if senior officers are approaching you, you're supposed to salute.' Pat, dishevelled and exhausted, in a duffle coat and slacks, struggled to make a decision: 'In the end I waved and said, "Hello! Good morning!" and they waved back and said "Hello!"' She grins at the memory.

'They walked on. I think it was all part of the ruse to make the Germans think we were going to land in Pas-de-Calais.'

To this day, Pat remains convinced that Britain's two most iconic wartime leaders and their military entourage were making a tactical visit to the Kentish cliffs that directly overlooked

Pas-de-Calais. The planned invasion of Europe via Normandy was imminent and Operation Fortitude was deliberately seeking to deceive the Germans into believing the landings would occur in Norway and Calais. And suddenly here were Churchill and Monty striding out in the bright morning light opposite the offending piece of French coast. Pat rushed back to her station to spread the word.

The Summer of 1944

Pat's voice speeds up. Her brief exchange of greetings with Britain's great leaders was just the beginning.

> Shortly before D-Day we were given a 20 mile limit, we were not allowed to go further than 20 miles from our station. Oh and I saw bits of the Mulberry harbour go by. The shipping had to go right past our cliffs. They looked like upside-down billiards tables!

If not seaborne at least Pat was sea-facing; the German war was in her headphones and the Allied response in front of her eyes.

The large chunks of Meccano-style concrete heading off to France were pieces of history in the making. The Mulberry 'B' harbour erected off the shores of Normandy landed over 2.5 million men and 4 million tonnes of supplies in the ten months after D-Day.

'I was an eyewitness to events that were to become very symbolic.'

Pat is far too gracious to draw a comparison with the girls stuck at Bletchley Park and she doesn't need to – BP's isolation is well known. But history tells us that the Park was also at the centre of the D-Day landings; providing confirmation that Hitler had swallowed Operation Fortitude's deception, delivering a thorough overview of German armed forces in the Normandy area and intercepting a staggering 4,840 signals a day. The giant code-breaking jugganaut, pumping the Allied high command with Ultra intelligence on all Germany's major decisions, was an invisible force about which the enemy remained ignorant. Meanwhile, back in Buckinghamshire, for the worker ants processing this information the long-planned invasion of Western Europe simply meant more (much more) of the same.

Ruth was one of the three thousand extra staff members recruited to cope with the additional workload. The minutiae of her daily tasks contributed to Bletchley's staggering statistics. 'Army and Air Force Decrypts are running at 2,500 per day from some 30 Enigma keys, together with 1,500 to 2,000 Naval Enigma decrypts per day.' The terrifying landings, the battle for the beaches, breaking out of Normandy and onwards to Brussels, the bloodbath at Arnhem, pushing for the Rhine – each manoeuvre on the Continent was matched by another plug inserted, a pin straightened, a wheel turned and a Bombe rattling and thumping home to its next vital 'stop'. Ruth was fighting the same war but in a north London outstation, Eastcote, and then another one, Stanmore.

'That was a kind of progression,' she supposes wistfully. At Eastcote almost every wing off the giant corridor was named after a country occupied by the Germans, and each Bombe after a town in that same country. 'Hello this is Norway checker. I have a good stop for you on Oslo,' Ruth would inform a member of Hut 6's Machine Room down the scrambler phone. Stanmore was a variation on the same theme; its rooms and Bombes were named after Commonwealth countries and their cities. These coded calls were simultaneously etched onto countless tired young minds back in BP's Machine Room. With the watch team breathing down her neck, at the other end of the line Ann took down 'stops' from Bombes called 'Auckland or Wellington, Warsaw or Krakow, Cape Town or Joburg'. Years later she admits to feeling a 'certain affection' for those countries whose names came to symbolise a potential breakthrough, a way into an Enigma key, a small victory for the girl whose D-Day invasion was fought on the flats of Buckinghamshire.

Despite the proliferation of German Enigma keys popping up on the Western Front, Ann doesn't recall a particular increase in her workload during the summer of 1944. But she was banned from visiting London. The Germans dropped their first flying bombs (V-1s) on Britain a week after the D-Day landings. Over the next fortnight nearly 800 doodlebugs hit the Greater London area; they arrived overhead 'with a curious shuddering movement . . . a shower of sparks emitted from the tail'. Bletchley Park could not afford to lose its most prized members of staff.

Ann's husband Angus proudly underlines this point. 'It was not the whole Park, only the people with valuable jobs who were not allowed to go to London.'

The days of German Blitzkrieg were long gone. Hitler described 15 August 1944 as the worst day of his life, but in fact much worse was to come. Within a fortnight Paris had fallen and Allied forces were crossing the Seine. The Führer issued instructions for the Germans to fall back up France, and Bletchley Park was on hand to read his message. The German High Command's strategy had never been so transparent: in the Newmanry some twenty-five Fish keys were broken in August, far more than any previous month. Computer power had come into a league of its own and Colossi were hatching at the rate of one a month.

No wonder Joanna was awestruck – her arrival coincided with the opening of Block H, a steel-reinforced building and the new home of the next six machines.

'I worked on number 5 and 7 and number 9. There was a discernible difference between all of them. They were always improving.'

For Joanna, the Colossus was more than an inanimate object, it was a responsive, pulsating being. All alone, without the assistance of her controlling father, she had become a proud nursemaid to Britain's first computers.

You had to make sure it's little eye was clean or it wouldn't be able to see . . . You would know if you got a positive result; it would tell you. It would go click click click whizz, the tapes would all run down and you knew you had a fit.

This was revolutionary stuff. The nineteen-year-old Wren was in charge of a machine that could read paper tape at 5,000 characters per second, with the tape travelling at 30mph. The later Colossus models she worked on were capable of handling messages up to 25,000 characters long. 'I was interested in how it did what it did, so I was determined to look after it and make life easy for it.' But the decrypts that Colossus helped unravel weren't Joanna's business and she didn't pry. Questions weren't permitted and towards the end of the war they weren't necessary. 'I knew we were winning because everyone was walking around with big grins on their faces.'

Death and Dislocation

He was missing. I was at BP and father rang up and said, 'Dick is missing.' I couldn't believe it. I can remember it now, this feeling: there is an extraordinary silence that surrounds you. You don't hear anything except a repetitive voice saying, 'Dick is missing, Dick is missing.'

Rozanne pauses. A painful silence fills the room. Dick was her only brother. It was September 1944, the Allies seemed to be winning the war but Dick was missing.

'The awful thing was I remember being told this with everyone else working around me.'

Rozanne had to do something, anything. She had to get out of the stifling block. 'I rushed, I rushed out of the room and down towards the station. Somehow to get away, have a cup of coffee perhaps. Just to get something – a ridiculous idea, really.' She was moving fast without really knowing where she was going, her stride disturbed only by her flood of tears, when she bumped into Paul Stevenson, one of the Park's thespian set.

I told him, 'My brother is missing!'
'Come on Zan,' he said, 'we'll get a cup of tea together.'
He was awfully kind. I will always remember the kindness of that man. The way he talked about there still being hope. But it was awful. I had a feeling there was no hope.
Dick was only nineteen, he was sweet. He was the second pilot in an unarmed transport aircraft. They weren't even armed; he was just delivering medical supplies.

The whole story tumbles out, strings of words and vivid detail, first about Dick's wartime degree at Cambridge, his training in Phoenix Arizona, and then the DC-10 he flew from the airbase in Down Ampney, Wiltshire.

They went straight into the battle without knowing it. They were just delivering supplies for the fight down below but unfortunately this Panzer regiment came up and had guns on them. It ploughed into them.

Rozanne moves forward in her chair.

Dick and his squadron leader were leading the whole squadron of aeroplanes. Their plane caught fire and they made NO attempt to jump out but they went on pushing these supplies out to the men below because they were going to save lives. Apparently they went around and around the battle area and they were flaming, the plane was on fire! The men on the ground were amazed by their bravery. We got masses of letters about this afterwards. Nobody jumped and then suddenly the plane blew up. There was a hush that fell over the battlefield. There was no shooting, not from the Germans, not from the British, everybody was amazed by their courage to stay in the plane so long. The squadron leader was awarded a posthumous VC. They were all killed.

Operation Market Garden, Montgomery's audacious plan to punch across the Dutch border into Germany and end the war before Christmas, cost Rozanne's brother his life. Arnhem has gone down in history as 'a bridge too far', an Allied defeat made all the more tragic through its proximity to ultimate victory. But for Rozanne Arnhem is not a piece of history, it is a wretched pain that has not faded with time. Aged ninety-one she is still trying to make sense of the loss.

There are silent tears pouring down her cheeks as she stares out of the window into the quiet of rural Oxfordshire. On the sill is a picture of Dick just before he joined up. Beside his proud parents he is standing tall and casual with a flop of hair combed back, revealing his handsome brow.

'It was such a waste of lives. Well, it wasn't a waste, no it wasn't a waste. It was a wonderful way they died. Dick gave his life for others.'

Her brother's death left a gaping hole in their family, but at least he was a war hero.

Today Rozanne is one of Bletchley Park's biggest champions. She loved her time there – the friendships, the camaraderie, the recreation, even the work – but after her brother went missing it was not the same. She admits,

I couldn't stop worrying, you can imagine if one of your brothers had disappeared. It was just so awful, missing is worse than dead. You don't know if they are terribly badly wounded or mentally damaged. I couldn't stop thinking about where he was, I always had this feeling of dread.

Rozanne was wracked with worry but she kept on working. One must not complain.

Two hundred and sixty-four thousand British men in active

service perished in the Second World War; one third of the losses of the First World War but more than enough to take a miserable toll on Britain. Rozanne's father, Air Chief Marshal Sir Charles Medhurst, never fully recovered from the loss of his only boy. Perhaps it contributed to his death at fifty-seven. 'It was dreadful for my poor father. Dick was his only son. He never thought he would be killed. Father was in the Air Force himself but he never thought his son would be shot down.'

When Charles Medhurst had flown in the First World War his comrades on the ground were six times more likely to die than he was. But twenty-five years later modern technology had changed the face of war; the smallest, youngest armed service – the RAF – was now also the most lethal. Seventy thousand air personnel never came home.

Gwen shakes her head. 'The loss of aircrews was colossal. But the Air Force was what all the boys wanted to be in. It was so romantic for men.' And for women. It is no coincidence that Gwen's first boyfriend was in the RAF; it was Gordon Watson with his dapper blue uniform who had persuaded her to join the WAAFs. But he didn't live to see Gwen progress to sergeant.

He was shot down over Holland aged just twenty-three in 1942. He was flying Halifaxes – they were terrible early bombers, very difficult to manoeuvre. I've got a lovely photograph of him. Would you like to see it?

Another young life severed, leaving another young bruised woman back in Britain.

I was busy writing poetically to him from the Gloucestershire Records Office, I was very much in love. They kindly sent me all my letters back. That is how you heard. I just got this pack of letters with a printed notice. 'We regret . . .'

Gwen doesn't feel sorry for herself; that is how it was. It was painful, but she learnt quickly. 'You shouldn't make boyfriends of aircrew because they were all shot down.' Emotionally Gwen grew up fast. What other choice was there?

> I hardly met a girl who hadn't lost some boyfriend. And not just from the Air Force. One of the girls in the Park, Eileen, her fiancé was a dispatch rider. These bloody kids had to come as fast as they could through snow and blizzards and rain from distant radio stations down to Bletchley. If you didn't get the codes within twenty-four hours there was no point. But the muddy roads weren't safe, there were no lights and the bikes were dangerous. Well her fiancé died and then she grew fond of his friend who came to comfort her. 'Don't do it,' I said. 'But I am very fond of him.' They got engaged and then he was killed too. I think she had a breakdown after that.

Gwen, who began the war cocooned in a safe Bournemouth school, was soon being ruthlessly bumped between her own heartache and that of her friends. Perhaps it is inevitable that Bletchley Park stands out as a monument to her youth, so much so that she wrote a book about her time there. This was where she and thousands of others grew up, holding on to life while all around trauma marked out its indiscriminate pattern.

Death was omnipresent but no one back in England was ever ready for it. Pamela thinks she was drinking tea in Bletchley when actor Owen Nares' name was dropped into conversation. 'Oh I saw that one of his sons has died. I think it was Geoffrey Nares.' What? Geoffrey dead? But Geoffrey was one of Pamela's close friends. He was also an actor and they had spent a lot of time together when she was in Rep in Bournemouth; now he was dead, snuffed out by sandfly fever in the North African desert. Making sense of such blunt news was never easy.

'I think on that occasion I wrote a letter to his mother.' What else could she do?

Charlotte was similarly stunned when Mark Glover, her colleague in the Japanese section, discovered his wife and son had been wiped out by a doodlebug (V-1).

'I shall never forget the look on that poor man's face. He came back on duty and said, "All I found was my boy's tie."'

Mark returned to work but for him the war would never end. The Blitz had been and gone four years earlier, only to return with devastating effect. Still no one felt safe.

Rozanne didn't discover her brother Dick had died until after the war. The pall of uncertainty lingered on, casting a gloom over her final months at the Park. The anxiety was intense but Rozanne is quick to contextualise her experience. 'I was not alone. There were lots of people at BP with relations being killed. There was a definite wartime atmosphere.' Loss and uncertainty were common bonds that the code-breaking community shared with the rest of Britain.

With the end of the European war in sight, Pat's anxiety showed no sign of abating. Her father wasn't missing but he might as well have been. Colonel Owtram had been sent to the Far East with his field artillery regiment in late 1941, where Pat concedes 'there was no way they could win. They were pushed all the way down the Malaya peninsular across to Singapore.' Within five months Pat's father was a prisoner of war in a large Japanese camp, his men dying like flies building the Burma railway. For the Owtram family, the next three years were a grim waiting game.

'My mother didn't know if Father was alive or not. It took something like a year and a half to get a postcard from the Red Cross.' Pat pauses, 'I always felt that for civilians like her, the war was much harder than if you were in a unit.' At least Petty Officer Pat could distract herself with work and friends. 'The idea that people might never come back, that you didn't ever know what would happen, I think that honed our ability to live in the moment. Yes, it did.'

For a whole generation, war gave life a sharper focus.

13

Capital Attraction

Shaken but not bowed by the Blitz, the Savoy Hotel remained a beacon of old-school elegance throughout the war. For six long years its revolving doors invited a privileged clientele into reassuring opulence encased in a seven-storey steel frame. A cacophony of politicians, actors, musicians and journalists took refuge in this icon on the Strand. (Churchill was a regular.) The once famous electric lights twinkled behind drapes of austere black, the wine cellar was a little less consistent but still remarkably palatable and smart waitresses successfully replaced the finest waiters with their salvers and servers. The Savoy was the ideal venue to wine and dine a woman in wartime London.

> It was very hard to get a table so Jim pretended he was an Irish Lord he knew wasn't in the capital. It was only later he discovered his friend Alan Price Jones used the exact same ruse with the exact same Lord. They both knew he was in Ireland.

Pamela smiles; her grown-up date in the Savoy with Wing Commander Jim Rose was worth the risk. The night formalised a relationship that began in a local hall just outside Bletchley Park.

'Baroness Trumpington asked me if I would go to a hop with her. I had been at the park about six months and I didn't really want to go out that night. It was just a gramophone in the village hall.' But Pamela (thankfully) relented. 'I remember Jim asking me to dance and thinking how attractive he was. I'd heard about him and he had a reputation for always being nice to people who were in trouble, so when he asked me I suspected the worst.'

Pamela fretted that her petticoat was on display, or perhaps a mutual friend, Lady Gater, had told him to dance with her. 'I couldn't imagine there would be another reason.'

But clearly there was. Jim and Pamela (the 'glorious vision of loveliness' he had seen on the Bletchley stage) were soon dating. On the subject of their blossoming relationship Pamela is a study of restraint but luckily the same isn't true of Rozanne, who still gets excited on her friend's behalf.

I lived down the road from Pam. I used to call in and see her and then suddenly Jim was in the offing. Pam was lit up, absolutely lit up! She had a little party. I remember the effect he had on her. She was so excited and thrilled because he reciprocated every-thing she liked. It was awfully sweet.

For Pamela, a 'worldly' twenty-four, there had already been several boyfriends including a German count, but Jim was different.

Again Rozanne is gloriously emphatic. 'He was the most attrac-tive man I ever met, really the most attractive. He was alive, on the go all the time.'

Pamela laughs out loud at her friend's testimony. 'Yes, I think Rozanne was more in love than I was!'

The head of the Air Section in Hut 3, Jim Rose – a charming, intelligent man from a wealthy Jewish family – stood out as exceptional to almost everyone who met him. But it was Pamela he fell in love with.

Their evening together in the Savoy was a carefully planned night out. Pamela's dress had short sit-up-and-beg sleeves and a dropped waist; it was cut from a pretty patterned pale blue silk. The colour picked out the startling turquoise in her eyes. Jim sat across the table in his Air Force blue uniform. This handsome couple had briefly escaped Bletchley for the capital's finest dining-room; Pamela was back in London with a dashing man eight years her senior. Prices capped at ten shillings, with extra charges for trimmings, even the Savoy couldn't fully disguise wartime fare, but it didn't matter. 'It was such a different world then. As a man you were expected to take a girl somewhere. At the Savoy you could have supper and there was a posh dance floor.' The sophisticated setting was perfect. They talked and talked and waltzed to live music and talked some more. And Pamela discovered what she probably already knew: Jim was the man she would like to spend the rest of her life with.

War's Aphrodisiac

No wonder Rozanne remembers Pamela's love story so vividly; her friend was dating one of the most appealing men at the Park. There weren't many others to choose from. Men at Bletchley were significantly outnumbered, considerably older and not to most young girls' taste. Celebrated Bletchley love matches – Mavis and Keith Lever, Shelia and Oliver Lawn, Shaun and Odette Wylie – were in the minority.

Lady Jean is characteristically upfront. 'There were no [suitable] men at Bletchley at all. They were awful types, I thought. I didn't have any interest in any of them.' A spattering of dishevelled professors could not make up for her two dead Commandos. The absence of any love interest at the Park merely served to exacerbate the monotory of her Buckinghamshire existence.

Doris Moller was equally struck by the absence of attractive men. By her own admission she was a good-looking girl; with flaxen hair and a peaches and cream complexion, men noticed her. In Lisbon, while her sister was goading German soldiers, Doris flirted with Paul, a British boy in the Merchant Navy. They played table tennis and he wrote her romantic letters but they never kissed – she didn't reciprocate his feelings. Crossing from Gibraltar to Britain Doris caught another man's eye – this time the Jewish wireless operator Alec Rabinovitch. He made a gentle advance and Doris remembers waving him away from her bunk bed. They met up in London to eat horsemeat before he was dropped back into France. 'You see, I think he was a spy. He died in France.' Doris didn't kiss Alec either and once she arrived in Bletchley there was no one else for the duration of the war. 'I know some did kiss men in Bletchley Park but I wouldn't have found my husband there.' Doris laughs. 'They were all so peculiar!'

She throws in an anecdote about Professor Hugh Foss, head of the Japanese Naval section, to underline her point. 'I have no idea why I went to see him but all he did was twiddle his hair. I remember thinking, "You're weird!"'

Beauty, however, is in the eye of the beholder and war had distilled emotions and derailed stability; romantic ideals had a potent hold over a generation of single women who were living an emotionally precarious reality.

Gwen was finding the dating game increasingly unreliable. Her first love, airman Gordon Watson, had died in service, and a second proved something of a cad.

'He was a flight engineer but I discovered he was going out with two other girls and I didn't like that. I said to him, "If you do that before you are married, you will do it a lot more after."'

Gwen came back from leave very upset; the relationship was over and her young heart (temporarily) broken. The eclectic group from the German Air Section tried to console her and none more so than poet Vernon Watkins. 'Vernon saw I was upset and depressed and tried to cheer me up by teasing me. He loved teasing people.' Distraction was planned in the form of a trip to the little fair in a field at the bottom of Bletchley village. 'It was so pathetic, there were pretend coconuts and a swing boat. An injured pilot sat in it all evening going around and around because he couldn't fly any more.'

Gwen and Vernon were making their way back to the Park together, it was dusky and there were no streetlights, when suddenly Vernon said, 'Wait a minute!' Gwen stopped.

'You know we have to get married?'

'Oh? No! I mean . . . Vernon, I really don't want to get married. I am only twenty-one.'

'No, I mean WE have to get married.'

'Well Vernon, I am very fond of you but . . .'

'Yes,' said Vernon, apparently oblivious to the fact that it was he who'd asked the question (which was really more of a statement). Perhaps the emphatic 'yes' was to reassure himself; after all, Vernon Watkins was a confirmed bachelor with high ideals. Aged thirty-six his guide through life had been the Danish Christian philosopher Kierkegaard. Kierkegaard had been told to abstain from marriage by God, so Vernon must do the same. But that was before he met Gwen – extraordinary, idealistic, brainy Gwen.

> It was so strange, so sudden, him just saying we have to get married. I now think all his life he had this hotline to God. I think that is who told him we have to get married and one doesn't like to say no to God. Not really.

The next day Vernon went to London and bought Gwen a beautiful engagement ring.

> I didn't really know what to do. Early on you could say to a boy, 'I don't want to see you', but Vernon was a proper man and I was very fond of him and I respected him a lot. I was overwhelmed, I was a little working-class girl of twenty-one. What in God's name had made him do this?

Now, sitting at the kitchen table, Gwen enjoys teasing out the emotional puzzle that once bamboozled her young mind.

> No, I cannot say I was in love with him but if you really think of it, who else was there at Bletchley Park who I might have even wanted to marry? And Vernon was a poet! That I should ever marry a poet had never occurred to me and I knew he was a very good man. So I thought, all right, I am not actually in love with him but I am never going to get a chance like this again. Never.

So Gwen said yes, she would marry Vernon. 'And I have to say I never regretted it.'

— ·◆· —

Bletchley Park pulled the fifteen women in this book into one shared historical trajectory. They are a handful of the Bletchley Girls, an elite group of veterans who will forever be associated with highbrow code-breaking achievements. But for most women at the Park war work was only ever an interlude, a protracted sojourn on a journey into adulthood where a good marriage was the ultimate milestone. If finding a bridegroom was not yet urgent for pretty young things in their late teens and early twenties, they still attached considerable importance to the opposite sex. Gwen's agreement to marry Vernon was prompted by yet another broken heart and Pamela knew Jim was 'the one' because she'd already had a number of boyfriends. However it is Ann's diary that really sheds light on a period so often shown through the prism of selective memory. With her Oxford maths degree she perhaps most closely resembles the 'bluestocking' Bletchley stereotype, and yet Ann too delights in the small dalliances and exchanges that took place with potential suitors. War had arbitrarily stolen the lives of thousands of young men; that meant boys mattered more than ever.

In Oxford a couple of months before her arrival at Bletchley, Ann indulged in a flirtatious game of cat and mouse with Henry, a fellow undergraduate. Did he lean heavily against her 'on purpose' at the Playhouse theatre? She thought so ('the darkness helps!'). There was a 'comfortable, warm, private, intimate' moment on a patch of grass when he queried the colour of her petticoat. And during an afternoon lying in a punt together, 'he more or less had his arm around me for nearly three hours, I'm surprised he didn't manage to kiss me'. But Ann wasn't convinced by Henry. 'I wish I could decide whether I liked him for himself or because I know him and there is no alternative man.'

Gerald, her other interest, was fighting in Italy. His two-year absence only heightened her ecstasy when she finally received a letter; it became a 'truly first rate day!' because he'd addressed her 'My Dear'.

'The mere omission of my name seems to have sped me on my way to seventh heaven.'

Emotionally Ann flitted between different men. Although no one in the Park took her fancy, by the time she arrived at Bletchley, Henry and Gerald had faded and her attentions were honed on Major Eric Reynolds, a Rugby housemaster she worked with during summer camp. She planned a visit to the town during her first two days of leave, during which she managed to talk with him in his study.

'Wonderfully comforted to see how genuinely pleased the Major was to see me again.' The second day was less of a success: 'saw him notice my bare legs – damn! Had decided not worth-while darning best stockings for today.'

'Yes that's right, that's how it was. We saw lots of different men. We could because it was so innocent.' Listening to the contents of her own diary, Ann is briefly jolted into a different era when young girls were like butterflies, flitting between suitors, enjoying their company and the idea of them but rarely settling for long. Physical contact was minimal, if it occurred at all. A cheeky exploratory hand in the punt was all Henry was permitted.

Ann's diary supports other veterans' memories of sexual restraint. Kathleen only remembers 'a wet kiss behind the huts' at WAAF camp and for Muriel, who loved chasing boys (even non-Jewish ones), it was nothing more than 'a bit of georgy porgy and petting. There was no contraception pill you see, so it was very touch and go.' Rozanne sagely nods her head.

Things are different now, everybody has sex early. But I promised my parents I wouldn't go to bed with anybody until I was going to marry them, because father said darkly, 'If you have a baby you will jolly well look after it yourself. We are not going to pay for it'! It was quite good to be tough, because it was a stigma; no man would marry shop-soiled goods.

The heady erotic charge of war did not touch everyone. Sex was a risk too far for most middle-class girls just out of school, parental threats still ringing in their ears. Gwen puts this pre-Bletchley world into context: 'My father would come in his car to a dance and pick me up. There was not a chance to snatch even a furtive kiss. We were very protected.' War propelled girls out of that parental orbit but an ingrained fear of a sullied status and unwanted pregnancy prohibited sexual freedom. Mistakes were costly and even at the Park, impossible to keep secret.

'One sad girl had a baby and hid it in a drawer, dead of course. That meant Police etc.'

On the whole it was women between the ages of thirty and forty-five who were responsible for the increase of illegitimate births during the war, not teenagers and twenty-somethings. Spinsters, many having accepted they would never marry, seized the moment to experience physical intimacy. Gwen can recall an 'easy and free-living group' at Bletchley Park, and Rozanne agrees that 'yes, there were people there having sex. I knew of three or four people with unwanted pregnancies. It was quite an education for me.' But this avant-garde set were a minority who enjoyed certain outstanding attributes – seniority, experience and confidence – that the vast majority lacked.

Still impressed with the daring of her own friend all those years ago, in her handwritten memoir Rozanne notes, 'Pam and Jim were lovers.'

'Well, yes we were,' agrees Pamela, very matter-of-fact, 'and there were many people doing much worse! People were swapping partners all the time.' (The avant-garde set, one presumes.) But 'no, absolutely not'. Jim and Pamela did not share a room in her final billet with the Calvocoressi family. 'That would have been very frowned upon.'

The unbuttoning of Britain's sexual contract remained a fairly discreet affair, even for Pamela, a few years older than the other women in this book and dating a man older still.

Footloose and Fancy Free

Censorious men opposed to female conscription had been quick to voice their concerns over the potential impact on public morality and parental authority. In Parliament there were apocalyptic warnings about the danger of removing women from the guidance of the home 'which has helped her to withstand all the temptations to which a girl of that age is subjected'. In 1941 female conscription was an unknown quantity and many commentators and politicians anticipated the worst.

But freedom from parental constraint and sexual freedom were polls apart. Every girl thrown into the orbit of war was still a product of her environment, only now she could make her decisions alone.

'A friend and I once hitched all the way from Gloucestershire to Birmingham and my aunt said, "God! You didn't realise what might have happened!"' But Gwen wasn't worried. 'If they saw you were a "come on and get me girl" then maybe they would . . .' She pauses mid-flow, old-fashioned decency sacrificing the end of the sentence.

> But on the whole it was not like that, especially if they saw you came from a good home. Most of the RAF men treated you how you wanted to be treated. If you were a loud tarty girl possibly it would've been different.

Gwen was not tarty, far from it. Thanks to Talbot Heath's School for Girls, she knew how to conduct herself.

Before Vernon decided her romantic destiny, she had enjoyed finding her way in this brave new world.

> You met people on trains going home on leave. I met my second boyfriend on a train going to Bournemouth. We were both standing in a very crowded corridor. It was so different from home – when you met people you could just get talking to them.

A uniform helped. 'On a train a service man would probably ask you where you are stationed. It was a very easy way of starting a conversation.'

The community of service men and women criss-crossing the country between postings leant itself to a relaxed conviviality. Even women who weren't in uniform enjoyed striking up conversations with men who were.

Returning from leave in Oxford, civilian employee Ann 'talked to a Polish airman from Bicester onwards – quite a sensible one too. Gave him my address!' The audacity of her own gesture took Ann by surprise.

No longer time-servers watching from the sidelines, girls like Gwen found the independence that accompanied their war effort exhilarating.

'It was very liberating, just being given a travel warrant and told, "Here you go!" One had not had that.' Nor had one been surrounded by such a variety of strapping uniformed young men – often far from home and with nothing to lose. One and three-quarters of a million American and Canadian men passed through Britain during the war, not to mention a host of other nationalities including Czechs, Poles and French. Just as the critics had anticipated, unregulated contact between the sexes increased. Only three hundred Americans were employed in Bletchley Park, but there was plenty of exotic eye candy nearby; in London, on trains, at dances.

'I remember some GIs were holding a dance and needed some girls so my sister and I put our names down.' Muriel, by now sixteen, needed no encouragement. The picture she pushes across the table says it all. The teenager has fixed the camera with a vigorous gaze – one arm raised for balance, her left leg is swung forward, exposing a shapely stockinged calf. Dainty wedge-heeled suede shoes complete the bold look. Behind their daughter stand her handsome parents, sharing a private smile.

Oh yes, I was lively! I loved those shoes, they were maroon suede and I wore them to the dance and a dirndl skirt. You know, with waistband and flouncy bits. Under the skirt I put layers and layers of different coloured net so when you jitterbugged around you could see the nets. I was a good dancer, a natural, an absolute natural.

Accompanied by her sensible older sister, Muriel recalls an Army truck with flaps, 'like in a film', that transported them to an airbase near Bletchley. Initially overawed by the men and music the two girls sat coyly side by side; a live big band ripped through the night, filling the air with buzz and crash. ('I didn't realise till later that it was Glenn Miller. He got killed shortly after that, I remember "Little Brown Jug".') But the ice only cracked when two Americans approached the sisters for a dance. 'Sitting down we was the same height but I was only 5ft and the tall soldier went for me! It was like little and large on the dance floor!' The rest of the night spun by in a medley of jives and swing-time tunes.

Muriel closes her eyes behind her red-rimmed spectacles. 'The Americans were good. Yes. The khaki uniform was lovely. I can still smell it.' She exhales and looks up. 'You could get close but not too close!'

Temptation was always there, but the sensible Bletchley Girls enjoyed it within existing social parameters.

'I had a wonderful time, it made up for the hardships. I met a very nice Polish soldier.' Ruth's hazel eyes soften as she recalls small simple rituals – fleeting indicators of mutual attraction between a young man and woman. 'I had his insignia on my handbag. You had to wear a navy blue handbag and you were allowed a boy's insignia or cap badge on your handbag.' There was also an American serviceman. 'We went arm in arm. He might have given me a kiss goodnight. It was all very modest.' But the patriarchy need not have worried on Ruth's behalf, she never felt compromised; quite the reverse.

I believe that having the Wren uniform did in some measure give me a protective covering as it were, because I found this did command a certain respect from newly-met service men. Also having the amount of restraint afforded by the rules spoken and unspoken regarding when we had to be back in Quarters, and how we had to behave in ways befitting our uniforms, gave me and maybe others, safe boundaries from which we could operate.

Beyond Bombe monotony and long shifts, Ruth remembers this as a good time; based at Eastcote, within sniffing distance of the capital, there was a frisson in the air.

'I freely admit I enjoyed being flirted with at socials, the cheeky banter with the technicians on watch, being asked, "Can I kiss you goodnight?" at the gate.' For Ruth these wartime courtships struck the perfect balance. 'Alas, how many girls today merit, or feel they merit, such a choice or such consideration? . . . Now it is "Your place or mine?" We have to watch our children and grandchildren and say nothing.'

But even back then, with war relaxing social and sexual mores, cocksure American GIs managed to rattle mothers' and fathers' conservative sensibilities. 'Over sexed and over here' Yanks claimed 70,000 blushing British brides. Canadian servicemen, however, were cut more slack. Loyally fighting alongside Britain since 1939, young Canadian boys were quick to follow up family contacts upon arrival in England.

Cora Pounds' mother was only too pleased to provide a refuge in Bournemouth; she had been lonely ever since her family emigrated to Canada between the wars. 'She played Scrabble by herself and took up smoking. She was very isolated and father was always working.' But if Mrs Pounds welcomed her young Canadian nephew's arrival, daughter Cora was incensed by the timing. 'Just as I joined the Wrens my cousin Doug Cole and his friend came over and stayed with Mother. Away I go for the first time in my life and all the men come! Damn it!'

Cora wasn't crestfallen for long; parachutist Doug Cole had no intention of spending his first winter away from home (and the last before the planned invasion of Europe) away from young female company. His pert blonde cousin got the surprise of her life.

I was on watch working in that big classroom checking Fish codes and the telephone goes. The leading Wren answers it.

'Wren Pounds there is a call for you.'

'What? No one knows I am here!'

Cora was astonished. Who on earth could it be?

'Hello, this is your cousin Doug from Canada.'

'Doug where are you? How did you get the call through?'

'I am at the office by the gate, I sweet-talked the telephonist.'

Even BP staff indoctrinated in the art of secrecy couldn't resist Doug's transatlantic charm. Cora couldn't believe her luck. 'I had such a crush on him!' Her mother had disclosed Cora's whereabouts. There was an exhilarating train journey to London – the seventeen-year-old sandwiched between two Canadian parachutists – followed by a dancing extravaganza in Covent Garden. Cora bopped, rocked and waltzed the night away. Like Ruth, she even received a memento to remember her man.

'Doug gave me his badge, silver wings because he was a parachutist, and I put them on the other side of my bag so no one could see it.' The Bournemouth girl had a weekend to remember and nothing to regret. 'I liked him very much. In those days you didn't get anywhere. It was very romantic if you held hands.' Or bopped. Courtesy of her Canadian cousin, the narrow confines of Cora's BP existence had briefly been prised apart. Then Doug was dispatched to Arnhem (he survived, his friend didn't) and Cora returned to her work. But the memory lasted forever.

—•—

Charlotte is midway through a piece of quiche; her words are hard to make out above the restaurant clatter so she patiently repeats her sentence.

'He was incredibly dishy, but I just didn't feel totally happy with the idea.'

Charlotte, like Cora, also met a Canadian serviceman through family contacts; John Sancton was an officer in the Royal Canadian Air Force based at Biggin Hill. Secure in the knowledge that their parents knew each other, John and Charlotte met in London on days off. There was lots of dancing and an exotic meal off Oxford Street in Veeraswamy, London's oldest Indian restaurant. 'I was a bit frightened as to whether I would like it or not.' Just like Cora's Canadian, John once tried to pay Charlotte a surprise visit only to discover the anonymous PO Box in their correspondence was not her actual address. 'He arrived to be faced with nothing more than a post box system.' Bletchley's obsessive secrecy extended to their mail.

As John also worked in Intelligence, neither could ask the other what they were doing, which left him all the more time to tell Charlotte what a swell life she would have in Canada. The handsome officer had fallen in love with this thoughtful, blue-eyed English girl; now he just needed to persuade her to marry him. They went to Herefordshire together to meet her parents ('Oh yes, we got that far') but Charlotte decided not to get engaged. 'I suppose I was rather immature and perhaps there was not a sufficient spark.' She puts down her fork and pauses. 'But I have since wondered about how my life might have been had I married him.'

A modest woman, not used to talking about her emotions, it is with dignified understatement that Charlotte picks her way through the memory of their relationship. Recently she has had cause to give it some thought; having read his late father's wartime correspondence, in which the intelligence officer's affection for Charlotte was made abundantly clear, John's son has been in contact from Canada. Charlotte has subsequently found the obituary of the man she might have married on the Internet; a warm intelligent face smiles back from the screen through owlish spectacles. After the war John got married to a different English woman, became a successful newspaper editor in Montreal and eventually died in 2004. Sketched out in the text is the life Charlotte did not share.

'I think it was that he lived so far away. From Canada travel to and fro was very difficult. I think that is what formed my decision.' But beneath Charlotte's anxieties over distance and travel lay a greater concern.

> I don't think my mother was at all happy about it, she never actually said anything but I think that probably coloured my decision. I even got the feeling she was a bit worried about me joining the Army.

Having lost her only son in infancy, by the time war broke out Mrs Vine-Stevens was fighting breast cancer. The radium treatment she received was pioneering but she never regained full health. Running their rural smallholding alone during the war took its toll.

Dutiful Charlotte couldn't bear the idea of leaving her ageing parents behind for a sparkly new life in Canada so John's offer was gently refused. 'I was very tied to my family but then lots of other people were too.' And with a nod of her head she neatly draws a line under the subject. Even at her great age, life is too short for regrets.

All too often parental intervention had a deflationary effect. Rozanne flinches. It was a difficult time. Her brother had gone missing in September of 1944 and she met Edo Kudrnka in the October. 'Yes, I was vulnerable, very vulnerable.' And out pours a story that still pains its narrator. It had all begun with so much promise. Several dashing older RAF friends ('something to do with intelligence work') invited her up to stay in London. They went to a dance where Rozanne met a Czechoslovakian airman: Edo.

> He was amusing and fun and immediately we clicked. We spent the whole evening under a table having a wonderful chat. The RAF people were looking everywhere for me and couldn't find me. They were very fed up. But I was having a wonderful time with this man, we were getting on so well.

It all happened very quickly – 'He asked me to marry him after about three weeks and I said, "Yes, I would love to!"' – but then war was an impulsive time. The relationship was rollicking along; Rozanne and Edo met up in London for meals and days off and he suggested the idea of a wedding in Czechoslovakia.

'Why Czechoslovakia?' Rozanne asked.

'Because it is my home and I want to get married there,' came the reply.

'It was all terribly exciting. I was young and wild. I was going to get on this aeroplane. He said he would organise a flight out there. It had just been liberated.' Edo had found the perfect English rose – Rozanne with her swan neck, youthful blush and impeccable class. The pair were in love. Excited, Rozanne broke the news to her incredulous parents.

'Who is this man you have got engaged to?'

Air Chief Marshal Sir Charles Medhurst promptly informed her it was a ridiculous idea, that she couldn't possibly rush off and marry a Czech; his son was already missing, he had no intention of losing a daughter. He made some enquiries into the Czech airman. The news wasn't good. Rozanne's father discovered that Edo was already married to a WAAF girl, they had a three-year-old child together and were separated.

'He never said he was married already! It was a shock, a terrible shock. It was awful, dreadful. I was in love with him. I did nearly faint, I could not believe it.' The emotion rises in Rozanne's voice. 'When in love one is blinded to anything else.' Then, brusquely, she pushes her thoughts aside. 'Anyway that is nothing to do with anything now. It is a past life.'

A few minutes later Rozanne calmly reflects on what might have been. 'I'm very glad I didn't marry the Czech. I might have been bumped off, one didn't know. The Russians bumped lots of people off. My life might have been totally different.' But despite her lucky escape, Sir Charles Medhurst's intervention still rankles. 'How annoying that father was right, how very annoying. I felt such a fool!'

London's Calling

'I always did my job to the best of my ability but at the time I had no emotion for the machines.'

Today Ruth is Bletchley Park Trust's model Bombe veteran, but back then they were just a noisy backdrop to something much more exciting.

> I was only interested in the fact we were a few miles from London. I always had a tremendous ambition to be in London. For me that was the place to be and the fact we could travel into London was wonderful. Both Eastcote and Stanmore were on the tube, they took you into town and that was where the fun really was.

Ruth articulates a real passion for this giant city under siege. No matter that London was the target of enemy aggression, and the indiscriminate grave to over 30,000 men, women and children. The capital retained its intoxicating urban appeal. Virtually every woman's testimony includes excursions, rendezvous and shows in nearby London: Cora with her Canadians in Covent Garden, ditto Charlotte, Rozanne falling for her Czech at a dance, Pam wined and dined in the salubrious Savoy, and Ruth, arm in arm with her beaus, taking in the shows.

Never had the Government worked so hard to keep the nation's theatrical lifeblood pumping, and at its heart was London. Capitalising on the free seats for service men and women, Ruth went to see Laurence Olivier in the Old Vic; she even queued for his autograph afterwards. 'I think I've still got it somewhere upstairs.' Others preferred the National Gallery, where displaced musicians led by Myra Hess played to packed lunchtime audiences in the empty building. There Pamela Gibson's mother sold sandwiches and Ann enjoyed the temporary War Artists' Exhibition. Even simple pleasures provided light relief: in the photograph Cora is on her haunches, grinning from ear to ear beneath her round naval hat and there are two fat birds squatting on her outstretched arm – she is feeding the pigeons in Trafalgar Square, flanked by three friends. The picture captures the joy on all four faces; it is 1944, there's a war on and these girls are having the time of their lives. The valuable one day off a week (which stretched to two every fortnight), was a chance to shake free of Bletchley's drab hold and enjoy London's unpredictable embrace.

Pamela, promoted to head of the Naval Index, had a constant battle with the rota – 'all the girls wanted to go up to London at the same time'. But she didn't grumble; upon arrival at Bletchley she too 'was constantly going up and down to London'.

Train travel was deemed so central to the Bletchley experience that today what was once Block C has been converted into the museum's entrance hall, where you step from a heavy metal train door into an experiential station with accompanying sounds and explanation. As a junction town, Bletchley's accessibility via train was well known, with London particularly well served. However for girls impatient to squeeze every spare minute from their treasured forty-eight hours off, there was always the option of the early-morning milk float or they could try their luck thumbing a lift on the A5 (petrol rations prohibited most independent car use). Lady Jean, emboldened by success stories of suave automobiles picking up her friends from the roadside ('it's so much easier and quicker!') decided to give hitchhiking a go.

Things did not quite pan out as she expected. Lady Jean recalls her shock. 'This can't be true! This cannot be true!' The driver of a vast cement lorry had seen Arran's Lady, thumb outstretched, and duly slowed down. So much for a quick easy ride to London. Jean was mortified by the cumbersome vision that had pulled up alongside her. The driver was quick to allay her fears. 'No doubt you are looking for a young man in a Jaguar. Well, you shouldn't be doing it,' lectured the driver. What followed, from between two solitary teeth, was a comprehensive explanation of why Lady Jean was much safer travelling in his lorry. How could she possibly refuse such a kind offer? She reluctantly clambered aboard and soon they were amiably shouting at each other over the roar of the engine all the way to London.

'And then he said, "Where are you going? I will take you there." I didn't like to say the Dorchester Hotel. I thought he might hit me over the head if he was a communist.' But the lorry driver was insistent – he was not prepared to offload his precious cargo at Oxford Street. So to Park Lane it was.

Eisenhower was so impressed with the Dorchester, he abandoned Claridge's and by 1944 had established his headquarters in this sumptuous art-deco goliath. Built from reinforced concrete, it had a reputation for safety – the Dorchester was where Lady Jean's parents, the Duke and Duchess of Montrose, always stayed when they were in London.

Jean knew the door porter well; a dignified man never seen without his officer's ribbons from the First World War, he did not welcome a cement lorry rumbling its way around the hotel's central fountain. He gave the lorry driver absolute hell (Jean heard words she didn't know existed).

Desperate to make things better she tried to intervene, 'leaning over the wretched engine, virtually hanging out of the driver's window. "Yoo hoo! It's me, it's me! Hallo! Hallo!"'

The porter had not seen Lady Jean. He quickly pulled himself together when he did. A gloved hand swiftly opened the door and helped her down as if she were stepping from a Rolls Royce. 'Good morning m'lady, I am sorry.' Her luggage was delivered to earth with equal grace. The driver meanwhile sat in silent astonishment. Jean shook him warmly by the hand. As promised he had delivered her safely right to the door of the Dorchester.

When her parents weren't in town Lady Jean still went up to London but stayed in the more modest international sports club attached to Grosvenor House Hotel. She was a member there and it provided an opportunity to catch up with friends and relax away from dreaded Bletchley. Others among her friends stayed in Claridge's but really the place to dance and be seen was the Savoy. 'I often went there, it was lucky I was rather a good dancer.' Like Pamela, Jean enjoyed waltzing on the famous raised dance floor. They weren't alone. In keeping with Bletchley's reputation as a station for smart girls, there are others who recall nights out at the Savoy.

The hotel itself was an afterthought; the owner D'Oyly Carte's initial love had been theatre – in particular Gilbert and Sullivan operas, which he orchestrated and staged in his first building project, the Savoy Theatre. In their honour, the neighbouring hotel boasted a string of plush private rooms named after popular Gilbert and Sullivan operas. It was in one of these – *The Gondoliers* – that Kathleen's grandfather held her twenty-first birthday party. (By October 1944 her father, Admiral John Godfrey, was away commanding the Royal Indian Navy.) For the two park friends, Kathleen and Rozanne, the pending party caused much excitement.

'I wore my first long evening dress; sparkling black net with yards of material in the skirt,' Kathleen recalls. Meanwhile Rozanne chose a stunning white chiffon number that fell to the floor and complemented her head of dark hair.

Rozanne had been to the Savoy once before, in 1940 to celebrate her then boyfriend's eighteenth birthday. (Just months later David was killed in the Mediterranean.) This time she was accompanied by her new Czechoslovakian beau, airman Edo. She wasn't alone; Kathleen writes, 'all the current boyfriends were in uniform and we danced away the evening in the adjoining ballroom'. There was no chance however of a surreptitious kiss: 'My grandfather presided over the feast at one end of the long table with my Bostonian great-great-aunt Mary Endicott sitting upright and immaculately coiffured at the other end.' Regardless, the night was one to remember – Rozanne and Kathleen were in the prime of their lives, shimmering across London's finest dance floor to a band that 'made us forget about the dangers and uncertainties of the real world outside'.

Three years earlier Gwen had meticulously planned her trip to London. Called up for a Bletchley interview, the Bournemouth teenager left her Gloucestershire barrack determined to make the most of a day in the capital. She walked down Regent Street seeking out the shop that sold undergarments of (German) parachute silk, visited a British restaurant, had a photographer snap her corporal stripes and enjoyed a concert at the National Gallery. Even bombed, the city captivated its enthusiastic visitor; Gwen relished its 'springtime dress of chickweed, speedwell, and scarlet pimpernel, where in autumn ragged robin and rosebay willow-herb would cover all the ruined sites'.

And now, three years later, she was more than just a visitor; in the bombed heart of this indefatigable city Gwen was getting married to her very own poet, Vernon Watkins. They escaped Bletchley in a hurry on a forty-eight-hour leave pass, a mere six weeks after he'd proposed.

Vernon was a romantic and nothing was left to chance. A devout man, he wanted to get married in St Bartholomew the Great, London's oldest working church. Inside this imposing Norman structure the Lady Chapel was the perfect setting – dramatic shafts of sunlight bathed a sheaf of golden roses Vernon had sourced that same morning. His young bride looked delightful.

'I had such a pretty dress, it was a pale sea-green with an embroidered bolero and plain halo hat. My sister-in-law took lots of photographs but not one came out.' Gwen had scrimped coupons from the air ministry, her aunt and her mother for a wedding dress. ('When mother met Vernon she said, "Oh dear, I am sorry he's older but he's very sweet, isn't he?"') Later there was a modest but perfectly adequate lunch at the Charing Cross hotel; 'ham salad, wine and meringues, it was quite well done I thought, but I was only twenty-one'. The day was almost perfect. Almost. Vernon's best man had failed to turn up. Dylan Thomas let him down; the couple had to make do with a colleague from Bletchley Park.

'May all the bells of heaven ring their wildest for you both.'

When Vernon had told his errant best man about his pending marriage, the response was stylishly ebullient. Gwen wasn't just marrying a poet, she was marrying into a fraternity of word-smiths among whom Dylan Thomas stood out as Vernon's most important friend. Before she ever met Thomas, Vernon serenaded Gwen with Dylan's work. In the sergeant's mess or on the grass by Bletchley's pond he read aloud, 'sometimes from Yeats, once the entire book of Job . . . but most often poems and prose of Dylan's'.

Now, telling her story years later, it is important for Gwen to strip away the legacy of Dylan's poetry and remember how it was back then – 'the freshness, the explosive originality of his prose, and the majesty and exaltation of his poetry after the political and sociological poetry of the thirties'. And it was this man, this edgy modern poet, who was going to be the best man at her wedding. But he didn't turn up. Gwen was not angry for herself, 'I preferred the Georgian poets, and I was worried about Dylan meeting father; he couldn't tolerate drunks.' But she felt miserable for Vernon, for whom she knew Dylan meant so much. Was Dylan jealous, perhaps, of Gwen's sudden arrival in bachelor Vernon's life?

'Perhaps. He always entreated Vernon for money, "If ever you have five shillings you hate, I shan't," but after we married he never asked again.'

Gwen didn't meet Dylan for another couple of months; it was December 1944 in London's Café Royal. He was late and drop-ping drinks, names and cigarette ash. Gwen was unimpressed – she wasn't a drinker. 'All alcohol tastes like cough mixture to me!' But how her life had changed. Here she was in a fashionable London bar making a judgement on one of the world's most cele-brated poets. Only a few years earlier her provincial public serv-ant father had been picking her up from dances at 10pm sharp, a trip to the library with her mother was an event to be savoured, and then there were the dullards at Gloucestershire's Records Office. No wonder Gwen cherishes her memories of the Park – it was her entry point into an extraordinary adult world.

14

V *is for Victory*

Ann was on leave in the Lake District visiting an aunt just weeks before Germany surrendered.

'I only remember sitting on a hillside, hugging my legs, thinking, "I know! I know the war is coming to an end, because there are fewer and fewer messages coming into Hut 6."'

But her husband Angus refuses to be swept up in the poetry of his wife's moment. 'You would have known anyway. It was obvious once we went over the Rhine into Germany that the war was at its end.'

Ann shakes her head, 'Well, I must have been very slow on the uptake because I didn't realise. Not until there were fewer Enigma messages.'

This marital tussle in a living-room in Edinburgh's Inverleith exemplifies just how removed many of Bletchley Park's personnel were from the dialogue of war. Continual reminders not to talk, not to ask, not to even understand, stultified curiosity and ensured that their work remained stubbornly detached from the realities of a war that was nearly over. A surge in Enigma traffic in the wake of the D-Day landing had, by the early spring of 1945, given way to a relative trickle as the German military shrank back within their own borders and resumed the use of landlines.

At the time, Angus was cutting his way across Western Europe in an armoured car regiment aged just nineteen ('Yes, it was an exciting time, I consider myself lucky to have been part of it'), while Ann, his future wife, continued to deftly turn cribs into menus for Bombe machines, as she had done for the last two years – only now there were fewer of them.

Up until this point, Betty had pictured the enemy as a 'great big bull-headed Gomorrah'. Like Ann she was clamped to a desk for the last two years of the war; sitting on the Yorkshire Moors plugged into the enemy's Morse communication, intercepting the unintelligible codes and sending them on to BP. And then suddenly she too got a whiff of the prostrate enemy's predicament.

'You did feel sorry for them – I did anyway, 'cos for the first time they came out with one or two plain language words and we knew then they were getting a bit panicky.'

Trapped between the Soviet war machine advancing in the East and the Allies pushing in from the West, the German soldiers reached out to each other in their own language. They were human after all.

'Of course I couldn't understand any of it, I couldn't read German, I just told the set room sergeant straight away.'

In the latter half of 1944 Gwen, working on her low-grade Luftwaffe ciphers, remembers the Germans unravelling as their airbases were overrun. 'In the confusion people had no time to look up their code books, and often sent their message in "clear" (plain) language.'

But despite the decoders' upper hand, there was no euphoria in the Air Section.

We thought wistfully of the days when the Germans, realising that the mere fact the ground controller of a bomber crew was on the air would alert interceptors to impending operations, used to operate their net at irregular times and pass 'spoof' messages simulating real ones . . . operators had no time now, and often no equipment, to send even pretend traffic.

The playing field was no longer level (with the odd exception, the Germans were being smashed on both sides)[1] and Gwen, who had

1. 1 January 1945: 900 German fighters attacked Allied airfields. The failure to give explicit warning of this was a blow to BP's reputation. 150 Allied aircraft were

taken such pride in her decoding role, mourned the passage of an even fight.

Likewise Ann in Hut 6 had relished her war work. She stopped keeping a diary four months after her arrival at the Park (what was the point when she couldn't write about what she was doing?) so it's impossible to recapture the exact moment when the end suddenly dawned on her. But today Ann is candid: 'The war had infiltrated my entire life, it made it more exciting I suppose.' For girls whose adult lives had been defined by a six-year conflict, the end was almost unimaginable.

Early Escapes

In anticipation of the D-Day landings, staff numbers rose at Bletchley Park by some 2,000 to 8,850 in the first half of 1944. After September that figure remained much the same until the end of the war in Europe. Only one category bucked the trend – civilian women. Their numbers were already falling and among the early departures was a euphoric Lady Jean.

There is no doubting this woman's verve. She thought nothing of partying on a London roof terrace with buzz bombs (V-1s) raining down.

> It was actually perfectly sensible because the engine of the buzz bomb cut out before it fell. Therefore if it was going to hit you, you wouldn't hear it anyway. So long as you heard it, it was going over your head and missing you . . . It was quite exciting.

Even the charred remains of London's Guards Chapel, the dust not yet settled, didn't put her off her driving duties. A hundred and twenty-one of the Chapel's congregation died on 18 June 1944 in the most lethal V-1 attack on British soil; the grim reality

---

destroyed and 111 seriously damaged; however German losses were far greater (about a third of their force). It was the last major Luftwaffe operation of the war.

was strewn across Birdcage Walk, but as a BP driver Lady Jean had messages to deliver in the capital and this was the shortest route. No matter that the sight was unpleasant. There was a war on and Jean, emboldened by her job in Bletchley's MTC, was determined to see more of it.

'Finally I left BP that summer. I was released. Yes, yes I was chuffed, absolutely! I joined the Red Cross. This time I didn't mention my TB history.'

Lady Jean had learnt her lesson; the truth doesn't always pay and nothing was going to get in the way of her long-awaited wartime adventure.

'I loved, absolutely loved my job as a welfare officer in India.' Her voice lifts and she shifts forwards in her chair, pleased that she can at last inject a bit of jeopardy into her story.

In her biography, Arran's Lady even writes with affection about the English countryside en route to Liverpool's docks, and 'wondered if and hoped that, one day I would see it again'. Stultifying Buckinghamshire wasn't given another thought, bar a quick prayer 'that the girls at Bletchley were working hard and had broken the code for that day', as the *SS Monarch of Bermuda* chugged across the Atlantic. The element of danger added to the experience – she was travelling across the Atlantic, the Mediterranean and the Suez canal, and all in uniform with fellow comrades signed up and ready for action.

'There were nine of us in a single cabin. Nine! Three tiers of bunk beds, one above the other! Somebody's feet below your head, someone else's feet above, right around the room!' Who said debutantes didn't know how to rough it? 'Each side of the ship was allocated one hour of water in either the morning or afternoon. The only way we could manage to wash was to fill our tin helmets, hot water bottles . . .' By the time they reached the Indian Ocean, Lady Jean had a severe attack of dysentery.

The arrival at her new posting was even more of a culture shock.

Most of the men were starving. They had to stay in the British military hospital for about a fortnight. They had had nothing but a cup of rice. And then maybe they could digest an egg or fish and finally, when they could digest red meat, they were ready to go home. They had Beriberi on their legs, they had to be de-wormed. And X-rayed for chest problems.

Lady Jean (still with dysentery) had finally arrived in Jalahalli near Bangalore. There the hospital doubled up as a recuperation centre for the survivors of Japanese labour camps. These hollow, broken men were her new charges.

Remarkably unfazed by the state of her male patients (no doubt life on a dour Scottish island helped), this young aristocrat found that her charges responded to her efforts at entertainment. 'Well, miss, what have you got for us today?' Leather work, knitting or just a good blether?

It is clear from the rich anecdotes that tumble out about privates, corporals and even a Scottish poacher that she rarely let them down. Lady Jean was at last in her element. Her boring work in Hut 8 may have helped locate wolf packs, sink U-boats and fire torpedoes, but she could not have been further removed from the vicious reality and heady kick of war. Stuck at Bletchley Park she had longed for a chance to prove herself, and now, at last, she was able to do just that.

———•———

It was on board the same requisitioned liner, *Monarch of Bermuda*, only a few months later in January 1945 that another female civilian made an early escape from Bletchley, this time across the Mediterranean to Cairo. The disappearance of her brother Dick and Edo's duplicitous marriage proposal had cast a long shadow over Rozanne's final few months at the Park. She would have toughed it out but when her father, Sir Charles Medhurst, recently promoted to Commanding Officer of RAF

Middle Eastern Command, suggested a transfer to Egypt, Rozanne agreed.

'Bletchley gave me leave on compassionate grounds, I got an intelligence job in Cairo, father's status helped.' After three extraordinary years in the familiar confines of the Park, Rozanne suddenly found herself alone, leaning over the railings of a giant ship, gazing down at the troops on the lower deck. 'I saw three men in cherry berets, they looked so young and brave and I thought it must be rather marvellous to be a parachutist.' At lunchtime that same day one of the trio sought her out in the dining hall. Up close, Rozanne was again struck by Halsey Colchester's youth and his uniform. 'He was very different from the people at BP, very much more down to earth and in the Army.'

Rozanne loved the Park almost as much as Lady Jean resented it, yet on their release both were equally impressed by the vulnerability and honest appeal of young British soldiers miles from home. It was early 1945, but for an isolated Bletchley Girl this was a new experience.

The convoy of ships was stuffed with military personnel; Rozanne and Halsey were part of a much larger mission heading towards the Egyptian capital. Cairo had been Britain's Middle Eastern headquarters throughout the war, where a large intelligence-gathering operation co-ordinated with BP to help the Allied defeat of Rommel's Afrika Korps. But now, on the verge of victory in Europe, imperial Britain had to come to terms with a very changed world order. Palestine was a colony, the Jews wanted a homeland and Egypt was an increasingly reluctant British military base. Caught up in their own moment, however, Halsey and Rozanne didn't give much thought to the geopolitics behind their postings – that would come later. Instead they made the most of their time together.

'We would climb into the lifeboat to learn Arabic. It was very innocent.'

Then, quite suddenly, to Rozanne's astonishment, Halsey asked her to marry him. 'We had not even got to Egypt!' (On hearing this story, Kathleen, Rozanne's Park friend, laughs: 'Yes, she was very popular with the boys!') Rozanne, raw from Edo's betrayal (and perhaps still a little bit in love with him), wasn't convinced.

'I was wary, but Halsey was very sure he wanted to marry me so we got semi-engaged!' Fully aware of how two engagements in less than six months must sound to contemporary ears, she laughs: 'I know, it was terribly impulsive, but war is an impulsive time!'

January 1945 was also the month when Gwen Watkins stopped working at the Park. However unlike Rozanne and Jean she did not go of her own volition and there was no mention of this early departure in her memoir about Bletchley Park – *Cracking the Luftwaffe Codes*. The book itself is a compelling celebration of a period that Gwen cherishes: 'there isn't one thing that hasn't changed since I was young, not one thing!' Except perhaps the staunch principles of the author herself. In an otherwise frank memoir, Gwen's new husband Vernon is modestly referred to as 'the poet', there is no reference to the couple's engagement and the marriage is given only a cursory mention.

> In October 1944, I had married our poet – Vernon Watkins. This caused a furore in the upper ranks of the camp, since it appeared that no Service man or woman could marry without the permission of the commanding officer . . . the Poet simply said, 'Well, sir I don't really see what business it is of yours when and whom I marry.'

In the 1940s the private sphere was just that, private, and had nothing to do with *Cracking the Luftwaffe Codes*. However, in conversation Gwen freely admits that her marriage had an almost immediate impact on her job at the Park. A blissful two-day honeymoon in St Albans ('we walked around the Verulamium Park, around the abbey and the pond having beautiful times') bore fruit. By January 1945 Gwen was three months pregnant.

'I was sorry to leave. I hoped I could stay working at Bletchley until I nearly had the baby but it was different then. Heaven forbid an ambulance might have to come to the gates!'

Although Gwen was devoted to her section and their team effort against the Luftwaffe, her early departure did not feel like a sacrifice. 'After I got married, Vernon and I moved out of the RAF camp and lived together at Mrs Henson's. I stayed there until the baby was almost born. I suppose I went on walks and read. I don't know.' Here she shrugs, momentarily lost in thought. 'There's one thing I notice now when I look back at myself, with a few exceptions I have always more or less accepted things.' And in this case there was little incentive to do otherwise; amid a global killing spree a fecund womb (within marriage) trumped all other female endeavours.

Victory in Europe

'I first came across the *Manchester Guardian* at Woburn Abbey; the Wrens there had daily newspapers on a table if you wanted them, so yes I was aware of the culmination of the war.'

For Joanna news of the steadily advancing Allied and Soviet troops was mirrored by multiplying Colossi (ten by late spring) and attendant Wrens – Fish decrypts reached their wartime peak in March 1945.

Amid the crush of her block, Joanna thrived on adrenalin and speculation.

'Germany was falling! I think we knew this at least a week before anybody else.'

On the night of 29 April a fraught Hitler telegraphed Field Marshal Keitel: 'Where are Wenck's spearheads? When will they advance? Where is the Ninth Army?' Stuck fast or encircled came the reply.

Communications like these were packed with such meaning for the reader back at Bletchley Park that euphoria was hard to suppress.

Somebody came into the room and yelled, 'It's over! Its over!'
There weren't many of us on shift but when we heard this we
grabbed the nearest thing to hand – loo rolls – and ran outside to
decorate a tree. We were throwing the paper up into the branches
when a top boss ran out and shouted, 'What are you doing! This
is dreadful! Shut up! Go back to work!'

Joanna shakes her head. 'There were only about half a dozen of
us but we got into an awful lot of trouble.'

The Wrens' timing couldn't have been worse. 'The overwhelm-
ing concern of Bletchley's management towards the end of the
war was security.' They were well aware the intoxicating idea of
victory could (and did) overexcite even the most judicious
members of staff. Joanna's loo-roll antics are a case in point.
Edicts were issued to counter exactly this type of behaviour. On
29 April Hut 3 was specifically told to severely restrict the issue of
decrypt information of a 'spectacular' type including: 'large
German capitulations' and 'the activities of prominent German
personalities'. So when Hitler blew his brains out the very next
day in a bunker under the Reich Chancellery, at Bletchley it was
business as usual.

After years of meticulous standards, complacency was not an
option. Britain was no longer under threat from direct attack;
air-raid wardens were stood down, fire-watching duties abandoned, but at the Park a war was still being fought against the
Japanese, with vast numbers of staff transferred into a rapidly
expanded department. Meanwhile closer to home and ominously
camped across the East of Europe was Stalin's Red Army; an
appreciation of their extraordinary tenacity against the Germans
soon transformed into a renewed fear of Bolshevism. Aware that
GC&CS's future would be increasingly defined against this
Soviet superpower, security at BP remained paramount. Echoing
Churchill's conviction that 'we have yet to make sure that the
simple and honourable purposes for which we entered the war
are not brushed aside or overlooked following our success',

Bletchley Park's Director Travis issued a 'special order' to his vast staff, reminding them:

> We and our American Allies are still at war with Japan, and we are faced with great responsibilities arising out of the preliminaries to peace in Europe. At some future time we may be called upon again to use the same methods. It is therefore as vital as ever not to relax from the high standard of security that we have hitherto maintained.

But if Bletchley's management were preoccupied with unfinished business and secrecy, for their young staff predominantly focused on a German foe, the declaration of peace in Europe, when it finally came, demanded a party. Bletchley's modest church bells and a chintzy gathering on the Park's front lawn did not suffice. Granted at least one of the two Victory days off, hordes of young workers headed for the train station or tried their luck on the A5 – London was the place to be.

Suitably chastened after her high jinks, Joanna saved her second celebration for Buckingham Palace. 'It was absolutely a seething mass of people!' There she saw King George waving on the balcony, flanked by doughty wife Elizabeth and Churchill, brandishing his famous V-sign. Joanna, keen for a better look, decided to launch herself on an imposing bronze lion.

'Ha ha, it was quite a thing in a Wren skirt and getting up was far easier than coming down!' By all accounts a sturdy girl, she was eventually picked off by a couple of willing men.

Ann thinks she also might have visited London for VE day but isn't certain.

'Did I? Did I go up to London?'

'Yes!' her husband Angus insists. 'It's in your photograph album.'

Sure enough between the sheaves there are five black and white snaps surrounding a central caption in Anne's own clear hand: 'VE day London, 8 May 1945.' With a Kodak Brownie Box

Camera, Ann joined the London celebration and recorded the moment for posterity. A sea of caps, military peaks and perms drifts through a shot of Shaftesbury Avenue. There is Admiralty Arch bathed in floodlight and a staring crowd flanks 'Whitehall a few minutes after Churchill had spoken from the Balcony'.

Again Ann isn't certain, but she thinks she went to London with her brother Paul, who was studying at Cambridge. Despite the throngs of people, her patchy recall and the sepia photos suggest that VE day perhaps didn't live up to expectations. This is in stark contrast to her mother Winifred's record of Armistice Day twenty-seven years earlier. Winifred was a VAD nurse behind the French front line. She sets down how the relentless hardship of the First World War ('awful leg, all gangrene gas, and a fearful smell') had finally given way to

> truly the most wonderful day in my life for it is the end of the war! . . . I was just starting out anyhow and finally got to Oxford Street. PACKED. Buses, taxis, lorries, private cars, crowded to overflowing with cheering, flag-waving mobs. Truly a marvellous sight.

But for daughter Ann the contrast between war and peace was less stark. Inside a sanitised Buckinghamshire Park there had been no bloodied men to mop up; her war work in Hut 6 was intricate and mentally challenging.

She had enjoyed herself thoroughly and now it was over. After VE day, civilian Ann would not return to her position at Bletchley – the end of the Enigma codes spelt the end of her job. There she was, young, free and single, standing in a shabby city disembowelled by war. No amount of ticker tape and bunting could hide the jarring scars – London was a giant metaphor for a future riddled with uncertainty.

Cora had been twelve years old, polishing her mother's dining-room, when she heard Chamberlain announce Britain was at war on the wireless. Six years later, again listening to the wireless, 'I heard the war had come to an end.' Cora's entire adolescence had been etched out against the backdrop of international conflict. A private girls' school had given way to a not entirely dissimilar life in the Wrens (uniform, routine, friendship) with shifts spent at 'boring Bletchley Park'. Cora did not really know what peace meant; no wonder she felt 'underwhelmed' by the portentous announcement. Her location didn't help. 'I was in Woburn village when I heard. Nothing really happened. It was a bit of a dump.' Pealing bells in a handsome Georgian village fell short of her eighteen-year-old expectations, but at least she had the day off work.

'No, isn't that odd? Now you come to mention it I can't remember VE day. No. Hmm, I wonder why not.'

Puzzled, Charlotte says she will sleep on it, but the following morning Victory in Europe day still doesn't resonate. 'I was probably working, maybe I heard it on the radio.' Charlotte's vague testimony is proof, if any were needed, that generalisations regarding an 8,000-strong organisation don't work. The now famous photograph of Hut 6 employees in tea dresses and military stripes on the lawn toasting the end of the war is no more representative of Bletchley's VE day than city streets lined with bunting and blancmange. For some in the Park nothing had changed: enemy codes still needed to be broken, and Charlotte, by now an accomplished paraphraser of Japanese messages, had a job to do. The industrious buzz down Block F's Burma Road did not stop; for some at least the war was still going on.

'I felt ambivalent. Father was missing.'

Pat stood amid a uniformed throng on London's streets but she didn't share their ecstasy. How could she? 'We hadn't defeated the Japs and Dad was in a Jap camp.' Pat shrugs; she might have given the VE day celebrations a miss but by now she was in London and it would've been churlish not to step out and breathe in the optimism. 'I left Abbot's Cliff once the German fleet capitulated. There were no more codes to intercept.' The Chief Petty Officer Wren was transferred to London. First there was a job translating the electric wiring of a German U-boat at the Admiralty and then a position in General Eisenhower's Headquarters on the top floor of Peter Robinson's department store. The job came with perks, including access to American rations. 'You would go along with a suitcase and fill it up with Hershey's bars and Camel cigarettes.' But the work was arduous and distressing.

> I had to understand and translate different captured German documents. Who was a spy? Who was an SS man? They had to work out who should be brought up for war crimes trials. And of course they got the concentration camp documents too.

The words hang in the air.

> They were capturing places like Dachau and Buchenwald concentration camps. It was quite horrific; I knew it was horrible but I had no idea how awful. We got the pictures before they became public knowledge, then they put on an exhibition. I was appalled to see people queuing up to look at these photographs.

Peaceful Europe was proving a hard place to make sense of.

———◆———

'In the spring of 1945 I had started working for the intelligence service in Cairo. It was all to do with the situation in the Middle East and what became the Israeli war.' Rozanne simulates a writing motion with her hand.

> It was quite administrative. I think I was doing the same sort of work as I did at Bletchley but dealing with the immediate Arab

situation and the intelligence coming from that. We were trying to stop too many Jews entering Palestine but all the refugees were coming from Europe because of Hitler. More and more kept coming because they had nowhere else to go. They'd had this awful experience. The concentration camps.

Although embedded in an exotic ex-pat lifestyle, as part of the intelligence service Rozanne was working on the edge of an unsolvable humanitarian catastrophe. 'They were kept on ships, they were desperate . . .' Her voice trails off. The Nazis' systematic attempt to exterminate Europe's Jewry led to an unprecedented exodus across the Mediterranean to Palestine. Boatloads of traumatised people kept coming, among them seasoned soldiers who had fought with the Allies. The Jews' demand for a new Israeli state in the ancient Holy Land was impossible to ignore. As far as the Zionists were concerned the Palestinians were in the way and, with the Mandate of Palestine, so were the British.

'We were in charge of Palestine and the Jews were saying they must come. They had to come.' Rozanne frowns; it's complicated. European brutality against the Jews bled into a Middle Eastern trauma that could not be written off with a bit of bunting and good cheer.

At last peace prevailed in Europe but within three years there would be a war in the Middle East.

Victory in Japan

Ha that was a funny thing about Pa! He came to see my Wren officers at Woburn Abbey and they gave him too good a time. When he drove out of the grounds worse for wear he saw one of the Duke's wallabies and thought, 'Heavens, I am hallucinating!'

Joanna laughs, but only briefly. It rankles that her controlling father once again put a spanner in the works. 'He came to check up on me and tell the Superintendent WRNS that I was not to be posted overseas, which I thought was jolly mean!'

Joanna had joined the Wrens to break free of Group Captain Stradling, yet still her father managed to interfere. After the fall of Germany a few Wrens were singled out for inoculations and fitted with white blackouts (unflattering white naval knickers) and white bibs for their circular hats. But not Joanna. The code-breaking outposts sifting Japanese traffic in Delhi and Colombia would have to manage without her.

Ditto Charlotte, although she did get as far as being interviewed for a posting to India. 'I was selected but I somehow knew I would not be going even though my name was on the deployment list. I had a strange premonition ... convincing me that Delhi was not to be my next destination.'

Instead, duty called on the other side of the Atlantic. Charlotte, who had turned down the offer of marriage to a Canadian, was now posted to the military centre of an emerging modern superpower. America's Pentagon, finished in 1943, was the world's biggest building; somewhere deep within it she was to join the British Army's code-breaking contingent in the Allies' war against Japan.

Despite teething problems, cross-pollination between British and American code-breakers had increased since 1942, with some of Bletchley's most famous names – Alan Turing, Frank Birch, Edward Travis – visiting the USA.

Charlotte, by her own confession nothing more than 'a natural administrator', was staggered by the invitation. 'I couldn't believe it! Me? A humble staff sergeant.' Years later and still mystified, she asked her head of section Captain John Burrows why he chose her.

He simply answered, 'I thought it was a good idea.'

But meet ninety-one-year-old Charlotte today (a parish councillor midway through the preparation for yet another lecture on her time at Bletchley) and it is immediately apparent why he selected her to work for Britain in America; he knew she wouldn't let him down. And perhaps it was also a reward for a meticulous performance over four long years.

'I thought it was marvellous to be going to America but I was also petrified.'

Throughout the war, gorgeous Hollywood stars (Veronica Lake, Rita Hayworth, Cary Grant) had bombarded Britain's straitened imaginations, showy GIs with flash teeth and coloured candy injected the drab home front (even Bletchley) with glamour and now quiet unassuming Charlotte was on her way to their land of plenty.

The journey began inauspiciously; 'unceremoniously clambering' onto the wings of a Sunderland flying boat she bumped and vomited her way across the Atlantic with a group of anonymous civilian men. 'I feared they might ask me what I was doing and where I was going.'

If the photograph on the front of her memoir is anything to go by, Charlotte kept her cool.

Ah that perm I had done specifically for America. Cypriots in Oxford did it. It cost an arm and a leg to get there and an arm and a leg to have it done. I paid four guineas! The whole thing was very laborious with lots of stinky chemicals.

But the end result was handsome. Charlotte's dark hair is scooped up in a gentle wave above her forehead, beneath which her direct gaze stares out from the picture. 'I was in America by the time that was taken. I'd been given a Canadian summer uniform.'

The light, man-made jacket and silky nylons had a transformative effect after years in a thick woven ATS jacket. It was just the beginning of a staggering cultural overhaul.

The bus from Washington DC that first morning took her over the Potomac River into the state of Virginia. The expanse of land, the accents, the racial segregation – Charlotte shakes her head: 'Yes, it was a lot to take in.' As for the Pentagon, how can she even begin to describe the enormity of it? It seemed even bigger then, uncluttered by later building projects, jutting proudly out of the landscape – an iconic reminder to the world that America had finally arrived on the military stage. 'And I was the only ATS girl in the whole building!'

Somewhere amid the giant construction, the thousands of workers like ants swarming in every direction, the countless escalators, the stringent security, the cool air-conditioned corridors, young Charlotte took her seat in front of a typewriter and resumed the paraphrasing job she had left behind at Bletchley. The Burma campaign dragged on; the Japanese stubbornly refused to surrender. For two months Charlotte worked nine to five on 'a constant flow of signals passing between Japanese forces'. At least her setting had changed; there were drinks in boats on the Potomac River, cockroaches in an overcrowded Washington hotel, jukeboxes that took a nickel in a slot, juicy watermelon and cottage cheese. Otherwise it was more of the interminable same. Would the war never end?

It was a ghastly noise, the whole of America erupted, went mad! People rushed about with their horns fixed. And steaks. There had been some rationing and then suddenly steaks seemed to drop from the sky!

Charlotte stumbled out into the shouting waving crowd.

'We want Harry! We want Harry.'

'Such excitement and the noise from hundreds of car horns drowning everything else.'

On 6 August 1945 America's new President Harry Truman authorised the use of 'Little Boy', the world's first atomic bomb, on Japan's Hiroshima. Three days later a second bomb, 'Fat Man', was dropped on Nagasaki. Japan surrendered; the war was finally over.

On one side of the Pacific people cheered and ate red meat; on the other there was unimaginable human suffering.

'I suppose the Japanese had to be stopped. In some ways they were worse than the Germans.' Charlotte is quiet for a moment;

the memory is a confusing one. 'But the effects of the atomic bomb were absolutely horrendous. It was the most awful thing for humanity.'

Only many years later did this realisation fully dawn on her. 'An Army officer brought a brick from Japan which had literally crumbled due to radiation and when you think of the effect that must've had on human flesh. It is indescribably awful.' A measured, sensible woman, Charlotte shakes her head. 'There will always be wars as the human race can't control itself. Terrible. The mind boggles.'

In her memoir *Secret Postings* Charlotte notes: 'The authorities intercepted a message indicating that Japan would never surrender and the decision was made to take action that would finally turn the tide of war.' Although a commonly believed line, in fact the reality was more complicated.

For some weeks before the atomic bombs were dropped, the Americans knew the Japanese had been extending peace feelers via Russia, courtesy of their own decrypts. In other words there might have been another way to end the war, but the Americans chose not to pursue it. Instead they pressed ahead with atomic attacks on Hiroshima and Nagasaki. In doing so they ended the war with Japan quickly and simultaneously let the world know they had built a lethal new weapon and (just as important) they were prepared to use it. America's rival new superpower, the Soviet Union, had been warned.

◆

Miles away in provincial Britain, twenty-one-year-old Gwen Watkins gave birth to her first child in a private nursing home in Kinson, a Bournemouth suburb. 'It was relatively easy for me. At the first sign of a tear I was given an anaesthetic.' Fittingly baby Rhiannon grew up to be 'the most sweet-natured and peaceful person' her mother ever knew. Perhaps it is no coincidence she was born on 15 August 1945, Victory in Japan Day.

In Britain, unlike America, juicy steaks did not suddenly appear in restaurants – rations prohibited such niceties – but for those not enduring childbirth, proclamations, royal appearances and rain-soaked bonfires marked the celebration. Neither the weather nor the chilly atmosphere between superpowers could dampen the spirits of a nation that had endured six long years of war.

For Pat, Victory in Japan Day on 15 August was far more important than VE day. Now, at last, she began to believe she might see her father again.

'I could have gone abroad at that time. They were looking for people to work in the military government in Germany or I might possibly have been an interpreter at the Nuremberg trials.' But German-speaking Pat didn't volunteer to go overseas. 'My mother said, "Your father will be awfully disappointed if none of you are home when he returns."'

Pat is now justifiably proud of her father's legacy; later testimonies confirmed that imprisoned in a Japanese labour camp and compelled to build a railway on the River Kwai, Colonel Owtram regularly took 'brutal beatings for his adamant and steadfast refusal to order sick men out to work'. With his lovely tenor voice he organised concerts for his men and sourced small treats, 'half a cigarette or something'; anything to make life more bearable. The feats of individuals like Colonel Owtram would later be immortalised by Hollywood, but that was in the future. When he finally docked at Liverpool in the autumn of 1945, his family welcomed home a changed man.

'Well, he hated the Japanese for one thing! He was very thin and there were some teeth missing.' But it was more than that. 'We hadn't seen my father for such a long time, it was rather like having a stranger in the house. He had been through a lot.' Adjustments were required on both sides.

I remember he came down to London and we were all staying at the Mayfair Hotel. There were drinks before dinner and my sister Jean and I said we would like a Scotch. Father said, 'Women don't drink Scotch, have a sherry!' But we had a Scotch.

Colonel Owtram didn't realise his daughters had grown up, that they too had changed. The secrecy of their war work compounded the problem. Pat had been a Y-station listener and Jean a cipher officer; neither sister could begin to tell their father what they had done during the war.

———•———

Once the war in Europe was over the numbers at Bletchley Park had started to fall fast, but GC&CS retained a 6,000-strong workforce until the end of July. For those not engaged in the Japanese section, a vast wind-down operation got under way. Pam, head of the Naval Index, recalls co-ordinating the shredding of paper among other administrative and tidy-up tasks.

For Joanna it was the cancellation of all night shifts that stood out; suddenly the Wrens in the Newmanry were crushed into a day-time schedule and left to work on historic messages.

The eldest Moller sister, Georgette, thinks that towards the end she and Doris were both working in Block F on the Japanese war, and after some thought Doris nods her head. Georgette is probably right. Either way whatever she was doing it wasn't nearly as exciting as her work on the Hagelin machine against the Italians in the middle of the night. The Park had an increasingly listless air – the European war was over and everyone, girls included, was keen to get on with the rest of their lives.

However there were exceptions. At Stanmore outstation Bombe operator Ruth was terribly excited; among her group of Wrens there was talk of white blackouts and a need for additional training at the Park itself.

'That was the rumour, that we were going to BP for ten days and then on to Colombo!' It wasn't just a rumour; some code-breakers and Wrens were already en route to the outstation in Ceylon.

'Believe it or not the day the atomic bomb dropped I was in a queue for jabs to go abroad.' The abrupt end of the Japanese war meant Ruth's inoculations weren't needed after all.

She spent the rest of the summer

sitting outside in the sunshine with a soldering iron unsoldering the hundreds and hundreds of little connections from bits of coloured wire. All the wires were put into boxes and the connections into others boxes and sold as Army surplus.

For over a year she had slogged night and day to serve and maintain the Bombe machine; now she was unpicking the ingenious workings of this giant electronic testing machine. Of the two-hundred-plus Bombe machines, soon only sixty remained. What they had ceaselessly achieved, chugging through innumerable Enigma permutations, was not the business of posterity. No one must ever know.

Ruth needed no reminder that she had a lifelong secret to keep but she was given one all the same. 'Everyone who had worked on the project was reminded they had signed the Official Secrets Act. We were told we must not breathe a word to no one, even though war had ended.'

Joanna is glad she wasn't part of the team that dismantled the Colossi. She loved them too much for that. But she did bid these mammoth man-made brains a fond farewell. 'I was told I could take part of one of them with me, as a souvenir. I got a switch and I kept it in my Wren belt-pocket for years.'

A small tangible object, meaningless to anyone else, travelled with Joanna to the next stage of her life; meanwhile back at Bletchley all bar two of the Colossi were destroyed. In a new streamlined GC&CS (moved first to Eastcote before finding its present-day home in Cheltenham in the 1950s), there was no place for unwieldy reminders of what Britain had achieved against the Nazis. As Bletchley's work had exemplified so well over the previous six years, knowledge was power. No one, could know what had taken place in an unremarkable estate on the flat plains of Buckinghamshire.

The evidence was destroyed and the silenced workforce dispersed.

15

'Let Us Face the Future'

'I got priority demob 'cos I was married.'

Betty has been talking for about two hours but this is the first time she has mentioned her marriage. There was her young life in Northamptonshire's Higham Ferrers, the council school, her exemplary 11-plus, her four much older siblings and the premature death of her mother. Then came her war – training at Northampton's racecourse, Morse code on the Isle of Man and shifts spent listening on a Yorkshire moor, but never at any point was there talk of a man. Now, suddenly, Betty announces she was married. 'Yes! Did I not say? I had to apply for leave for the wedding and tell them who he was and the like. It was right at the end of the war. May 1945.'

Once prompted, the story comes out. Betty had met Reg Randall six years earlier in the shoe factory and they had been an item ever since.

> He worked in the lasting room. So he took the uppers that we made and used a big heavy machine to put the sole on and make the finished article. Once we started making Army boots what Reg did became a reservist occupation so he didn't go to war.

Instead Reg stayed in Higham Ferrers and wrote to Betty every day. 'I think he chose me, yes I think so. Not the other way around. No, I can't remember our first date. It was not *Mills and Boon*. Ooh no! There was no flash of light but he was lovely.' Betty spreads out the few photographs that represent her young life and holds them up one by one. Marriage is the predominant theme. There's little Betty clutching a posy, standing proudly in pristine white socks and buckled shoes – the bridesmaid at her sister's wedding – then comes a repeat performance in a cotton hat for her brother Eric's wedding, and again for brother Dennis. Her final stint as bridesmaid came when she was sixteen for her second sister, Olive. 'It was very important to get married. That was part of your life, finding a husband. People got married, that was just it.'

So when Reg proposed to Betty during the war she said yes straight away. It didn't matter if she wasn't head over heels in love; girls like her couldn't afford to turn down the solid offer of a good man. And anyway 'there was enough love there 'cos he was a lovely fellow'. In their wedding photograph Reg certainly cuts quite a dash with his strong jaw and broad shoulders. He has large limpid eyes and a dark quiffed fringe. He is standing on the church steps arm in arm with his young bride smiling at the camera: it is the end of the war and Reg can finally look forward to his Betty coming home.

'Everything was borrowed. Even my dress belonged to my sister's husband's sister.' But Betty carried it off, draped in white lace clutching a bunch of touched-up red roses, her hair neatly waved under a veil, she looks every inch the blushing bride. After a modest celebration ('there was no wine, it was a Methodist wedding') Betty and Reg spent their first couple of nights together in a little hotel in Higham Ferrers' market square. 'I was a bit nervous. I had no clue what anything was about. Nobody ever told me. Ha ha! I soon found out. No, it was lovely, it was lovely. Yeah.'

Then, having used up her three days' leave, ATS girl Mrs Betty Randall returned to Harrogate.

Aged twenty-one, and having served just two years in the ATS, Betty did not anticipate an early demobilisation. She was originally in group fifty-two – hundreds of girls had been ahead of her on the list. But getting married changed that. 'I got priority demob. I was put forward to group one and came straight out just like that.' On 23 July 1945 Betty was discharged from the Army and sent back home to her husband in Northamptonshire.

A lot of girls did get married to get out but I didn't. I missed the Army, I really did. The closeness of everybody; you were one of them. I came back home to nothing. Reg and I had to move back in with my brother 'cos we didn't have a house and I went back to work at the shoe factory. Absolutely yes! It was very flat to be back in the shoe factory.

The low priority which Betty accorded her fiancé and wedding in the story of her young life suddenly makes sense. Although he was a decent man, marriage to Reg Randall cut short Betty's job in the Army.

Instead she returned to Higham Ferrers and the shoe factory and an everyday existence bereft of both money and opportunity. Married or not, life back in Northamptonshire simply offered more of the same; a monotony compounded by the couple's inability to conceive. 'Children just didn't happen, I don't know why not.'

In stark comparison was her service work as a wireless operator. Immaculately turned out in braided khaki, clamped to a headset for hours on end, it was during those two years on a cold Yorkshire moor that Betty felt she really counted for something.

'Oh yes. I loved it. I really did.'

Demobilisation

History remembers 1945 as a seminal year for Great Britain. The war ended and an extraordinary peace began. Just six weeks after VE day, in the first General Election for ten years, the Labour party celebrated a landslide victory. Churchill had won the war but the Conservatives lost the peace. An unprecedented six years of state control paved the way for a long-awaited postwar period of reconstruction and redistribution. Out of the bombed ruins (in six years a quarter of a million homes were destroyed and nearly four million damaged), new hospitals and houses mushroomed, a welfare state promised to look after the needs of the nation and an Education Act championed learning for future generations. Nothing was left to chance.

'Yes,' remarks Pam, in her unmistakeably grand accent, 'I seem to remember we almost all voted for Clement Atlee. It was time for a change.' (Not quite all – Lady Jean, working in imperial India, was much distressed to hear Churchill had lost the election: 'I thought it was terribly disloyal.')

However change, when it came, was targeted; in the postwar political discourse, redistribution should not be confused with equality. 'The principal address to women in the policies of the reforming Labour government of 1945 . . . was as a wife and mother.' After all, wasn't the preservation of domestic bliss – the comely woman lovingly tending to her husband and offspring – what every man had been fighting for?

A Ministry of Labour booklet baldly stated that 'married women have the right to claim priority of release over all other women'. No wonder Betty was sent scuttling back to the arms of her new husband in Northamptonshire. Gwen, clutching her firstborn in a Bournemouth nursing home, could relax knowing she had seamlessly transferred from wartime service to the 'vital work' of 'ensuring the adequate continuance of the British race'.

But if the ideological message was clear enough, reconstructing Britain in the wake of a devastating war required time and (a bit) of womanpower. In July 1945 over 400,000 women were still in the armed services; for the vast majority demobilisation didn't happen overnight. With commitments at home, in the Middle East, occupied Germany and the colonies, the three women's auxiliary services fought to control the release of their own staff, despite political pressure. Young and without jobs or husbands to return to, Wren ratings Joanna, Cora and Ruth would have to bide their time. Ditto WAAF sergeant (and former Bletchley indexer) Kathleen Godfrey.

'As soon as the war was over, we were all out of work but still in the Air Force . . . some went home and some, like me, were sent to new stations and different jobs.' Although now one of

Bletchley's most feted female veterans, Kathleen was not sad to leave the Park. 'No, I stayed on until VJ day and then it was time to go. Rozanne had already left.' As was the case at the beginning of the war, the end for Kathleen had a poignancy. In 1939 her family was dispersed, in 1945 it was her friends. And still she had very little control over her life. 'One was given so little choice. I don't ever remember being given any choice.'

Her next destination was 'a dull, ugly' Air Force station in Uxbridge where her administrative job consisted of 'marching around in charge of 150 women, inspecting barrack rooms and counting sheets and blankets'. She signed passes, scolded girls ('yes ma'am, no ma'am'), saluted in brown leather gloves and scrounged a tiny electric fire for her small ice-cold room. 'What a life.'

It was over yet another breakfast in the Officer's Mess that she noticed someone she had not seen before.

'He was strikingly good-looking, a Greek god newly flown down from Olympus. His face was lean and suntanned, showing that he must have recently returned from overseas . . . He attracted me immediately.' Kathleen had spotted a breed rarely enjoyed at Bletchley Park – a devastatingly good-looking airman. Suddenly time no longer dragged.

It was the German playwright Wolfgang Borchert on his return from the Eastern Front who observed that 'men serving on the front line are like puppets on a string'. Peace, he concluded, tore away those strings and gave rise to the bewildering experience of being in charge of one's own life, often for the first time. Although less acute for women, the sense of disorientation still existed. Young girls who joined the war effort straight from school had no experience of adult life outside the services.

Having spent a year tending a machine already rendered obsolete, Ruth quietly concludes, 'I didn't have any skills when I left the Wrens except perhaps a bit of rudimentary typing.' A bright girl who matriculated from school with impressive academic results, Ruth no longer wanted to go to university. 'After the war I wasn't in the frame of mind to study.' Instead, like Kathleen with her 'Greek god', Ruth had also met a man, more specifically the handsome American officer she was dating.

> I wanted to marry the American and he wanted to marry me. He was Jewish and very eligible and well connected but mother said girls who marry Americans go back to America and find they have told a load of lies and are not rich or well connected and might even be married already.

Off the back of a few ill-placed enquiries, Mrs Henry decided the matter on behalf of her nineteen-year-old daughter – Mr America was not to be trusted. Disappointed, Ruth made up her mind not to solicit her interfering mother's counsel in the future. She would find a husband all by herself and ideally before she was released from the Wrens.

During the war thousands of girls had left home and lived independently. For many the prospect of returning to the watchful gaze of their parents was not appealing. Some awaiting release didn't need the Government to persuade them – the obvious answer was to find a husband. But although keen to stay away from her overbearing father, Joanna was an unsophisticated nineteen-year-old. A man was not the answer, not yet anyway. She wanted a job and was determined to use the remainder of her time in the Wrens wisely. After a stint at the fleet mail office in Stanmore she applied to become an Educational Vocation Trainer in the Navy.

'I did not want to do a ghastly menial job.'

Her work on the Colossi left her impatient for a more fulfilling role. Thankfully she passed the Admiralty interview.

Joanna chortles; the memory of her young self teaching older service men and women how to adapt to a world still tied up in rations and coupons is an amusing one.

I had to dredge up my domestic science. I was training people to live on civvy street. But I had never lived on civvy street! I hadn't even seen a ration book and had to teach people how to use them! I was good with colour though. I enjoyed teaching people how to dye their uniforms.

Posted to a naval base in Staffordshire, she encountered a vibrant community life reminiscent of certain groups within the Park. 'We had a music department and we'd go off to concerts.' One night Joanna opted to stay behind (the naval van was full) when a voice piped up from the back: 'There are plenty of knees in here!'

'Well damn yes! Perhaps I will go,' thought Joanna and promptly sat on the organist's lap. His name was Dick Chorley. Within eighteen months they were married.

'Oh, my time at Southsea was much more fun; I was bored at BP and I couldn't go anywhere stuck in Woburn Abbey. At least when I was posted to Portsmouth there were lovely ships and sailors to look at!' Cora laughs; history's fascination with Britain's code-breaking legacy insists she relives her time at Bletchley when really it was Southsea that captured her imagination. But perhaps one needed the other. Bletchley gave Cora a confidence to match her blonde good looks; by the time she arrived at the coast she knew how to enjoy herself. There was a 'proper job' in the alimony office, a big marine barrack full of men and theatrical performances she could actually take part in. No more makeshift ballet moves in Woburn's icy halls, this eighteen-year-old Wren was finally up on stage. She didn't even have to worry about the future; after demob Cora was guaranteed a job back in Bournemouth in her father's firm, Charlie's Cars.

'It felt very small, I had the extraordinary feeling of being tied in.'

On her return to Britain, Charlotte came back down to earth with a bump. 'I remember going to London in a taxi and feeling very hemmed in. It was not comparable to America.' The States had rocked her senses; new friends, silk stockings, boating parties on the Potomac River, there was even an unscheduled stop in New York. But by October 1945 the adventure was over. Charlotte handed back her light Canadian uniform and, dressed in stodgy ATS khaki, she boarded a requisitioned English cruise liner. Any excitement she felt about her return to Britain soon dissipated on arrival. Back at Bletchley Park,

> I just remember the atmosphere one gets after everyone has gone from a party or a feeling of emptiness after packing a house up before a move . . . I was not required to help the few people left to pack up the site so I felt a little lost and, it is sad to say, it was almost an anticlimax in comparison to the bustle and focus which had filled the place during the war years.

Demob from a posting in East Grinstead came five months later. The intervening period was a difficult time for Charlotte. Army life within Bletchley's curious cocoon had suited her measured temperament. Routine, purpose, uniform and camaraderie propped up her days and nights for four long years. Then quite suddenly the centrifugal forces that governed her existence gave way to uncertainty. Charlotte was in limbo. 'You are all keyed up to do a job and it is not there any more. It was very flat.' But in her analysis seven decades later she is still careful to put her situation in context. 'Soldiers in particular felt worried and panicky about what they were going to do next.' To share such feelings might not be ladylike but Charlotte did worry. What was she going to do next? She had turned down the possibility of marrying a Canadian a year earlier. Did she ever regret rejecting a new life on the flashy side of the Atlantic?

'No I didn't. That chapter was closed and there is no point in regretting. You can't go back.' It is apt that, as Charlotte says this, she is peering through her windscreen at the road ahead, still driving forwards aged ninety-one. She is on her way to give a lecture in Bromsgrove about her time at Bletchley Park. There she later explains to an enquiring audience, 'as soon as I was demobbed I went home to mother and father, it had been a long war and they really needed my help'.

Marriage

'I didn't want to get married. The last thing I wanted was to get married!' Pat is adamant.

> Had it not been for the war I suppose I would've got married to some country gent who did a bit of shooting in Lancashire, but instead my life went down a totally different track. I had done intelligent work at a very young age and that changed things.

After early demob and a fascinating stint in the British embassy in Oslo, Y-station listener Pat clinched a university grant available to ex-service men and women. (Joanna was the only other Bletchley Girl who took advantage of this funding.) For Pat it was the first of three degrees.

> I was rather pleased that before the war my parents had said, 'We can't afford to send you to university,' but in the end I went to three of the top ones. I did meet a man I got very fond of, but he was going into the oil industry overseas and I couldn't see my desire to have a career fitting in with that plan at all.

Pat studied at St Andrews, Oxford and Harvard, before she landed a job as a journalist at the *Daily Mail*. 'The men were appalled that there was a female reporter!' It was the beginning of a stellar media career. Marriage didn't come until much later in 1968 when she was forty-four years old. Career girl Pat single-handedly bucked the prevailing postwar trend.

'Marriage is the aim, confessed or unconfessed, of the healthy, normal girl', *Woman* magazine pronounced in 1945 and the statistics suggest they were right. After the war, among civilian and service girls alike, there was an extraordinary matrimonial surge. In one of the great set pieces of the decade, former ATS girl, young Princess Elizabeth married her prince in Westminster Abbey on 20 November 1947; it was nearing the end of a record-breaking year which saw 401,210 couples tie the knot. Up and down the country bells tolled for the beginning of family life. Courtships were shorter and brides were younger than at any time between the wars. Only very occasionally did extenuating circumstance delay the nuptials.

'Oh didn't I mention it? Jim was already married. He had got married at the beginning of the war to a girl from a good Jewish family. It was a mistake from the start, they were totally unsuited.' Jim Rose, the distinguished airman and journalist Pamela intended to spend the rest of her life with, had, along with thousands of others, rushed headlong into marriage in 1939. He was already in the process of getting divorced when Pamela met him; in the meantime her own wedding would have to wait. 'In those days trying to get divorced was an absolute pantomime. Really it was a horrific affair.' Between the wars, the socially avant-garde increasingly accepted that marriage was not necessarily for life, but despite legal changes designed to facilitate divorce, 'proof' of adultery (or other severe misdemeanours)[1] was required before a couple could rid themselves of each other.

Pamela explains what happened next.

If you were a gentleman, even if it wasn't your fault you took the blame for the end of your marriage and had to go down to a

1. In 1937 Herbert's Act was passed, enabling divorce also for cruelty and wilful desertion after three years and insanity after five years.

Brighton hotel with a lady who you probably paid and it is presumed you chatted or played cards with her all night and then before the chambermaid brought you breakfast in the morning you nipped into bed together so she could give evidence that she'd seen you committing adultery.

Pamela stops and smiles. 'It is extraordinary really to think of it now.' Seventy years on, that Jim Rose, one of Bletchley's senior intelligence officers, slipped away for the weekend with a paid escort to be deliberately 'caught out' sounds almost too ludicrous to be true.

But MP Alan Herbert's 1930s satirical novel *Holy Deadlock* featuring a sympathetic young couple forced to concoct fictional reasons for getting divorced, is a reminder that things were very different then.

'I always thought how lucky the girl was who got to spend the night with Jim.' Irrespective of the circumstances Pamela was very much in love. 'I stayed on at the Park to tidy up until Christmas 1945. Jim went to London to do some work for the Air Ministry. I didn't mind. I was delighted I was finally going to get married to him. I much looked forward to it.'

The wedding ceremony took place in a registry office on the King's Road in February 1946 and Jim and Pamela began their married life in an attractive Georgian town house in London's Earls Court. It is in the same handsome four-storey home that Pamela shares her story nearly seventy years later.

Looking back, Pam admits that she was never particularly enamoured with life at the Park. A twenty-four-year-old actress, she had entered Bletchley reluctantly at the beginning of 1942, keen to return to the stage as soon as war ended. But her priorities changed again when she fell in love with Jim Rose. It was to be another sixty years before she returned to professional acting.

'Jim said, quite sensibly, "There is no point in getting married if you go back to acting because you will always be going out when I come in and that means the marriage won't last."' A highly intelligent woman, Pamela knows that the story of how she nearly rejected the demands of Bletchley Park for her acting career, only to sacrifice her dreams entirely four years later for married life, is surprising (even disappointing?) to contemporary female ears. But she has not been alive for ninety-six years without learning how to bridge the generation gap.

> I suppose I occasionally did have a sense of loss, but in those days it was more unusual to have a career of my sort and I did feel, quite rightly, that most of my friends who got married on the stage would get divorced and they did. I knew from the start I wanted to spend my life with Jim, I knew my life with him would be an interesting one and I thought you just can't have everything in life. So I gave up acting. I don't think I would have thought like that now. But one is conditioned by the way other people think and I was a product of my time, as we all are.

Muriel has kept the reference she was handed when she left Bletchley Park. Without giving any incriminating details away it confirms that she worked as a 'Temporary Woman Clerk, Grade II, from 27 April 1943 until 15 June 1945' for the Foreign Office. 'During this time her character and conduct were excellent and her duties were performed to our entire satisfaction.'

'Yep, it's good, innit?' Muriel grins, pleased that she had the foresight to keep her reference all these years. Today, amid the Bletchley furore, it counts for something, but back then it didn't occur to her to use it.

> I never worked again after Bletchley, my husband wouldn't let me. You see I married our landlord Mr Dindol's son. He came back from serving in Aden in 1945 all suntanned. We met at a local Bletchley dance in January 1946 and we was married at the end of the year. No, I didn't hang around. I was eighteen years

old and one month and all my married life I never wanted for anything.

She had kissed local lads during the war and she'd earned her own modest wage, but Bletchley Park was never more than a transitory phase, a quirky stage in Muriel's adolescent journey towards her ultimate destiny.

'He wore a flying jacket with his collar up, he looked like someone out of a film. He was good, he was the man for me.'

Ann has also kept her Bletchley job reference, and several others besides. Unlike Muriel she deliberately collected together a fistful of recommendations from Headington School and Oxford University as well as the Park at the end of the war. Ambitious Ann had her sights set on the Colonial Service. Today those same references are efficiently clipped into a leather-bound scrapbook. The most impressive is from her former boss, one-time head of Hut 6 and Principal in the Treasury, Stuart Milner-Barry.

> Miss Williamson was engaged on technical work which I should describe as high-grade routine. She proved herself very quick and keen with intelligence above the average. She was thoroughly composed and reliable in everything that she did and was fully capable of taking charge of the work of her room. She stood up well to rather exacting conditions of work – night work, working against time and so on.

Despite the lack of detail, no prospective employer could fail to be impressed. But Ann didn't get into the Colonial Office. 'They told me I was too young.' Her husband Angus objects and Ann agrees, 'Yes, perhaps it was also because I was a woman.' Determined to reapply, Ann found an interim job as a librarian at the Bodleian library. It was then, when she was killing time in Oxford, Ann met her future husband Angus. Suddenly the idea of an exciting job at the Colonial Office was no longer important.

Here Angus interrupts with loud good humour: 'Her career was not as important as my career was in my eyes, to be perfectly honest. And I had just got a job in the Scottish Education Department. We were feeling very optimistic about the future.'

The young couple got married when Angus graduated and moved to Edinburgh in 1948, Ann happy to forgo the prospect of a career in return for the ultimate trump card: Mr Right.

———— • ————

Although now considered a bastion for intelligent bluestocking women, Bletchley was no more a breeding ground for the (much) later Women's Liberation Movement than the rest of Britain's conscripted female workforce. Bit parts in the conveyor belt of code-breaking, most girls missed the camaraderie, not the secret work about which they never had been allowed to talk and still weren't. Only the Moller sisters were re-employed together postwar. Recognising a good team, Frank Birch sent the girls to London where (by now fluent English speakers) they proof-read Britain's official history of the naval war (minus any reference to Ultra or the role of Bletchley Park!) for the next two years. But it wasn't a career, rather another job until they found a suitable man. As Pamela so lucidly explains, the Bletchley Girls were products of their time; having dutifully and discreetly served King and country, those who were lucky enough to find appropriate men got married as quickly as they could, irrespective of their backgrounds. Austerity weddings were all the rage.

For Muriel the memory is vivid. 'I got wed in a synagogue on Egerton Road. My sister Anita had got married a year earlier so I borrowed her dress. She's tall and I'm short so Mother had to turn the hem up and do a bit of ruffing on the sleeves.' It didn't matter that clothing was still rationed; for girls who had endured wartime's utility fashion – in some cases a straight swap from school to military uniform – a wedding dress was a dream come true, irrespective of the fit. Christian Dior would infuriate the Board of Trade the following year with his New Look: flounce and hem, yards of silk and satin were nipped in at the waist and left to hang voluminously around the calf. However, for most girls it was simply a question of making do.

Ann's sight has faded but she still has fun poring over her wedding photos looking for the telltale signs: 'Yes see there! I sent it to the dry cleaners and hung it in the wardrobe and it mysteriously grew by nine inches. So on the wedding morning Mother had to get down on her hands and knees and tack it up.'

On closer inspection the hem of her borrowed wedding dress does look rather sorry for itself, but Ann, standing next to a strong-featured youthful Angus back in Oxford, is radiant. Aged twenty-three she had found her destiny.

Kathleen's mother got hold of a length of patterned satin, so her daughter had a 'proper white wedding dress with long sleeves and the prescribed row of covered buttons down the back'. Kathleen's 'Greek god newly flown down from Olympus' (John Kinmonth, a doctor in the Air Force) had won her heart with a stunning compliment: 'Did you know that your eyes have chrysanthemums in them?' After six months of courtship Kathleen and John got married in London's fashionable Holy Trinity Brompton Church in June 1946.

'No one seemed to think it was odd that two people who hardly knew each other should spend the rest of their lives together.'

Kathleen's best Park friend Rozanne had led the way five months earlier on the other side of the Mediterranean. The attractive parachutist Halsey Colchester, who'd astonished her with his premature proposal of marriage en route to Egypt, landed a job in the Secret Service upon arrival in Cairo. He was soon transferred to the same office as Rozanne. 'Then we saw much more of each other and very shortly we decided we were definitely going to get married as soon as possible! I was twenty-one when I met him and just twenty-two when we got married. People were young in those days. Lots of girls married at nineteen and that was normal.'

Ruth was just nineteen and still in uniform when she got married to an RAF squadron leader from Czechoslovakia. This time she wasn't going to wait for her mother's approval. 'My husband came over as a refugee before the war. He had beautiful amber eyes.' A Jewish man, her fiancé returned to his Czechoslovakian homeland before they got married in 1946 to confirm what he already suspected. Bar one sister, his entire family had been wiped out in the Holocaust. 'Everyone bears their crosses at the end of the war. I fell in love with his story and his eyes. I thought if he had a loving wife . . .' Ruth pauses and looks out through the window of her north London home. It is gently drizzling outside. 'I was going to make jam and have babies and love him. And he promised Mother he would look after me.'

Lady Jean was a seasoned twenty-six when she finally got married in 1947, eight long years after her presentation to the King.

'No, war did not excite a thirst in me to work. I was quite keen to settle down and get married.' Fearful of another TB attack, Lady Jean had returned from her 'terrific adventure' in India in 1945 and quickly supplemented it with a second: in an 'old banger of a car' she drove around war-scorched Europe with a friend. By the time she met John Fforde in 1947 she was a formidably independent woman, albeit one keen to find a husband.

> John was good-looking and very brave. I met him through my brother in London. He was a very good officer. But I suppose yes, in a way we hardly knew each other. Mother pre-empted the marriage because she was afraid of gossip.

After a traditional Arran wedding, Lady Jean began married life miles from her island home inside a cantonment in Palestine. (A little square of concrete with two windows on each side, 'it was the smallest house I had thought possible to live in.') Her new husband was head of the CID in the British-run Palestine Police Force and a prime target for Israeli terror tactics. 'We were hurled into an extremely dangerous situation and I knew nobody.'

But now a married woman, this time there was no early escape.

Of the fifteen women featured in this book, eleven were already married by 1950. They mirrored a nationwide trend. By 1951 just 22 per cent of women between the ages of twenty-five and twenty-nine were still single.

Spontaneous weddings were all the rage. Lady Jean was warned by her parents 'that I did not know him well enough or long enough', but like all young people I thought I knew best!' Rozanne admits that she was 'terribly lucky', the man she impulsively married turned out to be 'very nice'. And Cora laughs and explains, 'for the men we had to get married quickly, petting and kissing wasn't enough!'

After a six-year conflict, plunging into a lifelong relationship at breakneck speed was considered a risk worth taking. The young generation who had lived and fought through the war were impatient to embrace the moment and build their futures together. Few dwelt on the past. What was the point? Especially if you weren't allowed to talk about it.

The Baby Boomers

> I never wanted five children. I thought three was enough but I didn't say, 'I can't do this.' A doctor friend of mine offered to give me an abortion and I said, 'Good God no!' The house we lived in was terrible, no foundations, no running water. I had to cross a field to a standpipe with a jug every morning but when I look back I just seem to have accepted it. Plain acceptance.

After a year of marriage to Vernon Watkins, Gwen and her Welsh poet husband left Swansea and rented a wooden bungalow on the Gower Peninsular which opened straight out onto sea and sky. It was there that Gwen spent the next fifteen years raising five small children. There is black and white archive footage of the poet's wife feeding her offspring at an overflowing table;

biscuits, creamy milk, stripy crockery. Later repositioned by the fire, furiously darning a large blanket, she confidently proclaims to camera: 'I suppose you can say it is like being married to someone who all his life has a passionate love affair with another woman only it isn't another woman, in this case it is the muse.' Gwen shared her husband with his poetic craft. She took care of the home front while Vernon went to work in the bank every day before returning in the evening to contemplate and write. The glorious domestic chaos that sprang around this one-time bachelor immeasurably enriched his prose. Young Gwen was his saviour.

> Love, that in silence writes upon these eyes,
> The script of that sweet music her eyes bear,
> Whose light was born not, changes not, nor dies,
> But makes the living dumb, the dead aware.

By the time he died in 1967, Vernon was being considered for the next Poet Laureate. Bright, energetic, uncomplaining Gwen had served her man and her family, just as she had served her country before them. Friends made during those heady days of war in Buckinghamshire occasionally visited their bungalow in Wales; these were bright moments which demanded recollections and laughter. But Gwen's pithy books, including several on Vernon and his poet friends and one on Park life, would come much later. The postwar woman's primary role was in the home and Gwen with her large brood was no exception.

'Perhaps there was a feeling that one imbibed at that time. And contraception never seemed to work!' She laughs heartily and lingers over a picture of the oldest four playing in a tin perambulator. 'Don't they look divine? I do hope I had time to enjoy them.'

Rozanne was another mother of five.

It must have been all the killing during the war. I suppose that was in the background of one's mind. I started a baby within a year of marriage. Then I had a boy every three years, except for Chloe, she came much later when I was forty-two.

But war alone doesn't explain the phenomenal baby boom that took place after the Second World War. There was no equivalent birth rate surge after the First World War when fatalities were considerably higher. Post 1945, other factors came into play: vastly improved pre- and antenatal care, family allowances, free health care, green belts and new-build houses with surplus bedrooms, a general rise in the standard of living and (crucially) a glut of young wives who were used to working hard for small allowances and little thanks.

With her husband rising fast through the ranks of the Secret Service, Rozanne was not in Britain to benefit from the brand new National Health Service. ('We lived in Egypt, Palestine, Turkey, Switzerland, Greece, France. All over the place, it was great fun.') But she is quick to observe that unlike her mother she gave birth in hospitals, not at home. Also in stark contrast to her mother, Christabel Medhurst, Rozanne relied much less on nannies. She brought up her own children.

'My mother hardly saw us till we were six, but I loved little babies. I liked having them around me. Fortunately my husband did too!'

This new generation of women were 'hands on' parents. Encouraged by the liberal views of Dr Benjamin Spock, the public's attitude towards motherhood changed unrecognisably in the 1950s. The disciplinarian mantra of the past gave way to the belief that what children enjoyed was good for them, and if that meant more of Mother's love then so be it. Meanwhile across Britain the 1,500-plus nurseries that opened during the war closed and domestic help became increasingly hard to come by. The message was clear: a father went out to work as the breadwinner and a 'Good Mother was supposed to stay at home happily baking while her children played at her feet'. A large tranche of 1950s mothers were the first generation of middle-class, educated women to look after their children almost exclusively by themselves and the Bletchley Girls were no exception.

Cora had three children, ditto Joanna, Muriel and Doris. Kathleen and Ann both had four. Ann smiles knowingly. 'I was very occupied with four children in eight years.'

Her husband Angus joins in. 'Four is a lot of children, yes! But everybody was having lots. It was almost fashionable and part of the generally optimistic building of the new world.'

But the drudgery that accompanied the orchestration of numerous children was unavoidable. Doris, the younger Moller sister, who married a local Bedfordshire man in 1950, equates small children with 'very hard work'. It was so different from her mother's day with maids and smart parties on the Continent. 'But there was no choice. I had to give up my job in a bank anyway when I got married because of the marriage bar.' Just as she had in the war, Doris, along with millions of other women, simply got on with it.

Wartime Britain had actively encouraged married women to work, but post 1945 there was a return to the status quo: a lack of equal pay and the retention of marriage bars in numerous companies ensured the patriarch thrived in the conventional 1950s. Meanwhile in the home even smart girls had to find their domestic feet. Kathleen quickly realised that 'John's life as a surgeon and the care of his patients undoubtedly came first.'

'How I fed us remains a mystery, as John had no interest in cooking and left it all to me.' Time for herself was hard to find. She had always belonged to a choir, even at Bletchley, but once she became a mother Kathleen gave up singing. It 'coincided with the children's bathtime. John never came back home as early as that. Why didn't he just insist that we had extra help on those evenings? Or why didn't I, come to that?' Perhaps, like so many wartime women, she was not accustomed to putting herself or her own needs first.

Her daughter Margy nods. Brought up in the 1960s and now a successful film maker with three children of her own, Margy and her generation would enjoy empowerment and liberation that their mothers never even dreamt of.

Female conscription did not lead to a feminist charge against the barricades; quite the reverse.

There was no de facto 'women's liberation' during the 1950s, nor a prize equivalent to their enfranchisement in 1918. Girls invariably re-entered the domestic sphere. But during the Second World War they had enjoyed a degree of independence and easy companionship and that counted for something.

Cora is certain that her stint as a Bletchley Wren emboldened her subsequent behaviour. 'The war made me. Before that I was very very young.' It was a defiant trip to Canada post war that forced the man who is now her husband of sixty-four years to make up his mind about their relationship. On Cora's return from visiting dishy cousin Doug, Philip Jarman promptly went down on bended knee.

'The best decision of my life!' Cora giggles at her handsome husband. They are still in love. Not all were so lucky.

Plunging into marriage post 1945 the war girls had expectations of their relationships that previous generations did not share. After years of restraint, even the sex was supposed to be good. Some couples did not survive the strain. In 1955 the Morton Commission on the State of Divorce concluded: 'Women are no longer content to endure the treatment which in past times their inferior position obliged them to suffer. They expect of marriage that it shall be an equal partnership; and rightly so.'

By 1954 it was estimated that one in fifteen marriages would end in divorce (compared with one in sixty in 1937 and one in 500 in 1911). The laws lagged behind the reality and not everyone was prepared to wait. Lady Jean tolerated loneliness and danger in Palestine and Sierra Leone where she brought up her one son Charles, but ever the individual she struggled as John's dutiful colonial wife. His infidelity was the last straw and the proof she needed to leave the marriage. In 1957 Lady Jean blazed a trail for other likeminded women and divorced her husband. Against the odds, she escaped from her marriage just as she escaped from Bletchley Park.

Perhaps her noble birth gave her the courage to walk outside the lines? 'Maybe.' She won't say more. Either way, young Lady Jean was one of life's exceptions. And sitting in her attractive island pile, aged ninety-three, surrounded by her own paintings, having just reissued a second copy of her memoir, it's clear she still is.

Ruth's marriage lasted for thirty-nine years. 'But over time our very different backgrounds caused difficulties. It was the same for lots of couples who met in the war. So I tried learning new skills to become a more useful wife, and for my own development.'

Ruth goes on to list an astonishing string of accomplishments that complemented her work as a wife and a mother of two boys: award-winning gardening, teaching, pottery, sewing, charity shows, cooking. Then, suddenly, in 1978 their beloved son was killed in a road accident in America; the tragedy ended the relationship. Ruth and her husband were granted a judicial separation in 1985.

'I suppose if our son hadn't died we might've stuck together. My husband, he felt the pain he suffered over the Holocaust all over again. And I suffered too, terribly.' The words hang in the air. A proud upright woman, Ruth is a product of a pre-war upbringing. Despite the extenuating circumstances, for her the separation stands out as a failure in an otherwise exemplary life. 'Nice girls didn't get divorced,' she says and gives me a wry smile.

Early on in their marriage her husband said it would be better if they both earned a wage.

Keen to pull her weight, Ruth returned to work in 1948. She wasn't alone. If two million women left the workplace immediately after the war, by the 1950s 22 per cent of wives had jobs that supplemented their husbands' incomes. There was plenty to spend the extra money on. In the 1950s Britain was bedazzled by mod cons (Hoovers, televisions and twin-tub washing machines, for starters) not to mention rising house prices.

Ruth took a while to find her feet. 'First of all I worked in a primary school, I didn't like that, and then in an import-export firm in Barnet.' One job in particular stood out.

We decided to open a laundrette in Temple Fortune. I liked that. My husband would come at night and look after the machines. I thought it was symbolic in a way. During the war RAF men had tended the Bombes at night; in the same way my husband serviced the washing machines. And there was me sitting watching the drums go around and around, twelve in a row, just as I had watched the Bombe drums go around and around in the war.

Although unarticulated, memories of her high-tempo war work didn't go away; they were buried deep in the fabric of Ruth's identity. But she wasn't tempted to tell anyone; a young woman with two children and challenging husband, in the 1950s she was desperately trying to make a go of the future. What good could possibly come of dwelling on the past?

16

The End Game

'Adjusting to the postwar years was difficult.'
After Bletchley and then the Pentagon, for Charlotte life felt flat. There were familial duties with her tired parents in Ludlow and a government-funded secretarial course in London ('a dreadful winter – everywhere had frozen up, and the food and fuel shortage had not eased'). With no husband on the horizon, Charlotte had to make her own way in the adult world but options for women were limited and she had to contend with an additional obstacle.

> Due to my obligations under the Official Secrets Act, I was not allowed to tell any prospective employer what I had been doing for the previous four or five years. I went for one administrative job and they specifically asked what I did during the war. 'I can't tell you,' I said. Well that wasn't quite right so I didn't get the position.

Her opaque Park reference did not always suffice.
It was a Bletchley contact who got her a job in the local grammar school and then there was an administrative post with a window manufacturer. These were the limbo years; how could anything match her extraordinary wartime experiences? In her memoir it reads as a relief when Charlotte (again through a Bletchley colleague), eventually joined the Territorial Army in 1955. A model soldier, she had finally returned to uniform and soon accepted a full-time officer post.

> My time at Bletchley, Washington and the Army had given me the skills to communicate and engage with people from all backgrounds

with respect and compassion. It is all those experiences that made me good at my job and I never forgot the value of discretion.

Without a husband and children to distract her, and keenly focused on a renewed military career, Charlotte had more reason than most to dwell on what had happened during the war. But she never breathed a word, not even to the musical mother whom she adored. 'That saddens me terribly. She was a wonderful woman.' Mrs Vine-Stevens died not knowing the most important piece in the jigsaw of her daughter's life.

'I was shattered when she died.' But 'life does have to go on, we have no choice'. And for Charlotte there was a silver lining. 'I met a lovely man, Alfred Webb, and in 1970 we got married, those were happy times for me.' Although her husband died only nine years later, Charlotte had a chance to share her secret war with him when the story seeped out in the mid-1970s. 'It was very difficult to talk about it to begin with. When I did tell Alfred, he said, "That's funny, I was serving at a camp just down the road from Bletchley." But he didn't seem that interested.'

And there her story might well have ended had Charlotte, like so many other accomplished women, slipped quietly into invisible old age, taking her stories with her.

Secret Keepers

The man Rozanne married in Egypt 1946, Halsey Colchester, quickly rose through the ranks of the Secret Service to eventually become head of personnel for MI6. Moving with her husband every four years to a different international hotspot, Rozanne remained on the peripheries of a secret world. A stint in Palestine was quickly followed by intense Cold War paranoia; even Kim Philby flitted across their path.

'He was awfully nice, that was the awful thing about him.' For Rozanne, half a century on, the anecdotes emerge as chinks of light and memory. With a husband who was also restricted by the Official Secrets Act there were stories she never fully knew, but Halsey did permit Rozanne a vague idea of his work. It wasn't such a risk; after all he was well aware that his wife knew how to keep a secret.

'I told him I worked at a place called BP. That was all at the time. But later when he asked more about it I did tell . . .' Here Rozanne looks up, perhaps momentarily uncertain as to whether she should continue. Forty years have passed since Bletchley's secrets were cracked open on the world stage, but the Park's veterans are still feted for their astonishing three-decade silence. Rozanne very much considers herself one of them; however 'my husband was in the Secret Service so it was obvious he could hold onto a secret'. She tentatively continues, 'So I did tell him, I did say I was code-breaking,' and then adds quickly, 'but I didn't tell him any details about it. No sections or what I was doing or anything. I never told anyone else, just my husband.'

Such was the level of secrecy among Bletchley veterans that even this innocuous indiscretion marks Rozanne out as a rare exception.

Gwen is adamant:

> No, it was no trouble to keep BP secret after the war. We had been indoctrinated, and when we left we were warned that we had signed the Official Secrets Act and were still obligated to keep it. I didn't even talk about the work to my husband; we only talked about BP friends.

She had no problem keeping Bletchley's secret. It helped that her husband Vernon had experienced the same confidential environment.

Pamela is equally sanguine. She and Jim had met at the Park, but she didn't feel tempted to look back.

> Jim and I didn't talk about our work at Bletchley. No. Not even when we were at that Park together. You weren't allowed to. And it simply wasn't that interesting. It was no longer part of our life. What would we have said? 'Do you remember the night the *Scharnhorst* escaped?'

Even Pat, on track to become a journalist and television producer, kept shtum. 'My sister also signed the OSA. She was a cipher officer in Cairo but we didn't talk to each other about what we did. Never.' And after a while it didn't matter so much; Pat moved from the *Daily Mail* to Granada before settling at the BBC, 'so BP was not the only thing that happened in my life'.

Muriel, a young wife and mother of three, never worked again after the Park, but that didn't make a difference to her resolve.

> No, I never felt tempted to talk. It was so hush hush. I just never would blab. You just didn't and you couldn't and you wouldn't, it was imprisoned in your mind. Unbelievable, incredible when you think about it.

In our contemporary era of WikiLeaks and social media exposés, where the issues of transparency and disclosure controversially posture as the guardians of liberty and democracy, the unquestioning acceptance with which BP's staff kept their thirty-years' silence is staggering. It has been described by one veteran as a 'phenomenon that may be unparalleled in history'. Joanna is quite sure modern girls would not manage to 'keep their mouths shut'.

In 1941, during his only visit to the Park, Churchill described Bletchley as 'the goose that laid the golden egg but never cackled' and significantly, after the war, although the self-evident reason for keeping the Park's work walled off from public view had disappeared, the Joint Intelligence Committee (JIC) did not believe those same well-trained workers would breach their silence. They were not disappointed.

'Men of status' on the other hand, eager to leave a chronicle of their wartime experiences and achievements, posed a far greater problem. It was Churchill, not the Bletchley Girls, who nearly gave the game away. Out of office in 1948 and working on his six-volume history of the Second World War, the former Prime Minister declared he would 'find it difficult to complete his book without including at some point statements which implied that we were able to break codes and ciphers of enemy powers'. But he was given little choice in the matter and 'eventually succumbed to the "strongest possible appeals"; Ultra was completely removed from volume I'. The war leader was silenced.

No such arguments had to be pulled out to convince Bletchley's predominantly female workforce to keep quiet. The products of a deferential patriarchal society who went on to be, in Gwen's words, 'indoctrinated' at the Park, did what they were told. It wasn't always easy. Again Rozanne is honest. Dashing up the aisle in Egypt and throwing herself into motherhood in Palestine did not suppress her need for recognition outside the family. Bletchley had taught Rozanne she was an individual in her own right, but as far as her secret past was concerned, it could go no further than Halsey.

'My mother-in-law asked me what I did during the war. I said, "Oh something to do with government offices." She obviously thought I was a bit of a . . .' Rozanne stops here and her hand wafts past her face; it would be tactless to articulate what her mother-in-law really thought. Either way she left Rozanne bubbling with frustration. 'I wished I had joined the forces so I could really say I was doing something. I had no war story! No war story!'

But although domestic niggles such as Rozanne's were not uncommon, there was far less pressure on the Bletchley Girls than on their male equivalents to chalk up an impressive war story. By the 1950s, Britain, tottering on the precipice of a post-imperial abyss, distracted itself from an uncertain future with a nostalgic diet of military films. *The Cruel Sea*, *The Dam Busters*, *Reach for the Sky*, *Sink the Bismarck!*, *Bridge on the River Kwai* all reinforced the idea of a heroic masculine war.

Women weren't in the picture and most didn't expect to be.

I never really thought about getting attention. No one seemed very interested in what I did during the war. We did see it more as a man's war. On the whole, service women were not in immediate danger whereas men were going into danger.

Pat is candid; there was little incentive for women to talk about their war. And if anyone asked, at least Pat had tangible proof of her work; unlike civilian Rozanne she had been a Wren with officer status. But any further questions drew a blank. Her discretion was assisted by the Park's rigorous working practices, which had permitted no unnecessary knowledge and cordoned off staff in separate units. Before the 1970s Pat had little clue as to the value of her Y-station duties, and in this she wasn't alone. In a contemporary world where Bletchley Park has become a touchstone for popular culture it is hard to imagine how little the diaspora of anonymous veterans actually knew. Never entrusted with the bigger picture, very few Bletchley Girls had any idea just how significant their secret work had been.

Pat admits

Yes. It was surprising to hear that Bletchley had achieved such great things because at the time we never got any feedback. We sent material to Station X but it was one-way traffic. We didn't know how important we had been.

The impact of the Park's Ultra rich intelligence on the Allied war effort is now common knowledge, but before the 1970s some of Bletchley's staff weren't even aware they had been involved in a codebreaking mission. As the JIC had predicted, the Bletchley Girls didn't 'cackle', nor did they realise just how much they had to cackle about.

Revelations

Lady Jean had been extremely busy. The upstairs-downstairs era was over, but somehow her late parents' large sporting estate and castle on Arran had to be managed.

'People did not want to serve others any more. I think perhaps if I could have found the staff I would have kept the castle.' Instead she handed it over to the National Trust for Scotland and moved into neighbouring Strabane, the handsome sandstone house she lives in today. There she established a vibrant garden and threw herself into building up and trialling her Isle of Arran pointers. For Lady Jean this was a happy time; she was finally in charge of her own destiny on beloved Arran after years of dislocation and colonial living. Contact with a couple of Bletchley friends, including a champagne session at Claridge's with Jean Campbell-Harris (Baroness Trumpington by 1980), were her only reminders of the dull and distant Park.

Never a fan, she gave the place little thought, until quite suddenly an unexpected news item caught her attention.

'I was horrified when I saw there was a book on Bletchley Park! Horrified!' Lady Jean's voice peaks in indignation. 'I rang up Jean Trumpington. I said, "Do you know there is a book out?"'

'She said, "Oh yes, it is allowed now."'

Lady Jean tosses her arms up at the memory of this extraordinary *volte-face*. How could it be? They had signed the Official Secrets Act – surely that was the end of the matter?

Pamela and her husband Jim were equally astounded.

My memory is that there was a man who wrote a book about how we broke the code. I think one was quite horrified to start with that they had given away the fact we had broken the codes. We were shocked that that had happened. Yes.

Pat concurs. 'When the books started coming out in the seventies I was appalled! I thought nobody was supposed to write about BP.' The emotion with which this sudden revelation is remembered by so many women suggests a sense of betrayal – that they had kept their word only to be undercut by someone else.

Charlotte nods.

I had a friend from the Park, Leslie Stuart-Taylor. She was in the camp bed next to me but I still don't know what she did. Years afterwards when the veil of secrecy had been lifted I went to meet her and even then she wouldn't tell me what she'd been doing. She died with her secret.

Charlotte stops for a moment to consider what she has said before continuing. 'Maybe to have spoken would have been to undermine her life to that point. It took me a long time before I could speak about it.'

No one informed the disparate code-breaking community they had been freed from the bonds of secrecy. No one knew who they all were. Bletchley Park's achievements did not suddenly break across a nation's television screens – that would come later. Instead the story came out in November 1974 via Group Captain F. W. Winterbotham's revelatory book, *Ultra*. Since the late 1960s the Cabinet Secretary had been having increasing difficulty trying to keep unwanted disclosures by ambitious writers and journalists at bay. Fortunately, time and advanced technology had diminished the importance of 1940s code-breaking confidentiality and with several unauthorised references already in the public domain the Government hedged its bets and permitted Winterbotham to publish his first-hand account.

On 7 November 1974, in the Review section of *The Times*, a short article appeared under the title 'Enigma Variations, the Ultra Secret'. 'It hardly seems fair,' began the commentary.

> Last year John Masterman revealed that we controlled most of the German spies in Britain during 1939–45 and now it emerges that by obtaining the 'Enigma' coding machine, we were able to read most of their radio signals too.

Back then nobody could have guessed the momentum the Bletchley story would eventually gain. Not all the veterans even picked up on Winterbotham's groundbreaking book.

However former Bombe operator Ruth Bourne had always been an avid reader. Astonished by the news, she immediately 'got hold of the book and read it and then I told my husband, "This is what I did during the war." And he said, "Oh that's interesting," and straight after that he asked me, "What's for tea?"'

Y-station listener Betty fared even worse. Her first husband Reg had died prematurely in 1955; it was to her second, Walter, that she mentioned, 'I did something in Army intelligence, I worked for signals.' 'And I got laughed at. He scoffed!' Even Kathleen's husband, a successful surgeon who she had met while still in uniform, was nonplussed.

'I told him what I had been doing and immediately the subject was changed back again to medicine. He was not a bit interested in what had been going on. He grunted!'

Kathleen tips her head gently to one side and fixes me with her blue eyes. 'We were so used to no talking or talking about nothing that one could hardly talk at all.' She had been in the Index Section of Hut 3; like Pamela she used her German to translate scraps of information on to card. This job ('on the whole one would call it very dull, yes') hardly seemed to fit into the sensational series of 'what ifs' that Winterbotham's book threw up. Had it not been for Ultra might we have lost the war?

Kathleen didn't know. She didn't even know what Ultra was. And even if she had, as a well-brought-up woman she would not have blown her trumpet. 'Our generation doesn't know how to show off,' she explains simply. Is it presumptuous to wonder if she is referring to just the women?

At face value the Bletchley husbands' lack of interest in their wives' wartime achievements appears astonishing, but over the last forty years much has changed. In the 1970s the wartime narrative remained almost exclusively male. It would be another thirty years before the Queen unveiled a 22ft bronze statue in Whitehall to commemorate 'the vital work done by seven million women in World War Two'.

Meanwhile, one book lauding the achievements of (predominately male) corduroy number-crunchers in Buckinghamshire could not compare with the heroic feats of Britain's young men. John Kinmonth, Kathleen's husband, had carried out emergency surgery in a London basement with the Blitz raging overhead, and his brother Maurice had been in a Japanese prisoner of war camp. How could indexing in Buckinghamshire compete with that?

Ruth Bourne's Czech husband was an engineer in the RAF. 'Twice he was mentioned in dispatches for having the highest availability of flying aircraft. He was very good at his job. He serviced the planes all over North Africa, Tunisia, Palestine. He lived the war.' Ruth meanwhile tended an unheard-of machine in a cement block in the suburbs of London.

Seventeen-year-old Cora had toiled over inexplicable Fish codes right inside Bletchley's nerve centre (never 'cod or haddock') but the first series of revelations about Ultra left her none the wiser about her own small contribution. However, at least she could tell her husband where she had been working. And Philip could tell her. Still gregarious at ninety-one, he takes up his own story over lunch in their Haslemere home.

> I was in Signals Intelligence so I also signed the Official Secrets Act and I operated an Enigma machine. I took the first one into Burma in 1943. Part of my joining instruction was to see that this Enigma machine went with me. It was carried by a coolie on his head but it was so heavy he couldn't lift it off! In the end three people helped him.

Cora nods and smiles proudly at her husband.

When I ask her about her husband, Muriel laughs. 'He wasn't bothered about my work at Bletchley. He just wasn't! I am annoyed with him now, poor man, and he has been dead ten years! But that is how it was. He was a bit Victorian minded.' Mr Dindol's son, brought up in the village of Bletchley, had no interest in his wife's early achievements. And back then nor did Muriel. 'When the time came around in the 1970s it was too late. People were not interested. BP had gone to nothing, really. There was a period when there was just nothing.' Leased by a variety of government departments, primarily the General Post Office, the integrity of Bletchley Park had not been respected. Its modern streamlined successor, GCHQ, had long since moved to Cheltenham. Muriel was right: in the 1970s Bletchley Park was just another anonymous war site, perched precariously on the edge of a rapidly expanding Milton Keynes.

———•———

It is ironic that in the 1970s Muriel considered the arrival of Bletchley Park into the nation's consciousness 'too late', when it was in fact another twenty years before the Bletchley site and story really became a national phenomenon. Arguably in the 1970s it was too early for such a transformation, not too late. For a start, not enough was known. Only in October 1977, to coincide with the opening of the Public Records Office in Kew, was the first consignment of 70,000 intelligence documents relating to Ultra made available. Until then the trickle of books and commentary had relied on memory and conjecture. It would be another two years before Bletchley veteran and official historian of British history in the Second World War, Harry Hinsley, made the extraordinary claim that the Bletchley Park's code-breaking harvest had truncated the conflict by 'not less than two years' and probably four. Bletchley's legacy was slowly gaining ground among academics and journalists; history was being rewritten. Meanwhile most veterans, once they got over the shocking breach of confidentiality, simply carried on with their busy daily lives. In Gwen's words: 'that the former code-breakers were now released from restrictions on discussing their work made no difference to most of us'.

A Celebrity Finish

I am extremely pleased about Bletchley Park. Not very much happens to you when you are eighty-eight, believe me! You are almost an also-ran, invisible. You don't go dancing, you never get asked out in the evening and when your children grow up . . .

Ruth pauses to regroup her thoughts. 'Honestly you have to be extremely accepting and psychologically strong to get old, so to me, working at Bletchley is my second life.' With a smile, she adds, 'It's as if I died and was resurrected.'

It is the summer of 2014, forty years since the first Ultra story broke in the press. And during the last two decades Ruth, perhaps more than any other Bletchley Girl, has painstakingly relived her own history for the benefit of public consumption. Once a bright teenager doing what she was told in a outstation near London, she is now an authority on the Bombe machine and the history of the Park.

Her knowledge is encyclopaedic and her reputation at Bletchley Park's thriving heritage site impeccable. Ruth is a celebrity. Pop her into Google and there she is joshing with the Queen and Prince Philip over an Enigma machine, talking on YouTube about the perils of working night shifts and smiling out from a commemorative Bletchley Park stamp.

Her rising stock (and 'resurrection') is intimately linked to the recent rebirth of the Bletchley Park estate. 'The rebuilding of Bletchley is hugely significant to me. I have been there since the start. I was the first veteran who was a guide.'

Ruth is woven into the fabric of two very different Parks; one the secret hub of Britain's extraordinary code-breaking efforts and the other a museum that celebrates the ingenious and laborious efforts of thousands of men and women during the Second World War. The latter almost didn't exist. It was in the early 1990s when the sale of the tatty Buckinghamshire estate with its random clutch of huts and blocks was mooted; the prime location on the edge of Milton Keynes made the defunct Park a valuable commodity. But by then, a full eighteen years after the first secret revelations, the seed of Bletchley's legacy had been planted in the nation's popular imagination. This was the hallowed site where Britain did more than outsmart the enemy – we used our eccentric abilities to save lives, shorten the war and pave the way for an extraordinary computerised age. A clutch of veterans and interested parties grouped together to form the Bletchley Park Trust, and the estate was saved.

'I went to a very good play about Turing called "Breaking the Code". It was excellent.' Actress Pamela sampled one of Bletchley's earliest reincarnations in popular culture. Hugh Whitemore's 1986 award-winning play was soon adapted into a BBC documentary. The extraordinary narrative had started to grow beyond the broadsheets and official histories. Bletchley Park, with its ingenious homosexual hero, gave the nation an alternative war story that resonated with a technically savvy modern generation. The preservation of the Park a few years later was the vital next step on Bletchley's ascent into Britain's A-list of stellar wartime achievements; now the code-breaking phenomenon had a home.

'At first there was just a trickle of people and we were only open on a Saturday and Sunday.' But by 2012 Ruth was helping to herd over 120,000 annual visitors; here was a Bletchley Girl to tell the public how it really was.

Ann shakes her head. 'It's unbelievable. The interest has blossomed. So many people say, "Oh are you the Bletchley person!" Don't they?' She turns to her husband Angus for affirmation.

'Yes, yes and I am very happy that it should have all come out. Am I pleased for Ann? Of course I am!'

Angus, the proud possessor of the Military Cross after liberating a small town in Holland, knows that in the twenty-first century nothing can compete with a Bletchley story, especially one from Hut 6.

Across the carpeted floor in front of Ann are a series of newspaper articles and magazine clippings all featuring her wartime story. 'After one lecture I gave in Edinburgh a man came up and said, "Can I shake your hand? I want to shake the hand of someone who worked at BP." He was a medical doctor!'

'It has given her a new lease of life. She is now a semi-celebrity. It is exhilarating!' Angus beams and a picture of the Queen stares down at him from the mantelpiece. 'It's rather nice isn't it? You automatically get one if you've been married for sixty years.'

Once her four children were in school Ann, a formidably bright woman, worked as a voluntary marriage guidance counsellor. Fascinated by the subject she returned to university in 1980 and spent several years researching the impact of divorce and separation on family life. She has written numerous books on the subject – her texts are still recommended reading for contemporary students – but it is her eighteen months at Bletchley Park not her seminal academic research that have transformed her old age.

> It has been a fillip at the end of my life. Suddenly to have risen in importance, to go from being a nobody to a somebody. A whole past that nobody was interested in and suddenly lots of people are. It's very strange.

This charming couple recognise the surge in interest couldn't have been better timed. 'We are both disabled and we don't get out much, so to have people come in to see us is great.'

But the recent hype is not perhaps as strange as Ann imagines. By 1999 the Park's narrative was again recast by a successful Channel 4 documentary series, *Station X*; the accompanying book was a bestseller. Only a couple of years later, Robert Harris's fictional novel *Enigma* was reincarnated as a Hollywood blockbuster. Kate Winslet played Bletchley Girl Hester Wallace.

Not all the real Bletchley Girls approved. 'Yes I saw *Enigma*, it was terribly unlike Bletchley, entirely.' Rozanne pulls a face of mock surprise. 'They wandered around and took pieces of paper home, but you wouldn't have dreamt of doing that! I remember thinking, "Heavens!"'

Her friend Pamela agrees.

> It was rather a ridiculous film. It said that women were badly treated. I never felt that at all. Yes the more menial tasks were

done by women but that is because young men were properly fighting unless they had very special skills.

However, if the artistic licence afforded by directors and writers doesn't always meet with the approval of veterans, their cumulative effect on the public's imagination is undeniable. Fiction has blended with fact and the code-breaking story gets richer with each retelling (2014's pending blockbuster *The Imitation Game* starring Benedict Cumberbatch as protagonist Alan Turing is a case in point).

Meanwhile the precious band of survivors, the last living link to that secret past, is dwindling fast.

Less than 10 per cent of Bletchley's original workforce are still alive, and most of them are women. Ann shouldn't be surprised by the recent attention. She is a member of an exclusive club. There are very few veterans left to tell the real tale.

Not every veteran wants to tell that tale. After I spent the day on Arran and having heard (and read) her story, Lady Jean's initial reticence made sense. I had to concede Bletchley Park featured as no more than a rather sorry blip in an extraordinary life. Her stout refusal to romanticise the Park makes her testimony all the more powerful.

Pamela, steady and wise, was also keen to resist hyperbole and nostalgia.

'There is no doubt about it, we were well protected, comfortable and properly fed. We don't need to be glorified.' And then almost as an afterthought she adds: 'I think the Enigma machines should be at the Imperial War Museum not Bletchley.' Although she met her husband there, Pamela has never accorded the Park venerated status. As a couple their interests lay elsewhere and after Jim Rose died in 1999 Pamela returned to her first love.

'A friend said to me, "You can't just sit around for the rest of your life!" so I took up acting again.' Aged eighty-three, sixty years after Bletchley's demands forced Pamela to relinquish her youthful ambition, she finally landed a part on London's West End stage. The play was *Lady Windermere's Fan*.

'I loved it! It was also very frightening. At the time I had a great load of grief to bear because I loved my husband very much and there is nothing like fear for driving out every other emotion.'

Still devoted to her dear friend Pamela, Rozanne has a very different view on the Park's place in history. An enthusiastic romantic, for Rozanne, Bletchley will always represent the high noon of her youth and with characteristic zeal she has embraced all that the media attention has had to offer. The war feature in the *Guardian* was just the beginning; there has also been a stint on a Bletchley-themed episode of BBC1's *Masterchef* and recently she's been asked to appear in so many wartime documentaries her son jokes, 'There is a television van parked permanently outside the house!'

Rozanne is enjoying the moment, but her casual quip – 'I had to wait for it, I'm nearly in the box!' – is a reminder that the fleeting present should not distort the past; like all the other Bletchley Girls, Rozanne's work went unrecognised for most of her life.

'It was very important for her.' Kathleen's daughter Margy reels off a list of her mother's Bletchley exploits that span the last decade.

> First she met the Duke of Kent, he's the patron of Bletchley, and then it was Prince Charles and Camilla, wasn't it? And there was the Queen and Prince Philip, that was in 2011. Oh yes and she was given a lunch and sat at the top table with the head of GCHQ – that was a very big thing.

Kathleen smiles as photos and chatter featuring royalty and recently erected war memorials swirl around her. Margy takes time to again emphasise how important this recognition has been for Kathleen. The daughter of a formidable admiral and the wife of a surgeon, finally she has had her own moment in the sun and thoroughly enjoyed it.

Bold Gwen speaks for more than herself when she emails: 'To talk about oneself to an interested listener is among the most pleasurable occupations known to man (or more likely to woman).' It turns out when given half a chance the Bletchley Girls could show off after all. And about time too.

Together, old friends Rozanne and Kathleen loved exploring the site with their families trying to identify former huts. Cora took husband Philip on a weekend jaunt to Milton Keynes and enjoyed tutting at the inaccurate Wren's uniform ('In their mock-up room they had a gored skirt with panels but in fact we wore plain straight skirts!') and Muriel found herself wielding a red plastic folder at the head of an impromptu gaggle of star-struck tourists. But Gwen hasn't returned recently. Her husband Vernon died years ago in 1967, and the only subsequent visit she made to Buckinghamshire was a bitter disappointment.

> F Block has been razed to the ground. BP is now a kind of theme park. Where once we heard talk such as we shall never hear again – brilliant, witty, sparkling and always memorable – now, for us who went there when we were young, there is silence.

For this cerebral woman the memories cannot be found in haunts that no longer boast their former occupants. Instead the poet's wife has honoured the extraordinary memories of her war in words. *Cracking the Luftwaffe Codes* is the story of a young girl from Bournemouth whose wartime work changed her life forever.

———◆———

The current Bletchley craze has touched every veteran differently, but none is impervious to its impact. Most are flattered or at least intrigued by the level of interest. Former Colossus Wren Joanna has just zoomed into BBC1's *One* show on her mobility scooter.

'Every time you use your phone or your baby computer in your hand you are actually using exactly the same things as part of Colossus. It is still an amazing thing!'

Later she laughs out loud over her new-found celebrity status. 'It's all a bit ridiculous isn't it, really!'

For others the change has come through newly forged relationships. Georgette married an American and still resides in Texas, but I eventually get to meet her in England's Northampton. The ninety-four-year-old, ebullient with bright blue eyes and a glossy head of hair, is thoroughly enjoying her trip. Every year she stays with her sister Doris and together they attend a reunion at the Park.

'We've got new friends there now, ones who we didn't even know during the war! It's great, I'm known at Bletchley.'

Then Doris laughs. 'Don't take any notice of my sister if she says she was a cryptographer. We were decoders of messages in Italian. I know I am degrading myself a little bit but you didn't have to be very intelligent!'

Sometimes the attention sparks jealousies; a couple of the Bletchley Girls quietly confide in me that their contemporaries snipe over the extensive press coverage the Park now receives. Muriel shrugs. She doesn't believe Bletchley's legacy is over-hyped. 'The Park means a lot to me, I know I was young but whatever I did was important.' A gold commemorative badge shines on her dark jersey. 'It's nice isn't it?' A telltale blue lapel pin is also in evidence when Muriel finally puts on her coat after our four-hour chat in Starbucks. The gold badges issued by GCHQ, with 'We Also Served' inscribed on the reverse, weren't given to veterans until 2009. For some (Pamela, Ann), they didn't mean much. But others pushed for their right to wear a badge.

'Via my MP I wrote letters.' As a young girl Ruth had always loved wearing medals on her gym tunic; for her it mattered 'that the people of Bletchley hadn't got anything'. She received her badge five years ago but others have only just been recognised. Remote Y-station listener Betty Gilbert discovered she was an official Bletchley Park veteran very recently.

I went to the Park for the first time a few weeks ago. I got my salutation and my badge. I always said, 'All I want is a thank you for what I did.' I take nothing away from the code-breakers but they couldn't have done it without us, and finally I've got that thank you!

A sense of belonging, public recognition, a place to call their own, the opportunity to meet significant public figures: there are numerous reasons why Bletchley's impact on these women's lives has once again been both unexpected and transformative. Old age rarely yields such invigorating surprises.

———•———

Charlotte pulls the door of her white Hyundai to and straps herself in.

'Yes I think tonight did go well!' she says, before adding with a twinkle: 'It seems I have become something of a celebrity! And I must say I am rather enjoying it.' Only last month she was busy meeting the Duchess of Cambridge, Kate Middleton, and now Charlotte has just finished yet another very successful lecture; together we are driving back from Bromsgrove to her bungalow in Worcestershire. Aged ninety-one, Charlotte has given well over a hundred talks. Her next is scheduled in Bletchley Park's mansion, the house where she once worked. On stage as in life, Charlotte enjoys an understated presence. With graceful poise she tells interested listeners of her wartime past in BP and then the Pentagon. It is a fascinating story and afterwards there are questions.

Surely the war was the best time of her life?

'Oh no.' Charlotte shakes her neatly set head of white hair and smiles. 'I am having the best time of my life right now.'

Notes on Sources

Introduction

p.2 *on a wider stage* . . . Baroness Trumpington, *Coming Up Trumps: A Memoir*, Macmillan, 2014

p.2 The Lost World of Bletchley Park . . . Sinclair McKay, *The Lost World of Bletchley Park: An Illustrated History of the Wartime Codebreaking Centre*, Aurum Press, 2013, p. 67

p.4 *It was horrible and wonderful like a love affair* . . . www.theguardian.com/world/2010/nov/07/women-spies-second-world-war

p.4 *bestselling* Station X . . . Michael Smith, *Station X: The Codebreakers of Bletchley Park*, Channel 4 Books, 2001, pp. 138, 196–7

p.5 *entitled* Cracking the Luftwaffe Codes . . . Gwen Watkins, *Cracking The Luftwaffe Codes: The Secrets of Bletchley Park*, Frontline Books, 2013

p.5 Secret Postings *has attracted* . . . Charlotte Webb, *Secret Postings: Bletchley Park to the Pentagon*, Book Tower Publishing, 2011

p.7 *It was excessively boring!* . . . Lady Jean Fforde, *Castles To Catastrophes*, Help-Yourself.net, 2011, p. 199

p.7 *worth you coming up here* . . . Sinclair McKay, *The Secret Life of Bletchley Park*, Aurum Press, 2011

p.9 *announced the* Daily Mail . . . *Daily Mail*, 4 February 2014

p.9 *codebreakers – the final secret* . . . *Telegraph*, 4 February 2014

p.10 *with his female colleagues* . . . Asa Briggs, *Secret Days: Code-breaking in Bletchley Park*, Frontline Books, 2011, pp. 81, 85

p.10 *of all that we could do* . . . Ibid., p. 80

p.12 *way of thinking* . . . www.war-experience.org/history/keyaspects/wrns/default.asp

p.13 *much more out of her* . . . Martin Sugarman, *Fighting Back:*

British Jewry's Military Contribution in the Second World War, Valentine Mitchell, 2010, pp. 91–132

p.14 *written in her own voice* . . . Kathleen Kinmonth Warren, *Shared Lives*, 2001

Chapter One

p.18 *little England that I love* . . . J. B. Priestley, *English Journey: Being a rambling but truthful account of what one man saw and heard and felt and thought during a journey through England during the autumn of the year 1933*, Victor Gollancz, p. 416

p.19 *over the brow of a hill* . . . Stanley Baldwin, 'England' in *On England and Other Addresses*, P. Allan & Co., 1926, p. 7

p.19 *he worked for Lloyds Bank* . . . Webb, *Secret Postings*, p. 14

p.21 *'lads and lasses' who lent a hand* . . . Ibid., p.15

p.23 *steamed through the Panama canal* . . . Kinmonth Warren, *Shared Lives*, p. 5

p.24 *their children in the mornings* . . . Cited in Angela Holdsworth, *Out of the Dolls House: The Story of Women in the Twentieth Century*, BBC Books, 1988, p. 117

p.26 *without incurring wrath and displeasure* . . . Kinmonth Warren, *Shared Lives*, p. 10

p.26 *we were summoned* . . . Ibid., p. 11

p.27 *item purchased was a Rover for £115* . . . Ann Mitchell, *Winifred*, self-published biography, 2012

p.28 *clumsy, watch out for my wireless!* . . . Fforde, *Castles to Catastrophe*, p. 6

Chapter Two

p.33 *who can Never Become Wives* . . . Virginia Nicholson, *Singled Out: How Two Million Women Survived Without Men After the First World War*, Penguin Books, 2008 (e.269)

p.36 *pursued my chosen path* . . . Extract from Ann Mitchell's lecture 'Enigma, Breaking the Code'

p.37 *upbringing you might say* . . . Kinmonth Warren, *Shared Lives*, p.12

p.37 *hitting the highest notes* . . . Ibid., pp. 12–13

p.37 *taking chances at village dances* . . . Trumpington, *Coming Up Trumps* (e.48) p.38 *couldn't dance well enough* . . . Ann Mitchell's personal diary, 15 May 1943

p.39 *no smoking and no drinking* . . . Fforde, *Castles to Catastrophe*, p. 174

p.41 *Kathleen could speak German* . . . For more on interwar British / German relations see K. Robbins, *Past and Present: British Images of Germany in the First Half of the Twentieth Century and their Historical Legacy*, Göttingen: Wallstein, 1999

p.44 *toasts drunk to him* . . . Fforde, *Castles to Catastrophe*, p. 164

p.45 *committed against the Jews* . . . For an analysis of Britain's reluctant response to the Jewish crisis see R. Wallis, *Britain, Germany and the Road to the Holocaust: British Attitudes towards Nazi Atrocities*, I.B. Tauris, 2014

p.45 *in the British Library* . . . World Committee of the Victims of German Fascism, *The Brown Book of the Hitler Terror*, Victor Gollancz, 1933, Plate no. 11

p.46 *sympathy and kindness* . . . T. Kuschner and K. Knox, *Refugees in an Age of Genocide: Global, National, and Local Perspectives during the Twentieth Century*, Frank Cass, 1999

p.46 *Lilly had taken no chances* . . . Louise London, *Whitehall and the Jews, 1933-48: British Immigration Policy, Jewish Refugees and the Holocaust*, Cambridge University Press, 1999

Chapter Three

p.49 *pouring down their faces* . . . Fforde, *Castles to Catastrophe*, p. 179

p.49 *wait to take part* . . . Watkins, *Cracking the Luftwaffe Codes*, pp. 32–3

p.51 *out of being wealthy* . . . Marion Hill, *Bletchley Park People: Churchill's Geese That Never Cackled*, The History Press, 2004, p. 8

p.52 *out of his own pocket* . . . Michael Smith, *The Secrets of Station X: How the Bletchley Park Codebreakers Helped Win the War*, Biteback Publishing, 2011 (e.62)

p.52 *became increasingly fractured* . . . This information was discovered by Margy Kinmouth amongst her grandparents' private papers and diaries. She published the story in 'The Ladies Who Secretly Won the War,' in *The Lady*, 19 July 2011 p.53 *data for the Admiralty* . . . Ibid.

p.54 *much of a home these days* . . . Kathleen Kinmonth Warren's family archive

p.54 *Domestic Science School* . . . www.bbc.co.uk/history/ww2 peopleswar/stories/61/a2429561.shtml

p.54 *peace-keeping female* . . . Lucy Noakes, *Women in the British Army: War and the Gentle Sex, 1907–1948*, Routledge, 2006, p. 6 for more on the way society has valorised the combative male

p.55 *in the case of the WAAF* . . . Cited in ibid., p. 105

p.55 *the men are standing by theirs* . . . *Woman's Own*, 14 May 1940

p.56 *letter to* The Times . . . Cited in Mark Glancy, 'Going to the Pictures: British Cinema and the Second World War' in *Past and Future*, Institute of Historical Research, 8, Autumn/Winter 2010, p. 7

p.56 *through the provision of art* . . . Anselm Heinrich, 'Theatre in Britain during the Second World War', *New Theatre Quarterly*, 26(1), 2010, pp. 61–70

p.59 *matters into her own hands* . . . Webb, *Secret Postings*, p. 11

p.60 *but I was howling inside* . . . www.theguardian.com/world/2010/nov/07/women-spies-second-world-war

p.61 *decided that I too would join up* . . . Kinmonth Warren, *Shared Lives*, p. 34

p.61 *rushed into the fray* . . . www.bbc.co.uk/history/ww2peopleswar/stories/61/a2429561.shtml

Chapter Four

p.62 *leave and join the Wrens* . . . Fforde, *Castles to Catastrophe*, pp. 179–80

p.63 *of TB and one of colitis* . . . Ibid., p. 180

p.63 *long time to come* . . . Ibid., p. 18

p.63 *German-occupied coastline* . . . Winston Churchill, cited in www.combinedops.com

p.63 *Arran's rocks and shores* . . . Fforde, *Castles to Catastrophe*, pp. 191–2

p.64 *Johnny did not come back* . . . Ibid., p. 198

p.66 *Enigma decodes appeared* . . . Frank Lucas, cited in *The Bletchley Park War Diaries: July 1939–August 1945, Secret Intelligence and the Second World War*, Wynne Press, 2011, p. 22

p.66 *unexpected effect of carrier pigeons* . . . Nigel de Grey, ibid., p. 11

pp.67–8 *life is not suited for women* . . . Cited in Noakes, *Women in the British Army*, p. 117

p.68 *went wonderfully smoothly* . . . Mary Grieve, *Millions Made My Story*, Victor Gollancz, 1964, p. 129

p.68 *the fairer sex should do war work* . . . Virginia Nicholson, *Millions Like Us: Women's Lives in the Second World War*, Penguin Books, 2011 (e.2241)

p.71 *from British Secondary Education* . . . Hilary Footitt and Simona Tobia, *War Talk: Foreign Languages and the British War Effort in Europe 1940–47*, Palgrave Macmillan, 2013, p. 16

p.75 *the professor type* . . . Alastair Denniston, head of GC&CS, in 1939 when describing the type of recruit he was looking for, cited in ibid., p. 39

p.75 *grounds throughout the war* . . . For more on Bletchley Park's Oxbridge origins see Christopher Grey, *Decoding Organization: Bletchley Park, Codebeaking and Organization Studies*, Cambridge University Press, 2012, pp. 132–4

Chapter Five

p.80 *modelled exactly on the men's* . . . www.bbc.co.uk/history/ww2peopleswar/stories/61/a2429561.shtml

p.80 *money I had ever earned* . . . Kinmonth Warren, *Shared Lives*, p. 35

p.81 *singing all the way* . . . Watkins, *Cracking the Luftwaffe Codes*, p.37

p.81 *into the realm of private life* . . . Penny Summerfield, *Reconstructing Women's Wartime Lives: Discourse and Subjectivity in Oral Histories of the Second World War*, Manchester University Press, 1998, p. 45

p.81 *astonishing facts about radar* . . . www.bbc.co.uk/history/ww2peopleswar/stories/61/a2429561.shtml

p.82 *He was, of course, delighted* . . . Kinmonth Warren, *Shared Lives*, p.36

p.82 *RAF Records Office* . . . Watkins, *Cracking the Luftwaffe Codes*, pp. 36–8

p.83 *understand what needs to be done* . . . Ibid., pp. 39–40, 43–4 p.84 *would not have missed for worlds* . . . Ibid., pp. 44, 38

p.84 *the garden of the service girls* . . . A spoof poem in *The New Statesman and Nation*, 6 December 1942, cited in Noakes, *Women in the British Army*, p. 108

p.84 *range of occupations now available* . . . For a comprehensive overview of the ATS during the Second World War see Noakes, *Women in the British Army*, pp. 103–32

p.84 *had lived as I had* . . . Webb, *Secret Postings*, p. 27

p.88 *man nor woman can do more* . . . Queen Elizabeth, cited in John Drummond, *Blue for a Girl: The Story of the W.R.N.S*; W. H. Allen, 1960, p. 20

p.88 *which you firmly believe* . . . Address given by Thomas Crick, the Archdeacon of the Royal Navy on 11 April 1943, cited in Drummond, *Blue for a Girl*, p. 21

p.91 *Cook and Messenger type* . . . Alastair Denniston in a memo to the Admiralty, cited in McKay, *The Secret Life of Bletchley Park*, pp. 151–2

Chapter Six

p.93 *a basis for guess work* . . . Post-War Review in The National Archives, cited in Grey, *Decoding Organization*, p. 227

p.94 *German songs can you sing?* . . . Watkins, *Cracking the Luftwaffe Codes*, p. 55

p.94 *know what was going on* . . . Webb, *Secret Postings*, p. 29

p.96 *wasn't allowed in without a pass* . . . Watkins, *Cracking the Luftwaffe Codes*, p. 58

p.96 *of a WAAF officer* . . . Ibid., p. 96

p.96 *confirmation from the Park. 'Hurrah'* . . . Ann's diary, 4 August 1943

p.97 *as early as 1937* . . . The Chief of the Secret Service, Admiral Hugh Sinclair, cited in Footitt and Tobia, *Wartalk,* p. 39

p.101 *when everything changed* . . . Pat Davies, interview with author

p.101 *to what it was she signed* . . . Watkins, *Cracking the Luftwaffe Codes*, pp. 97–9

p.103 *do so you may be shot!* . . . Rozanne Colchester's unpublished recollections

p.103 *assume he was joking. He wasn't* . . . Watkins, *Cracking the Luftwaffe Codes*, p. 99

p.104 *the presence of a gun on the table* . . . Webb, *Secret Postings*, p. 32

p.104 *It's nice to smile to myself!* . . . Ann's diary, 30 September 1943

Chapter Seven

p.106 *Enigma machines in the world* . . . www.bletchleypark.org.uk/content/visit/whattosee.rhtm

p.106 *middle of the battle of France* . . . Stuart Milner-Barry, cited in Grey, *Decoding Organization*, p. 196

p.108 *large ugly house* . . . Webb, *Secret Postings*, p. 31

p.110 *could be trained to do* . . . Cited in Grey, *Decoding Organization*, p.159

p.111 *epoch is the 'information age'* . . . Ibid., pp. 220–1

p.112 *great big metal bookcases* . . . Mary Stewart, Bombe Operator, interviewed in 'The Men who Cracked Enigma', Documentary Series *Heroes of World War II*, UKTV History Channel, 2003

p.115 *have thick pea soup fog* . . . Fforde, *Castles to Catastrophes*, pp. 199, 198

p.116 *for advice by the other three!* . . . Ann's diary, 9 October 1943

p.116–7 *an elite within an elite* . . . Peter Calvocoressi's description of the small minority of people within BP who knew about Ultra. P. Calvocoressi, *Top Secret Ultra*, M&M Baldwin, Cleobury Mortimer, 2001, p. 23

p.117 *service could not carry deadwood* . . . For more on the training and recruitment of Y-station listeners see Footitt and Tobia, *War Talk*, pp. 34–9

p.122 *people and full of tobacco smoke!* . . . Rozanne Colchester's unpublished recollections

p.124 *than the breaking of the Enigma ciphers* . . . Shaun Wylie, 'Breaking Tunny and the Birth of Colossus' in Michael Smith and Ralph Erskine (eds), *Action this Day*, Bantam Press, 2001, p. 317

p.125 *so he didn't bother* . . . Grey, *Decoding Organisation*, p. 188

Chapter Eight

p.128 6 *o'clock news* . . . Fforde, *Castles to Catastrophes*, p. 198

p.129 *accommodated another 4,000* . . . Grey, *Decoding Organization*, p. 55

p.130 *else was explained* . . . Rozanne Colchester's unpublished recollections

p.131 *shock to Rozanne* . . . Ibid.

p.132 *helped me wonderful* . . . Watkins, *Cracking the Luftwaffe Codes*, pp. 119–20

p.133 *child from suffering* . . . Ibid., pp. 119–21

p.134 *our narrow beds* . . . Kinmonth Warren, *Shared Lives*, p. 35

p.135 *I gave her* . . . Ann's diary, 28, 30 September 1943

p.135 *time felt unhappy* . . . Ibid., 19 October 1943

p.136 *and we slept!* . . . Webb, *Secret Postings*, p. 30

p.137 *sort of people* . . . McKay, *The Lost World of Bletchley Park*, pp. 61, 63

p.137 *Looks quite nice* . . . Ann's diary, 20 December 1943

p.138 *some magazines* . . . Ibid., 29 December 1943

p.138 *be moved out* . . . Ibid., 26 January 1944

p.138 *to the patriot* . . . Cited in Grey, *Decoding Organization*, pp. 155–6

p.139 *ridiculous to salute them* . . . Watkins, *Cracking the Luftwaffe Codes*, pp. 101–2

p.140 *outset of war* . . . Ruth Bourne, 'Eastcote and Stanmore' in Gwendoline Page (ed.), *We Kept the Secret: Enigma Memories*, Geo. R. Reeve Ltd, 2002, p. 97

p.141 *and greedy mice* . . . Diane Payne, 'The Bombes' in F. H. Hinsley and Alan Stripp (eds), *Code Breakers: The Inside Story of Bletchley Park*, Oxford University Press, 1993, pp. 135–6

p.143 *to the war effort* . . . *Oxford Dictionary of National Biography*

Chapter Nine

p.144 *ship-to-ship communications* . . . John Pether, *Funkers and Sparkers: Origins and Formations of the 'Y' Service*, Bletchley Park Trust, 1998, p. 12

p.146 *which is good going* . . . Ann's diary, 1 October 1943

p.147 *back to the Clarkes'* . . . Ibid., 29 September 1943

p.147 *encounter with the law* . . . www.bbc.co.uk/history/ww2peo pleswar/stories/61/a2429561.shtml

p.148 *total 'black-out'* . . . Rozanne Colchester's unpublished recollections

p.148 *late for her shift* . . . Ann's diary, 9 November 1943

p.148 *out of the village* . . . Webb, *Secret Postings*, p. 38

p.148 *Well I hated it!* . . . Fforde, *Castles to Catastrophe*, p. 202

p.149 *those wartime songs* . . . Sinclair McKay, *The Secret Listeners: How the Y Service Intercepted German Codes for Bletchley Park*, Aurum Press, 2012, p. 187

p.150 *retrieval of information* . . . Rodney Brunt, 'Indexes at the Government Code and Cypher School, Bletchley Park, 1940–1945', American Society for Information Science and Technology, 2004, p. 297, www.asis.org/History/24-brunt.pdf

p.150 *retentive human memory* . . . Calvocoressi, *Top Secret Ultra*

p.151 *a concentrated silence again* . . . Rozanne Colchester, unpublished recollections

p.151 *stations were recorded* . . . Grey, *Decoding Organization*, p. 188

p.154 *but it was tiring!* . . . Webb, *Secret Postings*, p. 34

p.154 *still 'felt fine'* . . . Ann's diary, 29, 30 November 1943

p.154 *with these people* . . . Ibid., 1 December 1943

p.156 *running at over 4 per cent* . . . *Bletchley Park War Diaries*, p. 157

p.156 *middle age than youth* . . . Cited in Grey, *Decoding Organization*, pp. 162–3

p.158 *whole five days* . . . Ann's diary, 3, 4, 6, 12 December 1943

p.158 *brush of real events* . . . Calvocoressi, *Top Secret Ultra*, pp. 18–19

p.158 *loathed Bletchley Park* . . . Veteran, cited in Hill, *Bletchley Park People*, p. 136

Chapter Ten

p.164 *real world lived* . . . Rozanne Colchester, unpublished recollections

p.165 *a friend for life* . . . Ibid.

p.165 *FORMAL in those days* . . . Ibid.

p.167 *of Eastern Languages* . . . Watkins, *Cracking the Luftwaffe Codes*, pp. 107–11 p.168 *devoted to reviews* . . . Gwen Watkins, *Portrait of a Friend*, Gomer Press, 1983, p. 95

p.168 *what historians wrote* . . . Watkins, *Cracking the Luftwaffe Codes*, pp. 111–13

p.168 *the BP community* . . . Ibid., Asa Briggs, foreword p. 17

p.170 *company of men* . . . Rozanne Colchester, unpublished recollections.

p.170 *behind Bletchley's Bombes* . . . *Oxford Dictionary of National Biography*

p.170 *if he said 'thank you'* . . . Trumpington, *Coming Up Trumps* (e.601)

p.171 *during each month* . . . Hugh Sebag-Montefiore, *Enigma: The Battle for the Code*, Weidenfeld & Nicolson, 2000, p. 214

p.171 *the word 'tendencies'* . . . Andrew Hodges, *Alan Turing, The Enigma*, Burnett Books, 1983, p. 206

p.173 *'ever present pearls'* . . . McKay, *The Lost World of Bletchley Park*, p. 61

p.173 *another three weeks* . . . Trumpington, *Coming Up Trumps* (e.542–6)

p.174 *never had any money* . . . Ibid. (e.533)

p.174 *comradeship and collaboration* . . . Calvocoressi, *Top Secret Ultra*, p. 23

p.175 *well-educated women* . . . Briggs, *Secret Days*, p. 81

p.175 *no more of the war* . . . Ann's diary, 28 and 29 September, 4 November 1943

p.175 *elegance and education* . . . Nicholson, *Millions Like Us* (e.2393)

p.176 *the wrong doorstep* . . . Doris White, cited in Nicholson, *Millions Like Us* (e.2393–8)

p.177 *must-have party accessory* . . . Obituary, *Telegraph*, 3 May 2009

p.178 *Israel's Foreign Ministry* . . . Martin Sugarman, www.bletchleypark.org.uk/resources/filer.rhtm/595696/breaking+the+codes-+jewish+personnel+at+bletchley+park.pdf p.19

p.178 *knew what it meant* . . . Walter Eytan in Hinsley and Stripp (eds), *Code Breakers*, p. 60

Chapter Eleven

p.181 *culture at its best* . . . McKay, *The Secret Life of Bletchley Park*, p.245

p.181 *recreational facilities* . . . Grey, *Decoding Organization*, p. 138

p.183 *emotional undercurrents* . . . *The Times*, 2 September 1942

p.185 *pianist accompanying him* Ann's diary, 8 and 28 October, 24 November 1943

p.186 *your sketch isn't bad* . . . Smith, *The Secrets of Station X* (e.2502)

p.187 *had ventured to hope* . . . *The Times*, 13 October 1940

p.187 *nothing else to do* . . . Ann's diary, 29 September, 26 October 1943, 17 January 1944

p.187 *Electric Cinema Cafe* . . . Ibid., 20 January 1944

p.188 *powerful wartime imagery* . . . Glancy, 'Going to the Pictures', *Past and Future*, p. 8

p.188 *none were British* . . . Ibid., p. 9

p.188 *still burning nearby* . . . Ibid.

p.193 *glasses of beer* . . . Rozanne Colchester, unpublished reflections

p.197 *food was 'rotten'* . . . Ann's diary, 16, 27 October 1943

Chapter Twelve

p.199 *I could drive anything* . . . Fforde, *Castles to Catastrophe*, p. 202

p.200 *humdrum roles* . . . Cited in Grey, *Decoding Organization*, p. 157

p.201 *people grow older* . . . Ibid., p. 163

p.201 *it was NOT!!* . . . Webb, *Secret Postings*, p. 34

p.202 *give certain victory* . . . Churchill in a letter to his Foreign Secretary Anthony Eden, cited in Cat Wilson, *Churchill on the Far East in the Second World War: Hiding the History of the 'Special Relationship'*, Palgrave Macmillan, 2014, p. 67

p.202 *fleets were patrolling* . . . Michael Smith, *The Emperor's Codes: Bletchley Park's Role in Breaking Japan's Secret Ciphers*, Biteback Publishing, 2010 (e.2567)

p.204 *much more bureaucratic* . . . Rozanne Colchester, unpublished reflections

p.204 *a light went out* . . . Ibid.

p.205 *in the know* . . . Kinmonth Warren, *Shared Lives*, pp. 37–8

p205. *had blocked it* . . . Harold L. Smith, 'The Effect of War on Women' in H. Smith (ed.), *War and Social Change: British Society in the Second World War*, Manchester University Press, 1990, p. 215

p.205 *during the war* . . . www.striking-women.org

p.208 *decrypts per day* . . . *Bletchley Park War Diaries*, p. 132

p.209 *emitted from the tail* . . . Anthony Powell in Peter Ackroyd, *London: The Biography*, Vintage, 2001, p. 748

Chapter Thirteen

p.222 *stockings for today* . . . Ann's diary, 11, 18 May, 4, 23 June, 7 July, 8 November 1943

p.223 *That meant Police etc* . . . Hill, *Bletchley Park People*, p. 105

p.223 *experience physical intimacy* . . . Holdsworth, *Out of the Doll's House*, p. 146

p.224 *age is subjected* . . . MP Gordon McDonald in Noakes, *Women in the British Army*, p. 117

p.225 *Gave him my address!* . . . Ann's diary, 23 November 1943

p.226 *we could operate* . . . Ruth Bourne in Page, 'We Kept the Secret', p.98

p.234 *door of the Dorchester* . . . Lady Jean Fforde's interview with author; Fforde, *Castles to Catastrophe*, pp. 200–1

p.235 *real world outside* . . . Kinmonth Warren, *Shared Lives*, p. 37

p.236 *all the ruined sites* . . . Watkins, *Cracking the Luftwaffe Codes*, pp.53–4

p.237 *poetry of the thirties* . . . Watkins, *Portrait of a Friend*, pp. 109–10

Chapter Fourteen

p.239 *even pretend traffic* . . . Watkins, *Cracking the Luftwaffe Codes*, p. 156

p.241 *attack of dysentery* . . . Fforde, *Castles to Catastrophe*, pp. 205–9

p.244 *whom I marry* . . . Watkins, *Cracking the Luftwaffe Codes*, p. 170

p.245 *came the reply* . . . McKay, *The Secret Life of Bletchley Park*, p. 278

p.246 *war was security* . . . *Bletchley Park War Diaries*, p. 171

p.247 *have hitherto maintained* . . . Cited in Smith, *Station X*, pp. 272–3

p.248 *a marvellous sight* . . . Winifred Williamson's diary extract in Ann Mitchell, *Winifred*, self-published, 2012

p.252 *my next destination* . . . Webb, *Secret Postings*, p. 41

p.254 *war never end?* . . . Ibid., pp. 42–3, 45–8

p.254 *drowning everything else* . . . Ibid., p. 50

p.255 *tide of war* . . . Ibid., p. 49

p.255 *prepared to use it* . . . *Bletchley Park War Diaries*, p. 176

Chapter Fifteen

p.262 *wife and mother* . . . Noakes, *Women in the British Army*, p. 134

p.262 *the British race* . . . Ibid., William Beveridge cited.

p.263 *What a life* . . . Kinmonth Warren, *Shared Lives*, p. 39

p.266 *the war years* . . . Webb, *Secret Postings*, pp. 52–3

p.273 *rest of their lives together* . . . Kinmouth Warren, *Shared Memories*, pp. 43, 45

p.275 *I knew best!* . . . Fforde, *Castles to Catastrophe*, p. 245

p.276 *the dead aware* . . . 'The Silence of Love', in *The Collected Poems of Vernon Watkins*, Golgonooza Press, 1986, p. 472

p.277 *played at her feet* . . . Holdsworth, *Out of the Doll's House*, p. 124

p.277 *exclusively by themselves* . . . Ibid., p. 125

p.278 *come to that?* . . . Kinmonth Warren, *Shared Memories*, pp. 47, 51

p.279 *and rightly so* . . . The 1955 Morton Commission on the state of divorce, cited in Holdsworth, *Out of the Doll's House*, p. 147

Chapter Sixteen

p.282 *or five years* . . . Webb, *Secret Postings*, pp. 54–5

p.285 *unparalleled in history* . . . Calvocoressi, *Top Secret Ultra*, p. 14

p.285 *from volume I* . . . E. G. Hastings, cited in Christopher Moran, *Classified: Secrecy and the State in Modern Britain*, Cambridge University Press, 2013, p. 263

p.292 *and probably four* . . . H. Hinsley, 'The Enigma of Ultra', *History Today*, 43(9) (September 1993), pp. 15–20

p.292 *most of us* . . . Watkins, *Cracking the Luftwaffe Codes*, p. 176

p.298 *there is silence* . . . Ibid., p. 177

Acknowledgements

I owe an enormous thank you to Rozanne Colchester, Pamela Rose, Betty Gilbert, Cora Jarman, Doris Moss, Gwen Watkins, Georgette McGarrah, Muriel Dindol, Joanna Chorely, Pat Davies, Charlotte Webb, Ann Mitchell, Kathleen Kinmonth Warren, Ruth Bourne and Lady Jean Fforde. It is their stories, so generously shared, that made this book possible. It was with trepidation that I sent out their extracts prior to publication. Thank you for the candid feedback and grammatical overhaul! Thanks also to husbands Angus Mitchell and Philip Jarman, daughters Chloë Fithen and Margy Kinmonth and nephew Adam Raphael for input and support (and in Margy's case impressive historical sleuthing!). I reserve a special thank you for Lady Margaret Stirling-Aird and her important, albeit brief, appearance in this book.

I could not have unravelled much of what I was told without the unstinting expertise and support of Dr Joel Greenburg who was busy writing his own book about code-breaker Gordon Welchman, but always found time for my code-breaking questions. Thank you very much. Thanks also to Professor Bruce Collins for casting an invaluable eye over the manuscript. Any errors are entirely my own.

The gem of an idea from which 'The Bletchley Girls' sprang was brought to me by Charlotte Robertson, thank you for sharing it. And thank you also for finding the project's perfect match with editor Rupert Lancaster at Hodder & Stoughton, whose steady hand has overseen the scramble from idea to timely execution. Assistant editor Maddy Price has been an outstanding support, coping with last minutes changes and my constant queries, while

Karen Geary has enthusiastically championed the book from first (very rough) manuscript onwards.

For research assistance I would like to thank Stephen Fleming at the National Museum of Computing, Katherine Lynch and Jonathan Byrne at Bletchley Park Trust, Carrie Fehr and Oliver Mahony at Lady Margaret Hall, Oxford University, Anne Wickes at The Second World War Experience Centre, Nicola Allen at Woburn Abbey and Paddy Meiklejohn at home in Forres. The British Library and the London Library have provided me with a second home and my mother has, as usual, always said the right thing. Thank you.

Picture Acknowledgements

1. © Crown Copyright. Reproduced by kind permission, Director GCHQ (above, centre and below).
2. Reproduced by kind permission Ruth Bourne (above left), Reproduced by kind permission Ruth Bourne/photo Akira Suemori/Press Association Images (above right), Reproduced by kind permission Gwen Watkins (below).
3. Reproduced by kind permission Pamela Rose (above left), Reproduced by kind permission Rozanne Colchester/photo Guardian News & Media Ltd (above right), © Tessa Dunlop (below).
4. Reproduced by kind permission Charlotte Webb (above), Reproduced by kind permission Lady Jean Fforde (below left), © Tessa Dunlop (below right).
5. Reproduced by kind permission Joanna Chorely/photos Geoffrey Robinson/Rex Features (above and below).
6. Reproduced by kind permission Betty Gilbert (above left and right), Reproduced by kind permission Ann Mitchell (below).
7. Reproduced by kind permission Pat Davies (above left), Reproduced by kind permission Pat Davies/photo Ray Davies (above right), Reproduced by kind permission Murial Dindol (below left), Reproduced by kind permission Cora Jarman (below right).
8. Reproduced by kind permission Kathleen Kinmonth Warren (above left), Reproduced by kind permission Georgette McGarrah and Doris Moss (above right), © Tessa Dunlop (below).

Every reasonable effort has been made to contact the copyright holders, but if there are any errors or omissions, Hodder & Stoughton will be pleased to insert the appropriate acknowledgement in any subsequent printing of this publication.

Bibliography

Unless cited all references concerning the fifteen veterans featured in this book were taken from face-to-face interviews and subsequent telephone conversations, letters, email exchanges and visits throughout the course of 2014.

Supplementary sources relating directly to the 15 'Bletchley Girls' include:

Published Memoirs
Bourne, R., 'Eastcote and Stanmore' in Page, G., (ed.), *We Kept the Secret: Enigma Memories,* Geo. R. Reeve Ltd, 2002
Briggs, A., *Secret Days, Code-breaking in Bletchley Park*, Frontline Books, 2011
Fforde, J., *Castles To Catastrophes*, Help-Yourself.net, 2011
Kinmonth Warren, K., *Shared Lives*, Self-published, 2001
Mitchell, A., *Winifred,* Self-published, 2012
Trumpington, J., *Coming Up Trumps, A Memoir*, Macmillan, 2014
Watkins, G., *Cracking The Luftwaffe Codes: The Secrets of Bletchley Park*, Frontline Books, 2013
Watkins, G., *Portrait of a Friend*, Gomer Press, 1983
Webb, C., *Secret Postings: Bletchley Park to the Pentagon*, BookTower Publishing, 2011

Unpublished Memoirs
Colchester, R., Handwritten recollections
Williamson, A., *Personal Diary*, 1943–44

Poetry
The Collected Poems of Vernon Watkins, Golgonooza Press, 1986

Websites
www.bbc.co.uk
www.bletchleypark.org.uk
www.war-experience.org

Newspapers
The Daily Mail
The Guardian
The Telegraph
The Times

Bletchley Park and Code-breaking
There are an ever-increasing number of books, journals and memoirs on the subject of Britain's Second World War code-breaking efforts. This is in no way a comprehensive summary, rather a list of the publications that I found instructive during the writing of *The Bletchley Girls*.

The Bletchley Park War Diaries: July 1939–August 1945, Secret Intelligence and the Second World War, Wynne Press, 2011

Briggs, A., *Secret Days, Code-breaking in Bletchley Park*, Frontline Books, 2011

Brunt, R., 'Indexes at the Government Code and Cypher School, Bletchley Park, 1940–1945', *American Society for Information Science and Technology*, 2004

Calvocoressi, P., *Top Secret Ultra*, M&M Baldwin, Cleobury Mortimer, 2001

Greenburg, J., *Gordon Welchman: Bletchley Park's Architect of Ultra Intelligence*, Frontline Books, 2014

Grey, C., *Decoding Organization: Bletchley Park, Codebreaking and Organization Studies*, Cambridge University Press, 2012

Hill, M., *Bletchley Park People: Churchill's Geese That Never Cackled*, The History Press, 2004

Hinsley, F. H. & Stripp, A. (eds.), *Code Breakers: The Inside Story of Bletchley Park*, Oxford University Press, 1993

History of Bletchley Park Huts & Blocks 1939–45, Bletchley Park Trust, 2009

Hodges, A., *Alan Turing: The Enigma*, Burnett Books, 1983

Howard, K., *Dear Codebreaker, The Letters of Margaret Rock (Bletchley Park Codebreaker) & John Rock (Parachute & Glider Forces Pioneer)*, Booktower Publishing, 2013

Jackson, J., *Hitler's Codebreakers: German Signals Intelligence in World War 2*, Booktower Publishing, 2012

Jarvis, S., *Japanese Codes*, Bletchley Park Trust, 2009

McKay, S., *The Secret Life of Bletchley Park*, Aurum Press, 2011

McKay, S., *The Secret Listeners: How the Y Service Intercepted German Codes for Bletchley Park*, Aurum Press Ltd, 2012

McKay, S., *The Lost World of Bletchley Park: An Illustrated History of the Wartime Codebreaking Centre*, Aurum, 2013

Moran, C., *Classified: Secrecy and the State in Modern Britain*, Cambridge University Press, 2013

Page, G., (ed.), *We Kept the Secret: Enigma Memories*, Geo. R. Reeve Ltd, 2002

Pether, J., *Funkers and Sparkers: Origins and Formations of the 'Y' Service*, Bletchley Park Trust, 1998

Sebag-Montefiore, H., *Enigma: The Battle for the Code*, Weidenfeld and Nicolson, 2000

Segrave, E., *The Girl from Station X: My Mother's Unknown Life*, Union Books, 2013

Smith, M., *The Secrets of Station X: How the Bletchley Park Codebreakers Helped Win the War*, Biteback Publishing, 2011

Smith, M., *The Emperor's Codes: Bletchley Park's Role in Breaking Japan's Secret Ciphers*, Biteback Publishing, 2010

Smith, M. & Erskine, R. (eds.), *Action this Day*, Bantam Press, 2001

Smith, M., *Station X: The Codebreakers of Bletchley Park*, Channel 4 Books, 2001

Stubbington, Wing Commander J., *BMP Reports by the German Air Section*, Bletchley Park Trust, 2012

Walton, C., *Empire of Secrets: British Intelligence, the Cold War and the Twilight of Empire*, Harper Press, 2013

Wescombe, P., *Bletchley Park and the Luftwaffe*, Bletchley Park Trust, 2009

Winterbotham, F., *The Ultra Secret*, Weidenfeld and Nicolson, 1974

Young, I., *Enigma Variations: Love, War & Bletchley Park*, Mainstream Publishing, 1990

Websites
www.bletchleypark.org.uk

General Bibliography
It is hard to know where to draw the line when it comes to writing a bibliography of a book that spans the best part of a century. If it was to be truly representative it would even have to include my A level

textbooks on the rise of Nazism in Germany! I have therefore decided to limit the below list to texts that I have consulted during the course of writing *The Bletchley Girls*.

Ackroyd, P., *London: The Biography*, Vintage, 2001

Atkinson, R., *The Day of Battle: The War in Sicily and Italy, 1943–44*, (Liberation Trilogy, Book 2), Henry Holt, 2008

Baldwin, S., 'England' in *On England and Other Addresses*, P. Allan & Co., 1926

Bennet, T., et al. (eds) *Formations of Pleasure*, Routledge, 1983

Briggs, A., *The Birth of Broadcasting*, Oxford University Press, 1961

Corner, P., *The Fascist Party and Popular Opinion in Mussolini's Italy*, Oxford University Press, 2012

Drummond, J., *Blue for a Girl: The story of the W.R.N.S*; W.H. Allen, 1960

Footitt, H., and Tobia, S., *War talk: Foreign languages and the British war effort in Europe 1940–47*, Palgrave Macmillan, 2013

Gilbert, M., *The Second World War*, Phoenix, 2009

Glancy, M., 'Going to the Pictures: British cinema and the Second World War' in *Past and Future*, Institute of Historical Research, 8, Autumn/Winter 2010

Grieve, M., *Millions Made My Story*, Victor Gollancz, 1964

Harris, C., *Women at War 1939–45: The Home Front*, The History Press, 2010

Heinrich, A., 'Theatre in Britain during the Second World War', *New Theatre Quarterly*, 26(1), 2010

Holdsworth, A., *Out of the Dolls House: The Story of Women in the Twentieth Century*, BBC Books, 1988

James, C., & Porter, V. (eds), *British Cinema History*, Weidenfeld and Nicolson, 1983

Koonz, C., *Mothers in the Fatherland: Women, the Family, and Nazi Politics*, St Martin's Press, 1988

Kuschner T., and Knox, K., *Refugees in an Age of Genocide: Global, National, and Local Perspectives during the Twentieth Century*, Frank Cass, 1999

Jackson, S., *The Savoy: The Romance of a Great Hotel*, Muller, 1964

Jose, H., 'War and Social History, Britain and the Home Front during the Second World War', *Contemporary European History*, Vol. 1, No. 1 (March 1992)

Lamb, C., *I Only Joined for the Hat, Redoubtable Wrens at war . . . their trials, tribulations and triumphs*, Bene Factum Publishing, 2007

Langhamer, C., "'A Public House is for all Classes, Men and Women Alike": Women, Leisure and Drink in Second World War England', *Women's History Review*, Vol 12, No. 3, 2003

Light, A., *Forever England: Femininity, Literature and Conservatism between the Wars*, Routledge, 1991

London, L., *Whitehall and the Jews, 1933–48: British immigration policy, Jewish refugees and the Holocaust*, Cambridge University Press, 1999

Millgate, H, D., *Got Any Gum Chum? GIs in Wartime Britain 1942–45*, The History Press, 2009

Nicholson, V., *Millions Like Us: Women's Lives in the Second World War*, Penguin Books, 2011

Nicholson, V., *Singled Out: How Two Million Woman Survived without Men After the First World War*, Penguin Books, 2008

Noakes, L., *Women in the British Army: War and the Gentle Sex, 1907–1948*, Routledge, 2006

Priestley, J, B., *English Journey: Being a rambling but truthful account of what one man saw and heard and felt and thought during a journey through England during the autumn of the year 1933*, Victor Gollancz, 1934

Robbins, K., *Past and Present: British Images of Germany in the First Half of the Twentieth Century and their Historical Legacy*, Göttingen: Wallstein, 1999

Ross, S., *At Home in World War Two: Rationing*, Evans Brothers Ltd, 2002

Smith. H., (ed.) *War and Social Change: British Society in the Second World War*, Manchester University Press, 1990

Storer, C., 'Weimar Republic as seen by an English Woman: British Women Writers and the Weimar Republic', *German Studies Review*, Vol. 32, No. 1 (Feb 2009)

Sugarman, M., *Fighting Back: British Jewry's Military Contribution in the Second World War*, Valentine Mitchell, 2010

Summerfield, P., *Reconstructing Women's Wartime Lives: Discourse and Subjectivity in Oral Histories of the Second World War*, Manchester University Press, 1998

Taylor, A, J, P., *English History 1914–45*, Oxford University Press, 1965

Wallis, R., *Britain, Germany and the Road to the Holocaust: British Attitudes towards Nazis Atrocities*, I. B. Tauris, 2014

Williams, B., *Britain at War 1939–45*, Pitkin, 2005

Wilson, C., *Churchill on the Far East in the Second World War: Hiding the History of the 'Special Relationship'*, Palgrave Macmillan, 2014

World Committee of the Victims of German Fascism, *The Brown Book of Hitler Terror*, Gollancz, 1933

Websites
www.bbc.co.uk
www.striking-women.org

Index